Social Innovation in Latin America

The Latin American continent contains an incredibly rich diversity from which humans derive a range of ecosystem services (e.g. material goods, cultural benefits, climate regulation, etc.) that contribute to livelihoods and well-being. It has become critical to reconcile social and environmental issues in the region to ensure that development is sustainable and aligned with the Sustainable Development Goals.

To ensure the sustainable use and management of social and natural capital in the region, business, government, social enterprises and NGOs are engaging in different forms of social innovation that account for social, ecological and environmental values. This requires the integration of social and natural capital into decision-making at all levels. Latin America presents a useful scenario to explore social innovation in relation to social and environmental values and the management of local human and natural resources. This book presents social innovation initiatives that incorporate social and natural capital into decision-making processes in Latin America. This book aims to provide the reader with an insight into the relevance of social innovation for maintaining and restoring social and natural capital in Latin America.

Using case studies from Ecuador, Colombia, Peru and Mexico, this book provides an insight into the interactions between social innovation and social and natural capital in Latin America and will be of interest to researchers, academics and students in the fields of social innovation, management studies, environmental economics and sustainability.

Sara Calvo is the co-founder of Minca Ventures and the Director of the Master's in Cooperation and International Development at Universidad Internacional de la Rioja in Spain.

Andrés Morales is the co-founder of Minca Ventures and an Associate Professor of International Development and Social Enterprise at Universidad Internacional de la Rioja in Spain.

Routledge Studies in Social Enterprise & Social Innovation

Series Editors: Jacques Defourny, Lars Hulgård, and Rocío Nogales
Social enterprises seek to combine an entrepreneurial spirit and behaviour with a primacy of social or societal aims. To various extents, their production of goods or services generates market income which they usually combine with other types of resources. A social innovation consists of the implementation of a new idea or initiative to change society in a fairer and more sustainable direction.

Routledge Studies in Social Enterprise & Social Innovation seeks to examine and promote these increasingly important research themes. It particularly looks at participatory governance and social innovation dynamics in social enterprises and more widely in partnerships involving third sector and civil society organizations, conventional businesses and public authorities. In such perspective, this series aims at publishing both breakthrough contributions exploring the new frontiers of the field as well as books defining the state of the art and paving the way to advance the field.

Social Entrepreneurship and Innovation in Rural Europe
Edited by Ralph Richter, Matthias Fink, Richard Lang and Daniela Maresch

People Centered Social Innovation
Global Perspectives on An Emerging Paradigm
Edited by Swati Banerjee, Stephen Carney and Lars Hulgard

Social Innovation in Latin America
Maintaining and Restoring Social and Natural Capital
Edited by Sara Calvo and Andrés Morales

Social Enterprise in Western Europe
Theory, Models and Practice
Edited by Jacques Defourny and Marthe Nyssens

For more information about this series, please visit: https://www.routledge.com/Routledge-Studies-in-Social-Enterprise--Social-Innovation/book-series/RSESI

Social Innovation in Latin America

Maintaining and Restoring Social and Natural Capital

Edited by Sara Calvo and Andrés Morales

Routledge
Taylor & Francis Group
NEW YORK AND LONDON

First published 2021
by Routledge
605 Third Avenue, New York, NY 10158

and by Routledge
2 Park Square, Milton Park, Abingdon, Oxon, OX14 4RN

Routledge is an imprint of the Taylor & Francis Group, an informa business

Library of Congress Cataloging-in-Publication Data
Names: Calvo, Sara, editor. | Morales Pachón, Andres, 1984- editor.
Title: Social innovation in Latin America : maintaining and restoring social and natural capital / edited by Sara Calvo and Andrés Morales.
Description: 1 Edition. | New York : Routledge, 2021. | Series: Routledge studies in social enterprise and social innovation | Includes bibliographical references and index.
Identifiers: LCCN 2020043671 (print) | LCCN 2020043672 (ebook) | ISBN 9780367416881 (hardback) | ISBN 9780367823382 (ebook)
Subjects: LCSH: Infrastructure (Economics)--Latin America. | Sustainable development--Latin America. | Social entrepreneurship--Latin America. | Social movements--Latin America. | Competition, Unfair--Latin America.
Classification: LCC HC130.C3 S63 2021 (print) | LCC HC130.C3 (ebook) | DDC 338.98/07--dc23
LC record available at https://lccn.loc.gov/2020043671
LC ebook record available at https://lccn.loc.gov/2020043672

ISBN: 978-0-367-41688-1 (hbk)
ISBN: 978-0-367-72265-4 (pbk)

Typeset in Sabon
by MPS Limited, Dehradun

The editors would like to dedicate this book to all Latin American activists who have been killed fighting for a better continent maintaining and restoring the social and natural capital of the region.

Contents

List of Tables ix
List of Figures x
About the Contributors xi
Foreword xvii
Introduction xix
SARA CALVO AND ANDRÉS MORALES

PART I
Conceptual frameworks to understand social innovation and natural and social capital in Latin America 1

1 Buen vivir, a decolonial approach to development 3
ANDRÉS MORALES AND SARA CALVO

2 Global governance to address local ills: the universal periodic review aiding the creation of a third space in pursuit of land rights that support social innovation, biodiversity and natural capital in Latin America 37
LOUISA ASHLEY

PART II
Social innovation and natural capital 65

3 The environment through the regulation of emissions resulting from the automobile journeys in Peru 67
JOSE CARLOS SOLDEVILLA SAAVEDRA

4 The purepechas of cheran: community solidarity, public security and environmental conservation in Mexico 92
KAROL GIL-VAZQUEZ

5 The sustainable innovation of salinerito in ecuador 112
FABIÁN VARGAS AND MARIO CADENA LÓPEZ

6 Socio-technical regimes to understand grassroots innovations and natural capital in Chile 134
NANCY SARAVIA AND JORDI PERIS

PART III
Social innovation and human capital **159**

7 Entrepreneurship, associativity and social technologies in rural communities: a reading from the papal encyclical laudato si in Colombia 161
MARIETTA BUCHELLI AND JUAN FERNANDO ÁLVAREZ

8 Cooperativism in acapulco, México 174
ROBERTO CAÑEDO VILLARREAL, MARÍA DEL CARMEN BARRAGÁN MENDOZA AND DANIEL FRANCISCO NAGAO MENEZES

9 The relationship with knowledge, skills of entrepreneurs and companies' internal factors: findings from collective enterprises in Colombia 192
ANA MILENA SILVIA VALENCIA

10 Fair trade focus of social joint and engine for the sustainable local development: experiences in quito-ecuador with the American city of fair trade 205
CESAR AUGUSTO MARCILLO VACA, LAURA ANGÉLICA DE LA CRUZ GUERRERO AND JAIME RAMIRO FIGUEROA FRAGA

Index *223*

Tables

1.1 Development theory radiography 8
1.2 Sumak Kawsay/Suma Qamaña in other Latin American indigenous communities 12
1.3 Latin American practices based on solidarity and reciprocity 19
5.1 Organizational ecosystem of Salinas Parish, Guaranda Canton 120
5.2 Consolidated billing of Salinas community companies in 2018 128
7.1 Relation of interviews carried out between 2017 and 2018 167
7.2 Numerals of the Laudato Si that converge with the principles of the social and solidarity economy 168
9.1 Summary of linear regression results 200
9.2 Hypothesis contrast 200
10.1 Fair Trade exports in Ecuador 2017 *(value FOB Thousands USD)* 207
10.2 Exporters with fair trade certification 2017 208

Figures

1.1 The conceptualisation of Buen Vivir 15
3.1 Wiñaywayna, quechua settlement which merge with its environment 90
9.1 Factors determining the success of the creation of SMEs 196
9.2 Conformed cooperatives 199
9.3 Percentage of cooperatives 199
10.1 National Service of Customs of the Ecuador, SENAE 2016 207

Contributors

Sara Calvo is the co-founder of Minca Ventures Ltd. She is also the Coordinator of the Master in International Development at Universidad Internacional de la Rioja (UNIR). She is a certified coach and a social enterprise business consultant, with research experience in the field of social innovation, social enterprise and the social and solidarity economy. She has provided consultancy services for a wide range of organisations worldwide. She has been principal researcher for a variety of international research funding projects (e.g. British Council and Newton Fund) in Africa, Asia, Europe and Latin America.

Andrés Morales is the co-founder of Minca Ventures Ltd, a company that supports organisations that are interested in creating impact through education, training, consultancy and coaching. Andres is currently working as an Assistant Professor at Universidad Internacional de la Rioja. He has a wide experience working in leadership positions in social enterprises as well as a social enterprise consultant in several European, African, Asian and Latin American countries. Andres has also experience researching about social enterprise and social and solidarity economy in the Global South. He has a wide experience managing international projects for social impact in Africa, Asia, Europe and Latin America.

José Carlos Soldevilla Saavedra is an urban mobility specialist who has a balanced professional trajectory between technical practice and academic research. Having developed his experience between Asia, Latin America and Europe, he has focused on sustainable development from his architecture background to his urbanism transport and mobility speciality, recognizing different contexts, focuses and approaches in order to preserve nature and social environments. He has also a balanced experience between the private and the public sector, from where he has participated in the development of infrastructure, systems and programs related to sustainability from his mobility interest: projects like the Great Paris Express Metro, events as The Panamerican and Para-Panamerican Games of Lima 2019 and researches such as the development of a high-capacity surface tramway. Concentrating his efforts on urban planning and the public sector in Peru, he is now Planning co-deputy on the Urban Transport Authority for Lima and Callao in his homeland.

Karol Gil Vasquez was born in Mexico City. In the United States, she obtained her Masters in Sociology from the University of Central Missouri and PhD in Economics from the University of Missouri-Kansas City (UMKC). During her doctoral studies, Karol worked as a researcher for the UMKC's Institute for Human Development and participated in several projects related to immigration and community development. Upon graduation, Karol began her academic career at Nichols College as a professor of economics and finance in 2013. Her passion is research, which includes interdisciplinary topics related to Latin America-Middle Eastern studies, post-colonial studies, solidary economics, economic history of monetary systems, immigration, and the political economy of violence and crime. Her scholarly work has been presented around the world and published in books, academic journals and newspapers. In January 2019, the article titled "Bolivia's Institutional Transformation: Contact Zones, Social Movements and the Emergence of an Ethnic Class Consciousness" received the Editor's Prize for the best article published by the Journal of Economic Issues.

Louisa Ashley is Head of Law (Postgraduate) at Leeds Law School, Leeds Beckett University, with a professional background in legal practice and devised theatre. She is a solicitor of the Supreme Court of England and Wales (non-practising) who trained and then practised as an employment lawyer at a large corporate law firm in Leeds. Louisa's research interests include international human rights, equality law and labour law. Before becoming a lawyer, Louisa was one of the founders of award-winning UK based Unlimited Theatre. During her time with Unlimited Theatre, Louisa designed and delivered a variety of community arts projects, as well as devising and performing theatre for children and adults, funded by a variety of bodies including the National Lottery and the Arts Council. Louisa is a qualified coach and mentor and is also a poet who enjoys performing her poetry at festivals, events and open mic nights.

Roberto Cañedo Villarreal is the president of the Centre International de Recherches et d'Information sur l'Economie Publique, Sociale et Coopérative (CIRIEC), Mexico Chapter, Coordinator of the Master in Social Economy of the Universidad Autónoma de Guerrero (UAGro), member of the Governing Board from the Consejo de Ciencia y Tecnología del estado de Guerrero (COCYTIEG), and from the Register of researchers from the state of Guerrero and the

Node to Promote the Social and Solidarity Economy certified by the Instituto Nacional de la Economía Social (INAES). He is also a certified consultant for small and medium-sized enterprises (SMEs) of the Ministry of the Economy, both in standard consultancy and JICA, as well as in the formulation and evaluation of rural production projects and the training of trainers by the National Council for Standardization and Certification of Labor Competencies (CONOCER), member of different editorial boards of scientific journals and of different research bodies, both national and international.

María del Carmen Barragán Mendoza is a member of the scientific commissions of the Centre International de Recherches et d'Information sur l'Economie Publique, Sociale et Coopérative (CIRIEC), Mexico Chapter, coordinator of the research area and collaborator of the planning area at the Faculty of Economy of the Universidad Autónoma de Guerrero (UAGro), Coordinator of Tutors and Advisors of the Basic Academic Nucleus of the Master in Social Economy of the UAGro, member of the Register of researchers by the Consejo de Ciencia y Tecnología del estado de Guerrero (COCYTIEG) and of the Node to Promote Social and Solidarity Economy certified by the Instituto Nacional de la Economía Social (INAES). She is a member of different research bodies, both national and international, and participant in different scientific articles.

Daniel Francisco Nagao Menezes has a Law Degree (PUC-Campinas), Specializations in Constitutional Law and Civil Procedural Law (PUC-Campinas), in Didactics and Pedagogical Practice in Higher Education (Centro Universitário Padre Anchieta), Master and Doctor in Political and Economic Law (Universidade Presbiteriana Mackenzie)), Post-Doctor of Law (USP) and Post-Doctorate in Economics (UNESP-Araraquara). He is Professor of the Graduate Program in Political and Economic Law at the Mackenzie University School of Law and Member of CIRIEC-Brazil.

Mario Cadena López is a Senior Specialist in Social Management who has followed the process of the Salinas cooperative in Guaranda, Bolívar, province in Ecuador. He is involved in one of the salt entities, the Community Rural Cheese Makers Consortium Foundation, FUNCONQUERUCOM, where he has been President and is currently Vice President. He has worked in Rural Development as part of the Ecuadorian Populorum Progressio Fund, FEPP, acting as Livestock Technician, Regional Coordinator and National Deputy Director. In Popular and Solidarity Economy and Finance, he has been a founding member and director of the People's Development Savings and Credit Cooperative, now a bank (BANCODESARROLLO). He has also served as Executive Director of the National Network of Popular and Solidarity Finance of Ecuador, RENAFIPSE.

Fabián Vargas Chamorro is an entrepreneur, professional in Mechanical Engineering from the Polytechnic School of the Army and technician in agribusiness. He has 20 years of experience in rural development, productive linkages, popular and solidarity economy; experience in the private sector in the management of development projects and MSMEs (micro, small and medium enterprises) and experience in the public sector in management and technical advice. At present, he is involved in the executive direction of the Community Rural Cheese Makers Consortium Foundation, FUNCONQUERUCOM, which is part of the Gruppo - Salinas - Salinerito Corporation.

Jordi Peris Blanes is an Associate Professor at the Engineering Projects Department of the Universitat Politécnica de Valencia (UPV) and researcher at INGENIO. His research has been published in journals such as Habitat International, Sustainable Development, Journal of Urban and Regional Research, International Development Planning Review, Journal of International Development, Sustainability or Urban Transformations. He has been 2nd Deputy Major of the City Council of Valencia and councillor of citizens participation, innovation and climate change. Currently, he is the General Coordinator of Urban Strategies and Sustainability Agenda at the Major's Office of the City Council of Valencia.

Nancy Sarabia Mondaca is a researcher at INGENIO (CSIC-Universitat Politècnica de València) on issues of agri-food transition towards a new paradigm of sustainability. She holds a Master in Territorial Rural Development from the University of Cordoba in Spain, Degree in Veterinary Medicine from the University of Chile and Diploma in Agroecology from the Center for Technological Education in Chile. She has work experience of 15 years with rural families and indigenous communities in Chile, through the management and planning of government programs and local development projects (organizational, environmental and productive), focused on institutional coordination, technology transfer and project development.

Marietta Bucheli Gómez is a Business Administrator and Master in Rural Development from the Pontificia Universidad Javeriana and PhD in Administration from the University of Sherbrooke, Canada. She is a teacher with more than 20 years of experience in the Faculty of Rural and Environmental Studies. She has also been a visiting professor at the Université de Toulouse, France. She is a member of the Board of Directors of Ciriec, Colombia, Director of doctoral and post-doctoral theses in Colombia, Mexico and France and Editor of Booklets on Rural Develpment (Editora Cuadernos de Desarrollo

Rural). She is the author of dozens of articles and publications. She is currently Director of the Institute for Rural Studies at the Faculty of Environmental and Rural Studies of the Pontificia Universidad Javeriana.

Juan Fernando Álvarez is an economist from Universidad de los Andes (Venezuela), Specialist in Social Evaluation of Projects from University los Andes (Colombia), Master in Social Economy and Management of non-profit entities from the University of Barcelona (Spain) and Doctor in Social Sciences from the University of Lisbon. He is president of the Scientific Committee of CIRIEC-Colombia and author of studies published in editorials and magazines in Spain, Ecuador, Argentina, Belgium, Venezuela and Colombia. He is currently a full-time professor at the Faculty of Environmental and Rural Studies of the Pontificia Universidad Javeriana and director of his area of study in "Transformational Organizational Ecosystems".

Ana Milena Silva Valencia has a PhD in Business Management from the University of Valencia. She is Quality auditor with experience in constitution, entrepreneurship and strengthening of social and solidarity economy companies. She was part of the IDB-Bogotá Chamber of Commerce consultants' network on CSR. She is an Assistant Professor at ICESI. She leads several projects at the Univalle Foundation. She is Member of the CIRIEC-COLOMBIA Board of Directors and the network of researchers on solidarity economy UNICOSOL.

César Marcillo is an economist and specialist in Commerce and International Marketing who leads the Program "Solidarity Economy" of the Solidarity Observatory and The Cooperatives Training Area at University UTE, a Fair-Trade Latin American University in Ecuador. He is author of books in Spanish "Economía Solidaria", "Vive Comercio Justo", as well as articles in prestigious journals. He has trained in this field around 200 people including cooperatives executive leaders and college Teachers. He is a cofounder of Latin American Network of Universities for Fair Trade and of the National and Local Committees for Fair Trade in Quito. He is a keynote speaker, researcher and an official representative at the national and international levels. He actively makes proposals and participates in analysis for public policies with public institutions and organizations dealing with The Popular Economy of Solidarity.

Jaime Ramiro Figueroa Fraga is a professional in the area of foreign trade, with a specialty in Strategic Planning and Management. He is a former public servant at the service of control and surveillance activities in the National Customs Service of Ecuador and ex official of the Municipality of the Metropolitan District of Quito in the administrative direction. Currently, he holds the Chair at the UTE University in the subjects Social and Solidarity Economy, with issues of fair trade and responsible consumption; International Business Environment. In the academic management area, he is the Director and support teacher in multidisciplinary bonding projects of connection with society, in execution until 2022.

Laura Angélica De La Cruz Guerrero is a Professor at "Universidad UTE" where she lectures chairs related to the legal field of customs and foreign trade. She provided her services, for more than 18 years, at the National Customs Service of Ecuador - SENAE. Also, she was a consultant for companies offering her services in topics related to international merchandise traffic. She participated as a lecturer in a Master program at "Universidad Central" of Ecuador, teaching the chair of Customs Taxation. She develops research activities in the Faculty of Administrative Sciences with publications of scientific articles. In addition, she has participated as a speaker at the Ninth RACNI Congress of International Business in Nicaragua.

Foreword

Valentin Molina Moreno

I have been invited to humbly reflect on the contents of this interesting research work where eminent connoisseurs of the reality of the economy and social innovation have participated at a time when the majority of stakeholders and representative organizations of different economic sectors are aware that it is necessary to incorporate new instruments, methodologies, ideas so that our economic model of linear economy transitions towards a new paradigm where the production and provision of goods and services occurs on the one hand generating fewer negative externalities from the environmental and social point of view and on the other hand helps to generate a better distribution of wealth, enabling a new macroeconomic approach where efficiency and effectiveness in the use of productive resources should be a priority to tackle serious environmental problems and social issues currently our species is suffering from while prioritizing the sustainable development goals that have been set by the United Nations.

This book provides us with excellent information, data and ideas that are fundamental for those of us who believe that it is possible to improve the quality of life of citizens in Latin America and that incorporating social innovation as a transversal instrument in the design of public policies is possible to generate new spaces for the creation of capital and human wealth in the 21st century. Now more than ever, new contributions are necessary and the proposition that the social economy must also be understood as an economy that provides knowledge, experience and know-how so that it is restorative, regenerative and cohesive, contributing to generate a new sustainable economic model in the field. This has been established by both the UN millennium goals and the new 17 SDGs with the proposals of the 25 summits against climate change.

The case studies contained in this great academic work are a good reference that ideas and new philosophies can be carried out, which understands that there is a great interconnection between environmental, social and economic aspects that any action that aims to raise new Development models must internalize these three dimensions under the paradigm of the social economy that has always opted for the valorization of endogenous resources and the valorization of the value of human resources in rural areas.

Social innovation should not be just a specific idea and a specific action. It should be internalized as an instrument that helps to generate changes in a society and on a planet that now more than ever needs to be incorporated to face new challenges and solve structural problems that we continue to have. For this reason, I hope that this book will help us to think and consider what we can contribute from our different areas of academic knowledge and professional experience so that together we can generate a more caring, fair and sustainable society for both our generation and future generations.

This book aims to give the reader an idea of the relevance of social innovation to maintain and restore social and natural capital in Latin America. Using case studies from Ecuador, Colombia, Peru, and Mexico, this book provides insight into the interactions between social innovation and natural and social capital in Latin America. This book grew out of a Newton Fund project where researchers from Latin America and the United Kingdom met and discussed during four intensive days in Colombia about the role of social innovation in maintaining and restoring social and natural capital in Latin America.

Prof. Valentin Molina Moreno,
Expert in Social Innovation,
University of Granada

Introduction

The Latin American continent has an incredibly rich diversity from which humans derive a range of ecosystem services (e.g. material goods, cultural benefits, climate regulation, etc.) that contribute to livelihoods and well-being. It has thus become critical to reconcile social and environmental issues in the region to ensure that development is sustainable and aligned with the Sustainable Development Goals.

To ensure the sustainable use and management of social and natural capital in the region, business, government, social enterprises and NGOs are engaging in different forms of social innovation that account for social, ecological and environmental values. This requires the integration of social and natural capital into decision-making at all levels. Latin America presents a useful scenario to explore social innovation in relation to social and environmental values and the management of local human and natural resources. This book presents social innovation initiatives that incorporate social and natural capital into decision-making processes in Latin America.

Social Innovation and Social and Natural Capital: Connecting the Dots

Social innovation encompasses new social practices that drive social change. Social innovation is a reaction to societal problems that governments have failed to tackle, such as poverty, poor health care and education (Domanski et al., 2017). While economic growth contributed to lower poverty rates in some areas, growth did not improve inequality in Latin America, which still has the widest income inequality globally. Thus, social innovation provides the chance for beneficiaries to be active participants in their development, as opposed to passive citizens that rely on top-down paternalistic strategies of developers from the Global North. Whilst social innovation is growing, barriers are also expanding; for example, resources, technical assistance and government assistance are often lacking. In order for social innovation to advance further, social innovation ecosystems need to be facilitated by involving individuals from civil society, academia, the economy and the government.

Social innovation offers an alternative to the dominant neoliberal development model through its promotion of citizen participation and the engagement of both private and public sectors. As Carrasco et al. (2018) argued, social innovation offers a potential *sustainable* resolution for societal problems in Latin America. In their view, success of social innovation is determined by the engagement of the communities involved and as a possibility to restore and maintain social and natural capital in the region.

Social capital can be defined as trust, participation, reciprocity, civic activities and volunteering (Agudelo et al., 2018). According to Emmelin et al. (2018), social capital is a "public non-exclusive good". They establish that the benefits can overflow to reach those who socially participate less or not at all and those at the lower end of the social chain. They find that social capital can have a moderating impact on the correlation between socioeconomic status and health – for example, increased social capital tends to decrease stress levels regardless of socioeconomic position. They also highlight that social capital can have structural impacts, such as enhancing democracy and social inclusion. Contreras et al. (2019) highlight the links between social capital and labour circumstances, such as job satisfaction, prestige and income. They find that social capital tends to facilitate better outcomes in Chile and that network heterogeneity is positively linked to status attainment. By contrast, Puga and Soto (2018) establish that social capital is not an accurate predictor of whether women engage in paid work in Chile. From their perspective, promoting social capital to empower women is flawed as there are more significant factors, such as family roles, wage inequality, childcare, and so on, which need to be addressed first. They find that focusing on social capital diverts attention from more important factors and places responsibility for their exclusion with individuals.

In Colombia, violence has eroded social capital. They found that internally displaced people overcame community challenges, such as a lack of basic services, through cooperative action. The authors measured abilities associated with social capital, such as the capacity to control aggression. They found that dance therapies increase social capital. They, therefore, recommend the use of trauma-informed dance projects in vulnerable communities.

Rubio (2018) identifies that social capital is key to providing support for citizens of developing countries in adverse circumstances as state support tends to be limited. Her research demonstrates that social capital is correlated with better provision of communal goods and an enhanced fiscal, governance and entrepreneurship performance. Violence negatively impacts trust and participation levels and thereby erodes social capital.

She suggests the policy implications of this are that physical and human as well as social capital need to be restored in conflict affected zones, such as Colombia.

Natural capital is a way of thinking about nature as a stock that provides a flow of benefits to people and the economy. Guerry et al. (2015) find that including natural capital is essential in governance systems to achieve sustainable consumption levels, maintain life-support systems and end poverty – current systems are not up to the challenge. Gaiger et al. (2019) highlight the abundance of natural resources in Latin America. They suggest the divergence between the wealth of natural resources and the lack of diversification of production in the region. From their perspective, the availability of natural capital represents the potential to progress towards social justice and sustainable development. They believe social enterprises are key to achieving this progress. Across Latin America, water projects are being established and developed to improve water quality and quantity. They assert that there is a need for governments, businesses and civil society to cooperate. Private short-term objectives need to align with long-lasting societal objectives.

Perez et al. (2018) contend that inequality in access to natural capital in Latin America needs to be recognised to prevent interventions exacerbating them. For sustainable governance of natural capital, instruments need to be enhanced and focus on decreasing the inequality in access to benefits of ecosystems. They find that increasing public awareness is essential for promoting and legitimizing public policies targeted at lessening these inequalities. Banerjee et al. (2016) stress the importance of protecting natural capital for sustainable development. They contend that over recent years, Latin America has made progress in environmental sustainability issues by increasing citizen awareness and establishing institutional and legal frameworks. Yet, natural capital continues to deteriorate, such as the health of forests, biodiversity and coastal-marine ecosystems. They deny that economic development and environmental protection are mutually exclusive.

They highlight the taxes introduced on wastewater discharge in Colombia as a demonstration that authorities and companies can be incentivized to take effective action. They find that public information campaigns regarding air pollution have helped to reduce human exposure. They illustrate the interdependence of local communities on ecosystems that they maintain and that provide their livelihood sources. They point out the most marginalized populations are the most vulnerable to environmental degradation and natural disasters, signaling the need for environmental management that is socially inclusive and involves local empowerment. They find that environmental performance in Latin American is still below international standards and thus increases in public and private environmental investment should be prioritised.

Rich history of solidarity in South America is rooted in indigenous populations. Some indigenous populations maintain their ways of life, but this often results in marginalisation and poverty. We have seen in recent years different communities across Latin America seeking alternative ways to live. We believe that social innovation is a potential way of achieving an ecologically conscious and more socio-economically just system.

Structure of the Book

Following the introduction, the volume is divided in three parts. The first part of the volume (Chapters 1 and 2) introduces the conceptual frameworks to understand social innovation and natural and social capital in Latin America. The second part of the volume (Chapters 3–6) focuses on case studies connected to natural capital and social innovation in Latin America. Finally, the third part (Chapters 7–10) explores social capital and social innovation in the region.

In the first part of the volume, in Chapter 1, Andrés Morales and Sara Calvo present the Buen Vivir (BV) theory. The emergence and rationale of BV are explained, where the authors elaborate on the BV reasoning by employing the work of Cubillo-Guevara et al. (2014) and Hidalgo-Capitán and Cubillo-Guevara (2016, 2017), who identified the three traditions that influence the present concept of BV: (i) the indigenist approach, (ii) the socialist/statist approach, and (iii) the ecologist/developmentalist approach. Moreover, the authors identify the BV values and pillars based on an extensive and in-depth review of more than 300 bibliographical references of the BV's literature. Examples of Latin American countries (e.g. Ecuador and Bolivia) are invoked throughout the chapter to depict the advancements in the BV implementation. Later, the chapter discusses the main BV criticisms (Bretón, 2013; Caria and Domínguez, 2016; Correa, 2008, 2007; Esteva, 1992; Lalander, 2016; Stefanoni, 2010). Finally, a concluded BV's model is suggested based on the identified *values* and *pillars*.

In Chapter 2, Louisa Ashley considers the extent to which the Universal Periodic Review (UPR) aides the creation of a Third Space; via joint submissions to the UPR, individual civil society organisations coalesce to define and strengthen a collective voice. The UPR thus operates to support civil society recommendations regarding development, the environment and land rights via their adoption and validation on an international stage. However, the number of UPR recommendations regarding land rights is low; in 2018, Colombia received only 15 land rights recommendations out of a total of 279. This chapter concludes that the UPR's potential to support a Third Space in pursuit of the protection of land rights, and by association natural capital and biodiversity.

The second part of the volume begins with Chapter 3, where José Carlos Soldevila Saavedra discusses about the regulation of the emissions from the vehicle fleet in Peru. The approach that he raises is that the private sector can exercise its social responsibility, with an environmental focus, in public transport, managed and/or regulated by the public sector where civil society converges in its basic need to move towards its work centers, educational, among others. Under this approach, the development of strategies that link the three actors within the basic need of all, daily displacement, applied strategies on the three fronts mentioned initially: use of sustainable vehicles, traffic regulation with priority to sustainable transport is proposed, and awareness campaigns on vehicles with all the infrastructure related to public transport.

In Chapter 4, Karol Gil-Vazquez presents insights into the specific measures developed by the *p'urepechas* over the last years to successfully deter the presence of organized crime, enhance environmental conservation, and re-install the rule of law based on UN's 169 Convention on Indigenous and Tribal Peoples. In 2006, under the auspices of the Merida Initiative, the Mexican Government declared the War on Drugs. Over more than ten years, the measure generated a crisis of public insecurity across the country's regions. A situation that compromises political and economic stability in addition to environmental conservation. The ongoing conflict threatens the sustainability of marginalized municipalities, including rural indigenous communities that confront the illegal exploitation of natural resources. Nonetheless, some rural indigenous communities stand still to the challenges brought by Mexico's War on Drugs. Despite their disadvantaged positions, they have effectively innovated strategies to ensure public safety and environmental conservation. Located in the western state of Michoacán, the rural-indigenous municipality of Cheran presents a lucid illustration of this phenomenon. Based on qualitative data, this chapter analyzes the strategies and programs implemented at the community level to cope with public insecurity and environmental exploitation, shedding light on the measures taken to prevent timber deforestation, which represents Cheran's primordial economic activity.

In Chapter 5, the authors, Mario Cadena and Fabián Vargas, present the case of Salinas de Guaranda in Ecuador, a project that has enhanced sustainable innovation. Salinas process demonstrates that peasant communities are characterized by marginalization and abandonment by the State; they live in general conditions of high precariousness. They can achieve positive changes in their way of life, strengthening their identity based on the principles, values and methods of work, born from their own experiences of solidarity, combined and enriched with the practice of cooperativism, more specific, of the social and solidarity economy, having as outstanding elements of this identity path, the peasant effort and its openness towards innovation. The innovation is an outstanding component of Salinas identity evidenced in the community organizations and in family initiatives better known as Productive Economic Units.

In Chapter 6, Nancy Sarabia and Jordi Peris present a theoretical review of the Chilean agro-food system, using the theoretical framework of studies on transitions to sustainability. It allows a holistic approach to understanding complex problems. The multi-level perspective (MLP) framework is used to structure the chapter, describing the foodscape, the established regime and the emerging niches addressing different global controversies and challenges. Along the chapter, some disruptive and innovative niche initiatives are analyzed. On the one side, the Food Labelling and Advertising Act has been in force since 2016. It mandates a warning on the labelling of products according to their saturation of fat, calories, sugar or sodium, along with a ban on advertising unhealthy foods to children. These standards contribute to the democratization of decision-making and food purchasing and production behaviour. On the other, there is the important increase of collective disruptive initiatives that are framed under the concept of Social Solidarity Economies (SSE). They are related to contemporary global movements of responsible consumption, agro-ecological production, food sovereignty, circular economy and the common good. SSE are born from social movements responding to the social, economic and environmental needs of the agri-food system.

In the third part of the volume, in Chapter 7, Marietta Buchelli and Juan Fernando Alvárez show how some transformative organizational ecosystems define response strategies to the challenges of society in Colombia-nature relationship expressed in the Encyclical Laudato Si. The Magna Carta offers alternatives of action for this relationship to face the ecological state of the world. The responsibility for the causes of a planet in crisis is in debate: who are responsible? Laudato Si advocates a collective responsibility based on a change of culture and knowledge, emphasizes the local actor and goes to an alternative economy to protect the common house. To observe the response strategies to these debates, the practices followed by some solidarity organizations in Colombia based in rural areas are presented. The results show, on the one hand, endogenous and autonomous practices that have had an impact on the reconstruction of a territory and a concept of territory within the context of the armed conflict. On the other hand, the exogenous commitment of public organizations to achieve local development is evident, but with dire results. The chapter also demonstrates the endogenous reaction to this situation by local actors. Both perspectives are analyzed taking as reference the guidelines indicated by the Laudato Si, the debate about the social economy and the territory. It ends with the interpretation of management alternatives to support the common house built from local actors.

In Chapter 8, Roberto Cañedo Villarreal, María del Carmen Barragán Mendoza and Daniel Francisco Nagao Menezes show the gap between the theory and practice of the cooperativism in Latin America. They start from the philosophy of being sources (with a Heidegger perspective and the epistemology of the south), in particular looking at what solidary means in the cooperative sector. An argued dissertation of what is being, the human being and the cooperative being was made; a research instrument was created (a questionnaire) and semi-structured interviews were done in cooperatives from Campinas city, São Paulo and Manaus in the Amazonas. They were made by cooperativism experts and cooperative members of these regions *in situ*. Also, non-structured interviews were done in Pereira, Colombia, with experts from different countries. After processing the collected data, a text analysis with a phenomenological view was made and from that some findings are obtained: 1) There is a big gap between philosophical foundation of solidarity, with the cooperativism mainly, and the daily praxis of this social development perspective and 2) in case of the practical problems of the cooperative productive process, there may need of professional technical and financial assistance for the creation of new projects or for the support in the consolidation process, but there are deeper problems, of a philosophical and ideological matter, which shape the future of the company.

In Chapter 9, Ana Milena Silva explores the concept of entrepreneurship or entrepreneurs when forming social organizations during peace dialogues in Colombia, which began in 2012 between Colombian National Government and the FARC (Colombian Revolutionary Armed Forces). These dialogues took place in Oslo, Norway and Havana, Cuba. In this context, she identified social enterprises that were formally established as of 2012, which are initiatives of people who undertook or created processes for the benefit of a community, or of a group of people who came together to satisfy their individual needs collectively and generate sources of income, employment and work by producing some good or service. The empirical test was carried out in a sample of rural cooperatives in Colombia, using a research methodology with a quantitative approach, in which the Multiple Regression Analysis was used.

Finally, in Chapter 10, César Augusto Marcillo Vaca, Laura Angélica De La Cruz Guerrero and Jaime Ramiro Figueroa Fraga explore fair trade in Quito, Ecuador. They argue that fair trade has been the result of the efforts of the small producers' associations of more than 40 years in spite of their limitations of instruction. This development is framed in a context of local and indigenous social organizations, the support of the Catholic Church and the international non-governmental organizations. It has been without state support. It began the journey facing the great world trade dominated by the transnationals. The result of this was the construction of a model of own development fruit of a long learning process and organization that under factor Cs (cooperation, companionship, collaboration, communication, quality, camaraderie, community, etc.) promoted the actions of these solidarity organizations. Quito, one of the thousands of cities recognized for its support for fair trade, concentrates and becomes a standard bearer of this movement in Ecuador. Through a permanent campaign, it brings together national and international producers, marketers and consumers. The biggest challenge, facing the future, is the creation of networks of responsible consumers: ethical, ecological and supportive.

Research Implications and Future Research

There are limited studies that explore social innovation for maintaining and restoring social and natural capital in Latin America. Therefore, the main objective of the chapters featured in this volume is to illustrate with case studies this phenomenon in the region. The studies presented in this book adopted a multi-disciplinary approach and applied both theoretical and empirical analyses to delineate the capacities of social innovation projects in Peru, Mexico, Colombia and Ecuador. Indeed, the present volume documents a number of cases in which social innovation projects have been able to maintain and restore social and natural capital in their neighborhood and communities. However, the volume also discusses the obstacles and lost opportunities faced by these initiatives due to both external and internal factors in different spatial and historical contexts. Some questions for future research may include:

1. What does social innovation provide?
2. What are the potentialities and limits?
3. How can social innovation contribute to the development of natural and human capital in the Latin American region?
4. What strategies and policies have to be implemented in order to enable social innovations to access the natural and social factors they need to flourish?

References

Agudelo, D. M., Gomez, Y., Lopez, M. A., Martinez, G. and Quinones, N., 2018. Dance movement strategies training to help rebuild social capital in Colombia. *Journal of Mental Health and Psychosocial Support in Conflict Affected Areas*, *16*(2): 110–118.

Banerjee, O., Cotta, J., Corderi, D., Lopez, J. L., Perazza, M. C., Quiroga, R. and Watkins, G., 2016. *Environment and Biodiversity: Priorities for Protecting Natural Capital and Competitiveness in Latin America and the Caribbean.* Washington DC: Inter-American Development Bank.

Bretón, V., 2013. Etnicidad, desarrollo y 'Buen Vivir': Reflexiones Críticas en

Perspectiva Histórica. *Revista Europea de Estudios Latinoamericanos y del Caribe*, *95*(1): 71–95.
Caria, S., Domínguez, R., 2016. Ecuador's Buen Vivir: A New Ideology for Development. *Latin American Perspectives*, *43*(1): 18–33.
Carrasco, G., Ferreira Dias, M., Galego, D., Marlene, A, and Waldo, S., 2018. Embedding Social Innovation in Latin America Academic Curriculum. *4th International Conference on Higher Education Advances*. Valencia: Universitat Politecnica de Valencia.
Cohen, F., Hepburn, C. and Teytelboym, A., 2019. Is natural capital really substitutable? *The Annual Review of Environment and Resources*, *44*(1): 425–448.
Contreras, D., Diaz, J. D., Otero, G. and Suarez, N., 2019. Inequality in social capital in Chile: Assessing the importance of network size and contacts' occupational prestige on status attainment. *Social Networks*, *58*(1): 59–77.
Correa, R., 2007. *Discurso del Presidente de la República, Rafael Correa, sobre el Levantamiento en Dayuma. Orellana* , *1*.
Correa, R., 2008. *Discurso del Presidente de la República, Rafael Correa, pronunciado en la ceremonia de clausura de la Asamblea Constituyente. Ciudad Alfaro*, *25*.
Cubillo-Guevara, A. P., Hidalgo-Capitán, A. L., and Domínguez-Gómez, J. A., 2014. El pensamiento sobre el Buen Vivir: Entre el Indigenismo, el S ocialismo y el Posdesarrollismo. *Revista del CLAD Reforma y Democracia*, *11*(1): 1–35.
Domanski, D., Howaldt, J. Huenchuleo, C. and Villalobos, P., 2015. *Social Innovation in Latin America: The Chilean Case*. Santiago: Cieplan.
Domanski, D., Howaldt, J. and Schroder, A., 2017. Social innovation in Latin America. *Journal of Human Development and Capabilities*, *18*(2): 307–312.
Emmelin, M., Stafstrom, M. and Vincens, N., 2018. Social capital, income inequality and the social gradient in self-rated health in Latin America: A fixed effects analysis. *Social Science & Medicine*, *196*(1): 115–122.
Esteva, G., 1992. Development, in the Development Dictionary. Wolfang Sachs (Ed.), *A Guide to Knowledge as Power*. London: ZED Books, pp. 2–26.
Gaiger, L. I., 2017. *The solidarity economy in South and North America: Converging experiences. Brasilian Political Science Review*, *11*(3).
Gaiger, L. I., Nyssens, M. and Wanderley, F., 2019. *Social Enterprise in Latin America*. New York: Routledge.
Goclowska-Bolek, J., 2015. Fostering Economic and Social Innovativeness to Address Development Challenges in Latin America. *Cracow University of Economics*. 11th International Conference of ASECU. Accessed 5th April. http://www.asecu.gr/files/11th_conf_files/asecu_2015_proceedings.pdf#page=201
Guerry et al., 2015. Natural capital and ecosystem services informing decisions: From promise to practice. *PNAS*, *112*(24): 7348–7355.
Guttmann, A., 2019. The social solidarity economy: Discerning its theory to accommodate the commons. *Review of Applied Socio-Economic Research*, *18*(2): 43–57.
Hunt, C. A. and Marcinek, A. A., 2015. Social capital, ecotourism, and empowerment in Shiripuno, Ecuador. *International Journal of Tourism Anthropology*, *4*(4): 327–342.
Hidalgo-Capitán, A. L., and Cubillo-Guevara, A. P., 2016. *Transmodernidad y*

Transdesarrollo: El Decrecimiento y el Buen Vivir como dos Versiones Análogas de un Transdesarrollo Transmoderno. Huelva, España: Ediciones Bonanza.

Lalander, R., 2016. The Ecuadorian resource dilemma: Sumak Kawsay or development? *Critical Sociology*, *42*(4–5): 623–642.

Leff, E., Porto-Goncalves and Walter, C., 2015. Political ecology in Latin America: The social re-appropriation of nature, the reinvention of territories and the construction of an environmental rationality. *Desenvolvimento e Meio Ambiente*, *35*(1): 65–88.

Hidalgo-Capitán, A. L., and Cubillo-Guevara, A. P., 2017. Deconstrucción y Genealogía del Buen Vivir Latinoamericano: El (trino) Buen Vivir y sus Diversos Manantiales Intelectual es. International Development Policy. *Revue internationale de politique de développement* 9(9): 45–66.

Perez, A. et al., 2018. Linking inequalities and ecosystem services in Latin America. *Ecosystem Services*, *36*(1): 1–14.

Puga, I. and Soto, D., 2018. Social capital and women's labor force participation in Chile. *Feminist Economics*, *24*(4): 131–158.

Rubio, M., 2018. *The Effect of Violence on Social Capital: Evidence from an Exogenous Variation in an Illegal Market*. Gothenburg: University of Gothenburg.

Saad-Filho, A., 2015. Social policy for neoliberalism: The Bolsa Familia Programme in Brazil. *Development and Change*, *46*(6): 1227–1252.

Stefanoni, P., 2010. *'Indianismo y Pachamamismo'*, *Rebellion*, 4 May 2010, [Online]. Available at http://www.rebelion.org/noticia.php?id=105233 (Accessed on 14 August 2018).

Veltmeyer, H., 2018. *The social economy in Latin America as alternative development. Canadian Journal of Development Studies*, *39*(1): 38–54. DOI: 10.1080/02255189.2017.1294052.

Part I

Conceptual frameworks to understand social innovation and natural and social capital in Latin America

1 Buen Vivir, a decolonial approach to development

Andrés Morales and Sara Calvo

Introduction

This chapter presents the Buen Vivir (BV) as a decolonial approach to development (Tödtling, 2010; Lowe et al., 1995; Vázquez-Barquero, 2003; Clarke, 2001; Laurie et al., 2005; N'Kaschama, 2012; Zuñiga, 1995; AIPPF, 2012; Giovannini, 2012; Tauli-Corpuz, 1996). BV emerges as a consequence of the failures of development and is built upon the objective to identify '*alternatives to development*', rather than '*development alternatives*', as a concrete possibility through ecological and cultural transitions (Escobar, 2015; Acosta, 2013; Gudynas, 2011). Then, the emergence and rationale of BV are explained, where the authors elaborate on the BV reasoning by employing the work of Cubillo-Guevara et al. (2014) and Hidalgo-Capitán and Cubillo-Guevara (2015, 2016), who identified the three traditions that influence the present concept of BV: (i) the *indigenist approach*, (ii) the *socialist/statist approach* and (iii) the *ecologist/developmentalist approach*.

Moreover, the authors identify the BV values and pillars based on an extensive and in-depth review of more than 300 bibliographical references of the BV's literature. Although there is no explicit evidence of the existence of values and pillars in the current literature, the authors identified them by cross-analysing the main intellectual referents of the BV thinking, mostly based on the work of Cubillo-Guevara et al. (2014), Hidalgo-Capitán and Cubillo-Guevara (2015, 2017) and Vanhulst (2015). Out of this analysis, three values, namely, (i) *community*, (ii) *solidarity and reciprocity* and (iii) *harmony and complementarity*, and six pillars, namely, (i) *rights of nature*, (ii) *community well-being*, (iii) *decolonisation*, (iv) *plurinational state*, (v) *economic pluralism* and (vi) *democratisation*, were identified. Examples of Ecuador and Bolivia are invoked throughout the chapter to depict the advancements in the BV implementation. Later, the chapter discusses the main BV criticisms (Bretón, 2013; Caria & Domínguez, 2016; Correa, 2007, 2008; Esteva, 1992; Lalander, 2016; Stefanoni, 2010, 2011). Finally, a concluded BV's model is suggested based on the identified *values* and *pillars* to understand natural and social capital in Latin America.

The tales of 'development': the failure of its implementations

Development is a concept that is still under discussion and subjected to the myriad and manifold definitions of it. As Cowen and Shenton (1996) suggested, development can be categorised as *immanent development (*the spontaneous *development* as in the historical trajectory of capitalism) and *intentional development (*attempts to improve material conditions in response to the consequences of immanent *development*, for example, poverty and unemployment) (*ibid*: viii-xiv). Their argument is constructed under the basis of its classical origin, by which *development* was understood as a natural process in which phases of renewal, expansion, contraction and decomposition followed each other sequentially according to a perpetually recurrent cycle (*ibid:* viii). With this in hand, *development* in the context of the '*developing*' or '*least developed*' world represents the dichotomy suggested by these scholars, the implementation of *development*'s recipes (intentional development) to encounter the negative outcomes of the natural cycle of *capitalism* (immanent development) to generates a sort of endless perverse *development* cycle.

According to Fukuyama (2001), *development* is strongly associated with economic *development* based on the increasing GDP per capita and is built upon different dimensions: i) *Economic Growth,* ii) *Social Mobilisation (*expressed in two forms *Civil Society* that represents the whole society and *Political Parties* that represent parts of the society) and iii) *Political Development* shaped by the *State, Rule of Law* and *Democracy*. His argument is elaborated based on the claim that *economic growth* nurtures *social mobilisation* as it creates change in society and that change generates different forms of social organisation that lead to the eventual *political development*. The point that Fukuyama makes is crucial for the later elaboration of BV. He argued that economic *development* is in essence the orthodox objective that most of the work in *development* is based on to reach the living standards and decrease societal needs (Friedman, 2000; Fukuyama, 2001; Rostow, 1952, 1960; Schumpeter, 1961; Warren, 1980). Although later works on *development* suggest that development cannot be only measured or led by economic growth, thus human development is subjected to other forms that may enable the improvement of societal living standards (Sen, 2000, 2001; Sen & Anand, 2000), the economy of the society is still an important feature to determine the *development* of humans to reach the individual/societal well-being. In spite the fact that orthodox *development* approaches move away from only economy-based recipes towards a more humane and sustainably oriented methodologies, the enhancement of the human well-being is directed and guided by a *development* agenda to readdress the failures of the immanent *development* cycles[1] (based on economy-based development theories influenced strongly by economic factors but with a sustainable ingredient, see more in Hettne, 1983). As can be seen, *development* is claimed to be a key determinant for societal progress manifested in the enhancement of living standards and therefore is a mechanism generator of human well-being. *Development* in both dimensions, theoretically as an assumption and empirically as an implemented framework, has been a subject of debates and studies.

Latin America (LA) scholars from the Modernity Coloniality Group (MCG) located in the Global South[2] (GS) claim that *development* is the legacy of *colonialism* and is considered the landmark to bring about the conditions necessary to replicate other worlds (or the 'civilised' world) over the features that characterised the 'advanced' societies (mainly from the Global North), high levels of industrialisation and urbanisation, industrialisation of agriculture, rapid growth of material production and living standards, media communication, technology and the widespread adoption of modern education and cultural values (Acosta, 2012, 2013; Albó, 2009; Escobar, 1992, 2000, 2004, 2012; Gudynas, 2011; Huanacuni, 2010; Lander, 2000; Mignolo, 2001, 2010, 2014a; Quijano, 2000, 2011). The MCG group of scholars evokes 'epistemic disobedience', analysing historical processes in the region and agreed that to create another paradigm it is necessary to create a new epistemological system built on ancestral/cultural ontologies (Walsh, 2012). They argue, in particular, for the need to be moving away from a hegemonic Eurocentric '*universe*' (unique thinking) towards what they call a 'pluriverse' world (acknowledging others' views to observe the planet). From this perspective, BV appears as a theoretical challenge to create another system of philosophical and ethical principles inspired by LA ancestral ontologies (Dussel, 2011; Mignolo, 2000).

It is claimed to be a western invention, indoctrinated and institutionally imposed during colonisation, and it can be seen as a conceptual regime of sets of implicit or explicit principles, norms, rules and decision-making procedures around which colonised actors' expectations converge in a given (mostly coercively) idea of how society should be and live (Acosta, 2012, 2013; Escobar, 2012; Mignolo, 2014a; Quijano, 2000). *Development* is as Acosta (2013: 68) puts it '*the lighthouse to warn, mark or guide society to reach the ideal world, avoiding dangerous coastlines, hazardous shoals or reefs of the 'uncivilised' world. Development is a modern concept imported during colonialism, subordinating the colonised regions*'. Similarly, but less symbolically, Escobar (2012) proposes to speak of *development* as a historical and singular experience, the creation of a domain of thought and action, constituted by: i) the forms of knowledge that refer to it (*theories*), ii) the system of power that regulates its practice (*institutions*) and iii) the symbolic archetype-generator *mechanism* (*developed versus underdeveloped/developing*).

As observed, in the current LA context, *development* is critically approached and heavily assessed and scrutinised by the regional scholars, practitioners, advocators and intellectuals in a post-development[3] scenario as a result of the *development's* failure on its implementation (Acosta, 2013). Some criticise *development* from an institutional point of view, in which a system of classification was created to legitimise western hegemony and reinforce hierarchical differences worldwide forged since colonialisation (international institutions such as the World Bank, the International Monetary Fund or the World Trade Organisation). The fact that international development indicators are established to classify countries as '*developed*', '*developing*' and '*least developing*' determined by a variety of factors (i.e. life expectancy, education level, GDP per capita and so on) demonstrates that a global hierarchy determinant is designed institutionally to marginalise one country to another and demonise those who are not meeting supposedly '*development*' living standards for human well-being (Acosta, 2012; Escobar, 2012; Gudynas, 2011). Others condemn *development* from an epistemic perspective and are calling for an epistemic disobedience, as they claim that there are other forms of colonisation (i.e. knowledge) and the 'ex-colonies' still are slaved and dominated by the colonisers.

There are other criticisms by intellectuals, activists and academics and that emerged out of grassroots organisations and social movements, which are very critical to *development* and its recipes claiming that these benefit the few and worsen the situation of the majority. One of the groups that is against *development* formulas in the LA region is the indigenous people. Natural resource exploitation and land expropriation and divestment for *development* projects have been a few of the many negative outcomes of *development* formulas. The majority of these groups claim for a more inclusive, local-oriented and sustainably performed *development* project implementation (Albó, 2009; Huanacuni, 2010; Pilataxi Lechón, 2014). Grassroots organisations and social movements led by indigenous, Afro-descendants and peasants refer to '*the crisis of western civilisation model*' as the root cause of the global social, economic and ecological crises, thus suggesting a more efficient and sustainably long-term change, in some cases the creation of a new civilizational project (Escobar, 2015; Mamani, 2006). Others suggest a more radical change for *development* and perceive *development* formulas as a threat to their communities and society in general, and the environmental and social struggles around extractivism (strategic tool for economic growth) have triggered off a more radical approach to encounter *development* (Svampa, 2012).

The reality in the region, suggested by the existing literature, is that there is a significant and substantial work about the possibility of a new *development* paradigm, and BV is an example of it. However, the emergence of new approaches in contradiction of the existing *development* frameworks is not exclusive of the LA region, nor in the GS; there is a wave of other forms of thinking that are also challenging and offering an amalgam of solutions to either substitute or enhance *development* formulas. For instance, *degrowth*[4] (Kallis et al., 2012; Martinez-Alier, 2002; Schneider et al., 2010), often associated with work on 'commoning' and the commons (see the work of Bollier, 2014; Bollier and Helfrich, 2012). Although ideas to rechannelling the *development* curse of society are proposed from both the Global North (GN) and Global South (GS), it seems that a profound bilateral conversation and the creation of a binary collateral participation are needed (see the work of Escobar, 2015), particularly with the attempting of breaking down the barriers between the GN and the GS in regard to *development* thinking.

Table 1.1 is designed to succinctly describe the main *development* theories to simplify the understanding of BV and how can be interpreted. Therefore, it is crucial for the elaboration of this thesis to ascertain BV within post-development studies produced in the GS, assuring that BV will be seen from an epistemic view generated, debated and discussed by *development* actors in the LA region. The authors rather to illustrate and debate about BV from a LA spectacles, as well as to position BV within post-development studies, embracing the fact that BV is presented as a post-development project as a consequence of *development* failure (Acosta, 2013; Escobar, 2012; Mignolo, 2001; Quijano, 2011). Table 1.1 is divided into three categories: *classic theories, emergent theories* and *transition theories* (TDs).

Table 1.1 collides in a simple radiograph of the *development* theory, the frameworks that *development* has set to provide a systematic solution to achieve human well-being and meet societal living standards. The paradigms within the category of *emergent development,* still valid and promulgated institutionally and politically by states and international institutions (i.e. the Millennium Development Goals by the United Nations), are considered an improvement of the *classic theories* category. These *development* frameworks propose a more inclusive, participative and sustainably oriented path to achieve human well-being. This category is located chronologically at the second stage, as it seems to propose an alternative pathway to achieve human well-being, but subjected to traditional *development* economic principles (economic growth to lead societal transformation but with a sustainable ingredient). Although *emergent theories* propose novelty ideas and offer a set of inclusive and sustainably oriented menu, they hardly challenge the root of the *development* failures (Acosta, 2013; Huanacuni, 2010; Pilataxi Lechón, 2014).

Table 1.1 Development Theory Radiography

Categories	*Classic Theories*					*Emergent Theories*				*Transition Discourses*	
Paradigm	Market-oriented	Modernisation	Neoliberal Development and Globalisation	Dependency Theories and World Systems	Human Development Theory	Sustainable Development	Endogenous vs Exogenous Development	Ethnodevelopment	Development Aggression	Degrowth	Post-development
Region[11]	GN	GN	GN	GN/GS	GN	GN	GN	GN/GS	GN/GS	GN	GS
Key Concepts	-Market -State -Economic Liberalism	-Society -Primitivism -Modernity -Economic Growth	-Free-Market -Neo-liberalism -Deregulation -Structural Adjustment Programs (SAPs)	-Post colonialism -Economic dependency - 'Developed', 'developing' and 'least developing'	-Human capabilities -Human freedom of choice	-Natural resources -Ecosystem services -Reduction of carbon foot print -SDGs	-Localism -Local-economies -Bottom-up approaches -Participatory processes	-Ethnicity -Ethnocide -Marginalisati- Marginalisation -Bottom-up -Ethnic values and culture	-Mining -Extractivism -Indigenous peoples	-Post-growth -Post-human -Ecology-oriented economics	-Non-liberal -Post-non-capitalist -Biocentric -Post-extractivist
Object of the Study	It assumes that the best economic consequences will result if are free by any form of governmental	It refers to a model of a progressive transition from a 'pre-modern' or 'traditional' or 'primitive'	It is associated with the laissez-faire economic liberation. It claims that a global free market will enable all the	The hierarchical relations between the 'developed' and the 'under-developed' world. Economic dependency	The expansion the of human capabilities, a widening of choices, 'an enhancement of	The study of an environmentally oriented economy	Endogenous development is based on local peoples' own criteria of development, and takes into account the	The countering ethnocide by enabling ethnic, minority, and/or exploited groups to revive values of their specific culture with	The study of development projects that violate indigenous peoples' human rights	Strategies for down-scaling of production and consumption	Construction of other form of thinking to challenge hegemonic development ideas spread out by the west

(*Continued*)

	constraint to make their own economic decisions	to a 'modern' society	countries of the world to prosper		freedom, and a fulfilment of human rights		material, social and spiritual well-being of peoples	a focus on strengthening their ability to resist exploitation and oppression				
References	(Friedman, 2000; Fukuyama, 2001; Rostow, 1952, 1960)	(Arat, 1988; Aya, 1978; Bernstein, 1971; Rostow, 1952, 1960; Weber, 2002)	(Friedman, 2000; Fukuyama, 2001; Lemaître and Helmsing, 2012; Springer et al., 2016)	(Amin, 1978; Baran, 1952, 1958; Cardoso & Falletto, 1979; Dos Santos, 1968; Harris, 1989; Kay, 1998; Prebisch, 1994; Wallerstein, 1974, 1989, 1989)	(Sen, 2001, 2001)	(Giddings et al., 2002; Hopwood et al., 2005; Smit and Pilifosova, 2003)	(Tödtling, 2010; Lowe et al., 1995; Vázquez-Barquero, 2003)	(Clarke, 2001; Laurie et al., 2005; N'Kaschama, 2012; Partridge et al., 1996)	(AIPPF, 2012; Gedicks, 2001; Giovanni-ni, 2012; Tauli-Corpuz, 1996)	(i.e. Kallis et al., 2012; Latouche, 2009; Martinez-Alier, 2002; Schneider et al., 2010)	(A. Acosta, 2013; A Escobar, 1992; Arturo Escobar, 2010, 2015; Lander, 2000; Mignolo, 2000)

Arguably paradigms such as *Endogenous versus Exogenous Development, Ethnodevelopment* and *Development Aggression* are contemplated as confrontational schemes that problematize *development* pitfalls; these are located in the second stage of *development* theory. These paradigms highlight other ways to pave *development* (inclusiveness, participation and sustainability) in contradiction to those suggested by the classic ones (market-oriented, free trade) (see the work of Giovannini, 2012), but do not suggest a paradigmatic shift of *development* as the TDs. While generally the TDs propose a more radical approach by seeking a transformational society based upon a paradigmatic shift moving away from economic-oriented frameworks, *emergent theories* advocate for an improvement of the economic practices (i.e. green or blue economy). The TDs are constituted by *degrowth* and *post-development* frameworks and are separate regionally (GN and GS). Drawing on Escobar's (2015, 2012, 2004) work, whilst in the GN, societal struggles are expressed in post-growth, post-materialist, post-economic, post-capitalist and post-human, those for the GS are expressed in terms of post-development, non-liberal, post/non-capitalist, biocentric and post-extractivist theories. That is why BV is located within the post-development frameworks. This theoretical framework is explained in detail in the following section.

From where Buen Vivir concept is emerging?

BV is inspired and influenced by the Andean '*cosmovision*' (worldview) of indigenous peoples in Latin America. In fact, *BV* is the Spanish language translation of *Sumak Kawsay* and *Suma Qamaña* in the *Quechua* and *Aymara* languages, respectively (Albó, 2009; Huanacuni, 2010). Both *Quechuas* and *Aymaras* are indigenous communities spread out over the whole Andean region. The *Quechuas* peoples are distributed in Peru, Ecuador, Bolivia, Argentina, Chile and Colombia and in the case of the *Aymaras* peoples, they live in Bolivia (*Aymara* is the second and most widely spoken language in the country), Peru, Chile and Argentina (Acosta, 2013; Albó, 2009; Huanacuni, 2010). Notably, although both indigenous communities are connected to the *Inca Empire*, *Aymara's* ancestors may be traced back in the region before becoming a subject people of the *Inca Empire* in the late 15th or early 16th century, and later of the Spanish in the 16th century (Acosta, 2012, 2013; Albó, 2009; Gudynas, 2011; Huanacuni, 2010). The legacy of the *Inca Empire* is manifested in the current ways that the *Quechuas* and *Aymaras* people (and other indigenous groups such as *Pastos* and *Yanaconas* in Colombia) are organised and operate (i.e. social structures shaped by hierarchies, in which everybody participates and is involved in practices such as *Minca*, *Ayni* or *Mita* as well as in the decision-making for the benefit of the whole community).

Interestingly, *Sumak Kawsay/Suma Qamaña* is not an exclusive object-oriented project of society. Table 1.2 depicts that there are many versions of *Sumak Kawsay/Suma Qamaña* within indigenous communities across the LA continent nurtured by their own *Cosmovisión*. For instance, in the south of the continent, the *Mapuche* in Chile and the *Kolla* in Argentina refer to it as *Kümen Mogen* and *Vivir Bien*, respectively. These two share views with the Quechuas and Aymara communities in relation to *nature community*, both nurture society and pave the way to reach societal well-being (Coraggio, 2011; Razeto, 2000). The *Guaraní*, one of the largest indigenous community in LA, spread out in Argentina, Bolivia, Brazil and Paraguay, identify the *Sumak Kawsay/ Suma Qamaña* as *Teko Kavi* in their own language, the well-being is subjected to the harmony of human beings with nature and the jungle (Santos, 2007). In the North of the region, the COICA (in Spanish, *Coordinadora de la Organizaciones Indigenas de la Cuenca Amazonica*) in the Amazons and the Maya in Mexico have also coincided with the Andean principles (Acosta, 2013; Pilataxi Lechón, 2014). It is important to point out that these indigenous communities have not been involved in the development processes described earlier in Table 1.1 with the exception of post-development theories which include the BV and that highlights the important role played by indigenous people traditions and cultural values.

BV echoes the *Sumak Kawsay/Suma Qamaña* principles of (i) *community*, (ii) *solidarity and reciprocity* and (iii) *harmony and complementarity*, principles that will be addressed later in this section (Acosta, 2013; Huanacuni, 2010; Pilataxi Lechón, 2014; Simbaña, 2012). Existing literature suggests that BV is considered within post-development theory and is a consequentialist project built upon Andean indigenous peoples (Escobar, 2010). Following the post-development approach, BV emerged out from what the authors call *development's fatigue*,[5] the evident *development* failure in the LA region, particularly the negative consequences of extractive projects (see the extensive works of Coraggio, 2011; Escobar, 2010; Razeto, 1984 about *development* and its pitfalls) and the interlinked connection with the environmental crises (see Gudynas, 2011; Martinez-Alier, 2002; Shiva, 2008) triggered off BV. Although BV advocates to re-flourish ancestral indigenous people's practices, particularly these related to the environmental care, it does also attempt to integrate (at least in its discourse) the struggle of other groups in the LA region, such as peasants, Afro-descendants, environmentalists, students, women and youth.

In practice, *BV* stems from the social periphery of the global periphery (Toledo, 2009 cited in Acosta, 2013). *BV* constitutes a new horizon of historical meaning, emerging from the long history of the indigenous resistance against the Eurocentric modern/colonial world system. As Acosta (2013) states, *BV* grew out of several decades of indigenous

Table 1.2 Sumak Kawsay/Suma Qamaña in other Latin American Indigenous Communities

Indigenous communities	*Mapuche*	*Aymara*	*Kichwa/quechua*	*Kolla*	*Coica*[6]	*Maya*	*Guaraní*
Country	Chile	Mostly Bolivia, but presence in Peru, Chile and Argentina	Mostly Ecuador but presence in Colombia, Bolivia Peru and Argentina	Argentina	Colombia, Peru, Ecuador, Brazil, Venezuela and Bolivia	Mostly Mexico and some presence in Belize	Argentina, Bolivia, Brazil and Paraguay
Terminology Used	Kümen Mogen	Suma Qamaña	Sumak Kawsay	Vivir Bien	Volver a la Maloka	Ronojerl K'o uchak upatan (RKU) and Ronojerl jastaq ki chapon kib' (RJCK)	Teko Kavi
Description	- A permanent relationship with nature - Harmony and balance with Mother Earth - Living without violence - Living with affection and empathy	Suma: fullness, sublime, superb, magnificent, beautiful Qamaña: live, live well, good life -Fullness of life -Live good	Sumak: fullness, sublime, superb, magnificent, beautiful, top Kawsay: life, be still - The process of the fullness of life	-Living in community -Living under the principles of harmony and balance -Growing with nature and not against it -'The human being is a land that goes'	-Return to ourselves -Value the ancestral knowledge -Live in harmony with the environment -Enjoy the feeling that links between the body and the spirit	(RKU): all have a role and a reason for being (RJCK): Ronojerl Jastaq ki chapon kib: all elements of the universe are connected and interconnected -To recognise that Earth is the mother, who give birth to life, feed us, shelters us, listens to us and take care of us	-Respect life -'You are right when you're well with nature, with the spirits, with the elderly, with children and with everything that is around you, that is to live well'

(*Continued*)

		-Know how to live -how to live. -Live in balance and harmony	- Life in material and spiritual balance -the sublime magnificence is expressed in harmony, in the internal and external balance of a community		-Protect our wisdoms, knowledge and sacred places -Community over individual -Live in a cyclical time of the great return, where the future is always behind	-The human being is an element of the universe	
Key References	(Razeto, 2000)	(Albó, 2009)	(Acosta, 2013; Huanacuni, 2010)	(Coraggio, 2011; Gudynas, 2011)	(Acosta, 2012, 2013)	(Pilataxi Lechón, 2014)	(Santos, 2007)

Source: Compiled by the authors.

struggles as they articulated with manifold social change agendas by peasants, Afro-descendants, environmentalists, students, women and youth. Thus, *BV* appears at this stage as an opportunity for the collective construction of a new form of living.

The conceptualisation of Buen Vivir

BV has been defined earlier in Chapter 1 as an ongoing project to build a different society sustained in the coexistence of human beings in their diversity and in harmony with oneself (identity), society (equity) and nature (sustainability), based on the recognition of the diverse cultural values existing in each country and worldwide (Acosta, 2013; Gudynas, 2011). In the attempt of building BV's concept, or at least making BV more understandable for this thesis, BV has been conceptualised in the work of Cubillo-Guevara et al. (2014) and Hidalgo-Capitán and Cubillo-Guevara (2015, 2017, 2016) with three traditions: (I) the indigenist approach, (II) the socialist/statist approach and (III) the ecologist/developmentalist approach (see Figure 1.1).

First, in the *indigenist* approach, the ancient indigenous thought is the core of the BV, particularly the thought of the Andean indigenous people. This tradition prioritises indigenous identity and aims for a more plural and inclusive society in which indigenous people legalise self-determination in their territories and propose a transformation from nation state to plurinational state (Dávalos, 2011; Huanacuni, 2010; Pilataxi Lechón, 2014; Simbaña, 2012). Indigenous people intellectuals, indigenous social movements and social actors/advocators/intellectuals that are sympathetic with the indigenous world are supporting this approach (Hidalgo-Capitán & Cubillo-Guevara, 2017). They advocate for the recreation of the life conditions of the *AbyaYala* people, a term which in the Kuna language means 'lands in its full maturity'. The term AbyaYala is used by those people in America to refer to their continent before the colonisation took place (Dávalos, 2011). This approach gives great importance to the self-determination of the indigenous peoples and proposes the conversion of the LA nation states into plurinational states. In fact, plurinationality is the ultimate purpose of the use they make of BV (Simbaña, 2012).

Second, in the *socialist/statist* approach, societal equity is prioritised and is strongly influenced by *neo-Marxism*. This tradition is led by the intellectuals involved in the institutionalisation of BV echoing indigenous ontologies in the countries of Ecuador and Bolivia (Coraggio, 2011, 1994; García-Linera, 2010; Ramírez-Gallegos, 2011, 2010; Santos, 2010). Through this revolutionary concept known as *citizen revolution* in Ecuador and as *democratic and cultural revolution* in Bolivia, these intellectuals propose to implement a new development model that essentially seeks to improve equity. This conception of BV has spread from

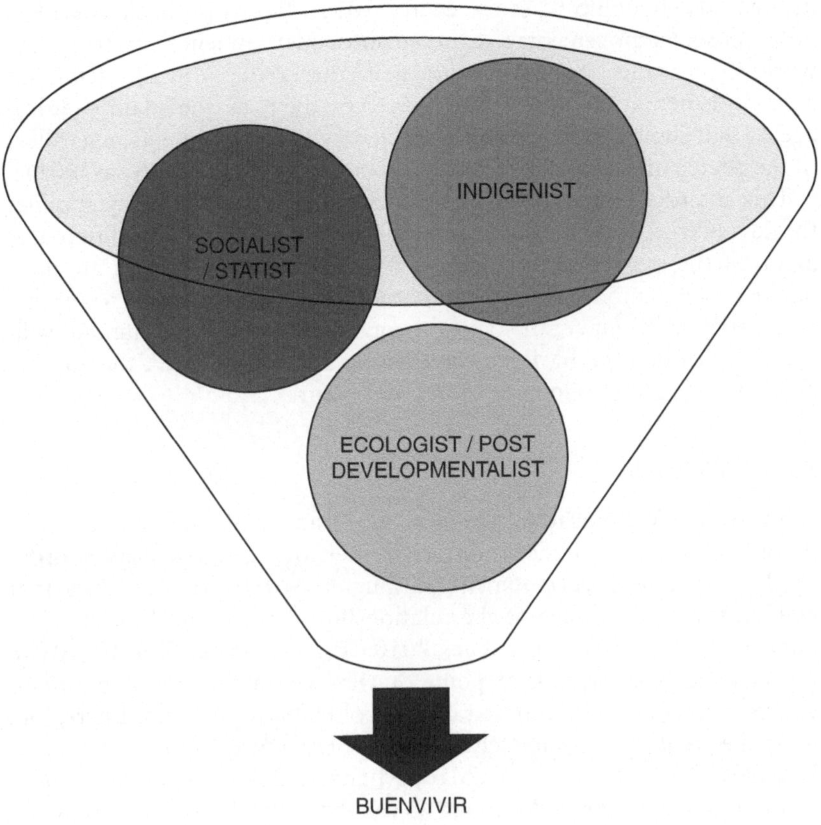

Figure 1.1 The conceptualisation of Buen Vivir.
Source: compiled by the authors.

the intellectual circles of the governments of Ecuador and Bolivia to the intellectual circles of other LA left governments, many of which have incorporated in their political discourse the socialist and statist notion of BV (Ramírez-Gallegos, 2010).

Third, in the *ecologist/developmentalist approach*, development theory and praxis are strongly criticised and biocentrism is the final objective (Acosta, 2013; Escobar, 2010; Gudynas, 2011; Walsh, 2012). This BV tradition relates to the ecological and post-development thinking of intellectuals linked to the critique of development and LA social movements. This approach attaches great importance to the role that civil society must play. These intellectuals propose the creation of local processes of social participation, so that each community can define its own BV (Cubillo-Guevara et al., 2014). This approach considers different social movements (e.g. indigenous, environmentalists, feminists, workers, peasants, pacifists and/or solidarity groups) in the definition and implementation of BV and perceives them as the main political agents that should be heard and respected by LA governments, regardless of the degree of political representation they may reach (Gudynas, 2011).

This interdisciplinary and interdimensional combination exemplifies the advancements on the conceptualisation of BV. Despite the differences amongst the suggested approaches, BV can be categorised as an alternative or a neo model that offers another *development* vehicle to reach a completely different set of societal living standards to gain human well-being. By examining in-depth the existing literature on BV, the authors have identified the following values and pillars.

Buen Vivir's values

While some BV advocators, the most moderate ones, suggest that a new set of values must be either transferred or encouraged to society in order to shift to a new development paradigm, particularly the ones that highlight the importance of the relationship of the human society with nature (Acosta, 2013; Escobar, 2010; Esteva, 1992; Walsh, 2012), others from a more radical point of view claim that modern *values*, which were coercively imposed during colonialisation in the LA region, must be replaced completely, as they legitimise *class* and *racism* (Dávalos, 2011; Huanacuni, 2010; Mignolo, 2014b; Pilataxi Lechón, 2014; Quijano, 2000). Although it can be difficult to establish what modern *values* are (as there are many) and whether everybody in the so-called west universally aligned with them, the BV literature suggests that the BV *values* are different from the modern ones and distant themselves from *individualism*. The following set of *values* are invoked to describe the *Sumak Kawsay/Suma Qamaña* and are demanded to be the ones which a society must departed from to arrive to a more biocentric and socially fairer society.

Community: Ayllu

Community or *Ayllu* is an essential aspect of indigenous people in the Andes and the exercise of *community* cohesion is inherited by their ancestors (particularly the Incas). On the one hand, *Community*, in its more practical expression, is a social group determined by their kinship and is located in a common territory that has its own form of government. On the other hand, *Community*, in its more spiritual dimension (cosmovisión), is constituted by human beings, the spirits of their ancestors and their deities (physically represented in nature) (Huanacuni,

2010). In fact, the head of the *Ayllu*, for the Aymaras, is denominated *Mallku*, a condor, and represents the top of the hierarchy (Albó, 2009). *Community* or *Ayllu* is strongly related with nature and therefore the importance of protecting the environment; that is why the rights of nature have to be demanded (Acosta et al., 2007).

Indigenous peoples distance themselves from western perspectives in many ways (i.e. cosmovision, relationship with nature, beliefs and so on), but *community* is of utmost importance as it is conceived as one particle of the whole system, above the individual and married to *nature*. For them, western societies are disconnected from non-human domains as well as separate from *community* and the spiritual aspect (faith and reason). The ontological conclusion of modernity that the BV advocators differed the most from western perspectivesis that while an individual is protected by the universal declaration of equality in the social contract, nature has been forgotten and has been, in their perspective, over exploited and abused (Albó, 2009; Aylwin, 2013; Guandinango Vinueza, 2013; Huanacuni, 2010; Pilataxi Lechón, 2014; Simbaña, 2012). Therefore, their claim to reconnect with each other and with the non-human world, as their ancestors and the upcoming generations are interconnected spiritually (Huanacuni, 2010: 146; Pilataxi Lechón, 2014: 58).

Although there are several ways to conceive and understand *community*: by their geographical place (Willmott, 1986), their common interest and communion (Crow and Allan, 1994; Lee and Newby, 1983; Willmott, 1989), as a symbol (Cohen, 1982, 1985), as a social network (Lee and Newby, 1983) or as a value (De Tocqueville, 1994; Frazer, 2000; Putnam, 2001), it is claimed that in the formulation of what *community* is and operates, the voices of indigenous people are needed to appear, particularly in the way that *community* is constituted. For them, it needs to transcend from an anthropocentric point of view. So, the necessity to include natural rights as an essential part for societal construction.

Solidarity and reciprocity: Yanapay and Ayni

Solidarity (*Yanapay)* and reciprocity (*Ayni)* are fundamental values of BV and have been rooted within communitarian and collective practices that are pivotal for the analysis of the BV. *Ayni* is referred to the reciprocal and mutual practices performed by the *Quechuas*' and *Aymaras*' ancestors. *Ayni*, as practiced, was ruled by the idea that everything in the world (human beings, the spirit of their ancestors and deities: materialised in nature) is interconnected and therefore rules the everyday life of the indigenous communities. *Ayni* was naturally enforced as it was embedded in the Andean culture (Simbaña, 2012). The members of a community or *Ayllu* are mandated to participate in *Ayni* tasks when a member of a community is in need; tasks such as agricultural work, housing construction and economic emergency are examples of *Ayni*'s tasks (Pilataxi Lechón, 2014).

Yanapay can be equalised with neither collaboration nor cooperation (words that do not even exist in Aymara and Quechua languages). *Yanapay* is claimed to be a spontaneous/natural behaviour, as it is an embedded cultural value and extended to the *Pachamama* (Huanacuni, 2010). BV advocators suggest that both *Yanapay* and *Ayni* are cultural values that dictate every action in the Quechua and Aymara society, thus the spontaneous behaviour to protect every member of the community and the natural environment (see the work of Guandinango Vinueza, 2013; Leon, 2010; Pilataxi Lechón, 2014). For instance, their agricultural system is dictated by the weather conditions and land exploitation is subjected to time cycles. Generally speaking, Andean indigenous communities are self-sustained and produce at small scale, and thus land rests till is ready for production. The members of the community are self-conscious of this and let the land rests as an act of solidarity (*Yanapay*) with nature (Huanacuni, 2010). *Solidarity* and *reciprocity* are claimed to be dictated by biocentrism and anthropocentrism rather than encouraged structurally (i.e. policies, institutions or legal forms) (Acosta et al., 2007; Escobar, 2000; Gudynas, 2011; Huanacuni, 2010). Table 1.3 illustrates some indigenous people's practices that still exist in the contemporary society and are guided by the principles of solidarity and reciprocity (Meléndez, 2005; Pilataxi Lechón, 2014; Santos, 2007; Huanacuni, 2010; Temple, 2003).

Harmony and complementarity: Turaq and Hunt'ay

Complementarity (Hunt'ay) is generally defined as a relationship or situation in which two or more different things improve or emphasise each other's qualities, and *harmony (Turaq)* is seen as a consistent, orderly or pleasing arrangement of parts (Oxford Dictionary). Harmony or *Turaq* (as there are no direct translation in Quechua) is understood as the action of maintaining the world in equilibrium and balance. *Harmony* relates directly to the interrelation between humans and their deities (materialised in nature). *Pachamama's* natural cycle dictates indigenous communities' calendar, which is built upon the equinoxes and solstices corresponding to the path of the sun (Huanacuni, 2010). Indigenous communities try to examine the *nature*'s behaviours and then make decisions accordingly and determine the social order (the way that Andean indigenous communities organise) (Guandinango Vinueza, 2013). The *winter solstice*[6] is a key date, as it marks the beginning of the new cycle of life. *The winter solstice* is considered as the *rebirth* by indigenous peoples, as it is the time of the year when *nature* renews itself (Pilataxi Lechón, 2014). Within the indigenous peoples' literature, the

Table 1.3 Latin American Practices Based on Solidarity and Reciprocity

Practices	*Tequio*	*Yunki*	*Guelaguetza*	*Minga*	*Ayni*	*Mutirão*	*Maloka*
Region	Mexico	LA Region	Mexico	The Andes Region	Ecuador, Bolivia, and Chile	Brazil	Colombia and Brazil
Indigenous Peoples	Zapotec Culture	Quichuas, Aymaras, Mayas, Mapuches, Misak, Guaranies and etc.	Zapotec Culture	Quichuas, Aymaras, Misak and etc.	Quechuas and Aymaras	Tupi	Amazon Regions
Description	Community members contribute materials or labour to carry out construction work for the community.	Exchange (goods or services) for other goods or services without using money In some of the LA regions is very popular to swap seeds (seed-swapping) to fight against the genetically modified GM[12] seeds	A reciprocal exchange of goods and services. Its practice is woven from the reciprocal relations that tie people together. It's the starting point for family and even village and territory-wide cooperative networks In its broadest conception; the *Guelaguetza* represents not only cooperating, but a whole attitude or quality with which each individual is born. For instance, respect and love for the Zapotec inhabitant and having attitude of respecting nature and life	An ancestral mechanism for collective work. The common objective is always more important than any individual benefit	It is a term with a meaning that's closely related to minga. It is a reciprocal practice when a member of a community gives something to another and is entitled to receive something back Means reciprocity in Quechua	An expression originally used in field work for the civil construction of community houses where everyone is a beneficiary and offers mutual help through a rotating, non-hierarchical system	It is an indigenous communal house found in the indigenous Amazon region of Colombia and Brazil. These are cohabited by different families Property is collective, as in Europe's squatter communities

Source: Compiled by the authors.

harmony with nature is frequently cited and can be seen as a principle that departs from their interrelation and the non-hierarchical relationship with the natural environment. The over exploitation and contamination of the *Pachamama* constrain a harmonious relationship between community and nature (Huanacuni, 2010; Leon, 2010; Pilataxi Lechón, 2014; Simbaña, 2012).

Likewise, *complementarity* is the one value that equalises and brings equilibrium to this equation to achieve *Turaq*. Thus, for indigenous peoples, *complementarity* is the acknowledgement of the pluriversal relation amongst human beings and *nature*; that is, each element within the *community* is different, but they complement one another. There is no power play in such a relationship, but there is a horizontal non-hierarchical and interrelational (natural and spontaneous) connection between each entity in the *community* (Albó, 2009; Huanacuni, 2010). For indigenous communities, all members of the *community* play a role in the social cohesion and they are all active contributors for the status quo of society (including *nature* as an active member of this *community*). Hence, none would be able to exist without the existence of the other and the link that is woven for *community* creation (Pilataxi Lechón, 2014). For instance, in the *Ayni* practice, for any societal transaction of either *Yunki* or seed swapping, there must be different societal actors considered experts to achieve these objectives. If there is a seed for *quinoa* that grows effectively and better in x location for the local conditions (height, weather, soil) and is produced by the x community, it might be possible to exchange the seed with the other community that urged the production in exchange for another type of seed (coca, maize, araucaria).

Buen Vivir's pillars

As mentioned earlier, the BV's identified *values* are a set of principles influenced by the *Sumak Kawsay/Suma Qamaña's cosmovisión*. As BV is considered a project that echoes indigenous principles, BV's *pillars* are meant to be regarded as reliably providing essential support for the BV model. The following are the BV's identified *pillars* according to the existing literature. They are established in a non-particular hierarchical order as they are all interconnected and, most importantly, interrelated to each other.

Rights of nature

One of the innovations of *BV* is the advocacy to establish *nature* as a living entity to be protected and equally treated. Most notably in the case of Ecuador and Bolivia, the *rights of nature* has been constitutionalised in the Constitutions of 2008 and 2009, respectively (SENPLADES, 2009,

2011, 2012). The identification of *nature* with *Pachamama* goes beyond environmental political correctness, given that the *pachamama* cannot be easily fitted into the philosophical structure of the modern constitution, within which *nature* is seen as an inert object for humans to be appropriated respect (Escobar, 1992). *BV* advocators claim for a holistic transformation of the system and the search for an ecological – non-dualistic – self that reconnects with all beings. *BV* implies an expanded ecological notion of the self, in which the liberal notion (claimed to be rooted in the GN) sees the self as deeply interconnected with all the living beings and ultimately with the planet as a whole (Acosta, 2012; Gudynas, 2011). That said, *the rights of nature* influenced by the cosmovisión of the indigenous peoples of the region is meant to be one of the pillars for the *BV construction* and it relates to the threefold set of *values*.

BV advocates a plural type of citizenship involving cultural and ecological dimensions which requires both environmental justice and ecological justice for the protection of people and *nature*. For instance, in this sense, *BV* intersects with other global thoughts, mainly associated with TDs. Examples of this include TDs based on 'deep ecology'[7] and the view of the ecological self (Gudynas, 2011; Macey, 2010); post-carbon and post-fossil fuel economies to maintain and invest in the environment for the long-term societal project (Shiva, 2004, 2005, 2008); the governance of natural resources in favour of society (Ostrom, 1990); the inclusion of the spiritual dimension to society based on a deep transformation of values considering *nature* as the principal *axis* of change (Hanh, 2008); or self-sufficiency (i.e. away from the oil dependency) generated by local communities or small groups called *transitional towns* (Hopkins, 2008). Here, the BV *pillar* of *nature* appears as a very serious multidimensional proposal that emerged from the LA region and is traversed with other TDs by ecological issues.

Community well-being

This BV *pillar* essentially suggests building up a new society based on different notions of living standards (moving away from the ones suggested by modernity that are strongly subjected to economic growth) influenced by the Sumak Kawsay/Suma Qamaña, in which *nature* is respected and sustainably treated (Huanacuni, 2010). As can be seen, *community well-being*, environmental protection and cared are dimensions of the living standards of society: (see the example of TIPNIS in Aylwin, 2013). Another important dimension in the *community well-being* is participation. This pillar suggests that community must participate and be included in the decision-making process at local, regional and national levels. Hence, the need to create spaces of participation different from the electoral system (a referendum took place in the elaboration of the constitutions of Ecuador and Bolivia and local authorities played an important role in organising community meetings). For instance, indigenous people's authorities endorse members of their communities to attend local events and be part of conversations that matter to their regions. They usually referred to it as '*Minga of Knowledge' (in Spanish Minga de pensamiento)*, in which all members of the community discuss and debate about relevant matters and play an important role for future decisions (see the Misak's example in Gow and Jaramillo, 2013). In sum, this *pillar* envisions a *community well-being* based on BV's *values*.

At a practical level, progress in the objective of achieving *community well-being* with other 'standards' can be found advanced in the institutional developments of *BV* in Ecuador and Bolivia. In the context of Ecuador, the *development plan* named '*El Plan Nacional del Buen Vivir 2013–2017*' (national plan of BV) was planned and designed following the BV's constitutional standards and proposed to deliver an enhancement of living standards by encouraging the business sector and the population in general to get involved in a new model of generating products and services that help conserve the environment and to decrease the use of natural resources as a raw material for export. Cross-sectoral (i.e. universities, business) financial investment was budgeted to ensure inclusive and participatory strategy to achieve advancements in the sustainably oriented *development* project of BV (Yánez, 2015, p. 105).

The economic growth is still an important dimension to enhance the living standards of the society, thus the need to transform its practice to reinforce that *community well-being* is important. Improvements in economic frameworks such as the Social and Solidarity Economy (SSE) are seen crucial for the construction of another *development* paradigm. For instance, in Bolivia, the SSE has been empowered, reinforced and strengthened. Previously, it contributed to the 25% of the GDP, but now it is reaching 35% (INE, 2016).

Decolonisation

Although is an early stage, *decolonisation* has become a key component for the *development* of the BV theory (see Acosta, 2013). In its more radical way, it is claimed in the literature that only by detaching from the western modes of production and worldview, indigenous peoples, Afro-descendants, women and *nature* will be recognised and will dismantle hegemonic social structures (based on race and class) (Celiberti, 2010; Escobar, 1992, 2010; Leon, 2010). Decolonisation is considered essential to transform society from universality to 'pluriversality'. A shift to a new cultural and economic paradigm is globally recognised both as needed and as actively under construction (Escobar, 1992).

In the Government of Bolivia, led by president Evo Morales since 2006, *decolonisation* has been the main concept in its political discourse (see the example of the Movimiento al Socialismo (MAS) that influenced Morales' political ideology in Paco, 2007). Political *decolonisation* has been institutionalised and constitutionalised, bringing cultural value to the *voiceless* or marginalised groups (Leon, 2010; Vanhulst, 2015), particularly as in modernisation theory, *indigenous peoples* are considered either an obstacle to '*development*' or a 'primitive' entity to be civilised (*inferior communities*). In the process of modernisation, indigenous communities are claimed to be socially marginalised and demonised as enemies of the *development* recipes, particularly as they inhabit in regions rich in natural resources (Pilataxi Lechón, 2014). In this respect, indigenous social movements flagged with decolonisation approaches have played an important role in the region bringing about some degree of justice to their communities (Mueses, 2012; Paco, 2004, 2007; Ulloa, 2004).

Plurinational state

Plurality is a key concept of the BV project and is cited frequently in the BV literature, particularly the authors that are more related with the *indigenist* approach (Dávalos, 2011; Huanacuni, 2010; Pilataxi Lechón, 2014; Simbaña, 2012). BV advocators coincide that only with a more plural (inclusive and participatory) society the construction of a new paradigm would be possible. In the perspective of Escobar (2012:24, xxiv), BV calls for a non-hegemonic system and can be considered as a transformational, intercultural and plural project proposal for society to reach a more symmetrical relation among cultures. Hypothetically speaking, *BV* project demands an acute consciousness of the rights of communities upon their territories and resources, of the marked uneven patterns of global consumption, environmental impacts and structures of exploitation maintained by capitalism, and of the concomitant need for social and environmental justice. However, there is no other technique yet to pave the way securely, but acknowledging other perspectives, civil and communal participatory approaches will be crucial to achieve societal well-being (Acosta, 2013, 2012; Calvo and Morales, 2013; Escobar, 1992; Gudynas, 2011).

A *plurinational state* is formulated in the BV literature as a political mechanism operated by a decentralised political and administrative system that must be culturally heterogeneous and allows the participation of all the social sectors and groups within society (Escobar, 2010; Paco, 2004, 2007). A *plurinational state* must ensure societal well-being by taking into account everyone's living standards. High urban standards of living are very different from the ones in the rural areas, so as that of indigenous peoples. Thus, a plural-viewed is suggested by BV, in which living standards are neither guided nor determined by western criteria (i.e. the SDGs) (Gudynas, 2011; Leon, 2010; Santos, 2003). Indigenous peoples, peasant and Afro-descendant worldviews are presented as particularly important sources for the debate on alternative civilizational models and to recover the meaning of what life is; therefore, state must be organised (Escobar, 2015). This pillar is strongly related to politics and how the government should function. In fact, Ramírez-Gallegos (2010) assured that BV is redefined in the political projects of Bolivia and Ecuador. He claims that plurality in both the state and the economy enables the last stage of BV: a 'bio-egalitarian republic'[8]. This term derivated from *bio*, as the rights of nature are recognised as social-egalitarian because it is concern about the future generations and expands democracy (political and economic inclusiveness based on pluralism). It uses the term 'republican' as it tries to interconnect the state and the citizens based on rights and responsibilities.

Ramírez-Gallegos (2010) also states that *BV* should be seen in the panoply of pioneering constitutional innovations, particularly as it is proposing a different idea of nation from the orthodox view of '*one flag, one land, one hand, one nation*' (Holmes, 1895). BV in this respect pursues an intercultural and pluri-ethnic nation that recognises not only the native people but also others such the settlers, the mestizos, Afro-descendants and Romans, but with the right to be autonomous and self-determining their own destiny. For example, in Bolivia, the state is declared as an 'unitary, plurinational, communitarian, free, independent, sovereign, democratic, social decentralised state, with territorial autonomies' that is founded on political, economic, judicial, cultural and linguistic pluralism as well as being assembled by *autonomy*, *communal democracy* (non-representative) and *plural participation* (García-Linera, 2010; Paco, 2004, 2007).

Economic pluralism

Economy is one of the main areas that the BV project is challenging and is attempting to modify from its perspective (Hidalgo-Capitán & Cubillo-Guevara, 2016; Hidalgo-Capitán & Cubillo-Guevara, 2017). The majority of the BV literature concerning economy tends to focus on post-extractivist (Gudynas, 2011), post-neoliberal (García-Linera, 2010; Ramírez-Gallegos, 2010), biocentric (Dávalos, 2011; Huanacuni, 2010) and alternative economies (Acosta, 2015; Coraggio, 2007; Razeto, 1984). That is why economy is considered plural. The economic approach within the BV literature is argued to be the result of processes of reflection of many intellectuals who have received many and diverse influences from other intellectuals both in the LA region and in other parts of the world (Hidalgo-Capitán & Cubillo-Guevara, 2017; Vanhulst, 2015).

Cubillo-Guevara et al. (2014) and Hidalgo-Capitán and Cubillo-Guevara (2017) have identified a manifold of elements which have influenced the BV's economic plural approximation and those include: the happiness economy (Coll and Ferrás, 2017), the subsistence feminism or care economy (see León-Trujillo, 2009), the indigenous-community-based economy (see Mutuberria and Chiroque, 2011) and the SSE (Coraggio, 2007; Escobar, 2015; Razeto, 1984; Unceta, 2014).

The history of *development* in the region demonstrates that all intended/implemented recipes of economic recovery are made to resume economic growth, but yet nothing has been proposed out of the 'orthodox-*development* box'. LA regional policies have rather followed foreign indications and guidance (mainly from the GN) and have outsourced assistance to deal with local issues (Santos, 2003). With this in mind, *economic pluralism* appears as a critical topic to be developed in the BV literature. Hence, the main objective of the pillar is to move away from mainstream economics, which in the region is determined by the private sector, towards a more inclusive and interdisciplinary approach to economics and promote heterodox sectors within the region guided by the BV (Acosta, 2013; Escobar, 2010; Gudynas, 2011; Lander, 2000; Razeto, 1984).

Democratisation

BV advocators claim that there is no other away to create another *development* paradigm unless *democratic* processes are revised and make participation accessible to everyone. This pillar is essentially constructed by the objective of dismantling representative democracy[9] and taking forward practices of communal democracy. *Aymara* leaders have referred semantically to Bolivia's representative *democracy* as *q'aracracia*', a term that combines q'ara' (plucked, bare or hairless, in *Aymara* and white person in *Quechua*) with *democracia* (democracy in Spanish). Building on these concepts, Evo Morales claims that Bolivia's democracy is imported and does not represent the local cultural values of the population (García-Linera, 2010; Paco, 2004, 2007). Hence, *communal democracy*, which as Toledo (2009) claims meant to emerge from citizen movements, would not be possible without the right of autonomy for indigenous groups. *Autonomy* in the case of Bolivia is legal and can be described in terms of a very radical democracy, cultural self-determination and self-governance.

Communal democracy (legally recognised in *Art 11, 1* in the Bolivian Constitution), as one of the most concrete proposals, builds upon values of communal solidarity, equality, and consensus and differs fundamentally from the individualistic principles that lie at the root of the liberal representative democratic model (individual freedom, limited government, popular sovereignty and plurality involve a commitment to settling disputes through political discourse and engagement). In the case of

Bolivia, assembly union democracy and communal indigenous democracy work as exemplary models of direct, unmediated representation, where all deliberate until they reach a consensus and a decision is made (*Minga of Knowledge*). These forms of *democratisation* do not reduce participation to voting, nor representation to delegation of power and representatives (*psephocracy*) (García-Linera, 2010; Paco, 2004, 2007). Unlike conventional *democratic* purposes, *participation* is an obligation linked to the economic, political and ritual duties of the members of the *community*. *Leadership* is another important aspect, as is a duty, and it is rotated among all *community* members. In a *communal democracy*, all participants must abide by collective decisions, which are reached through long deliberations aimed at reaching a consensus (Huanacuni, 2010; Macas, 1991; Paco, 2007, 2004). Thus, with this intention, *individual* rights are subordinated to collective rights, as in indigenous communities *democratic* rules do not apply, but there is a form of *authoritarianism* based on *consensus*. Consequently, the members of the *community* who oppose and do not respect and follow collective decisions are considered defectors, a crime punishable by measures such as monetary fines, ostracism and occasionally by means of physical penalties, such as whipping (Paco, 2004, 2007; Pilataxi Lechón, 2014).

Critiques of Buen Vivir

There have been a number of criticisms of the BV theory (Bretón, 2013; Caria & Domínguez, 2016; Lalander, 2016). BV theory is indicated to be rooted within different traditions (Cubillo-Guevara et al., 2014; Hidalgo-Capitán & Cubillo-Guevara, 2017). In fact, many of the contributions of the BV respond to very different thinking logics (Vanhulst, 2015). As some scholars have argued, BV is a concept that is under construction and has passed through many different stages and can be seen as a polysemic concept that is evoked depending upon different positions (Bretón, 2013; Caria & Domínguez, 2016). The critical discourses towards BV (and often central in the LA academic network) are generally the least performative at the level of public policies.

Drawing on Cubillo-Guevara et al. (2014) and Hidalgo-Capitán and Cubillo-Guevara (2017), the three approaches of BV that are discursively opposed contribute to the BV criticisms from their perspectives. For instance, the *indigenist approach supporters are* described by some intellectuals of the other two traditions as *pachamamistas*[10] (Stefanoni, 2010, 2011) trapped in a discourse of '*childish indigenist*' and without capacity to implement and achieve the BV (Correa, 2007, 2008). The supporters of the *socialist/statist approach* are considered by some intellectuals of the other traditions as practitioners of a *senile development*, referring to orthodox or GN approaches to development (Lalander, 2016; Svampa, 2011, 2012). There are advocators of this approach who are accused of having replaced in their political discourses the term 'development' by the term 'BV', emulating the same development recipes and creating a 'socialist version' of it (Acosta, 2015; Caria & Domínguez Martín, 2014; Caria & Domínguez, 2016). Finally, the supporters of the *ecologist/post-developmentalist approach* are accused by some intellectuals of the other traditions of lacking political pragmatism, of being trapped in a discourse of a romantic 'ecologism' (Correa, 2007, 2008). They claimed that they have distorted the original meaning of BV by complementing it with GN contents that are alien to the Andean cosmovision (Oviedo, 2011). Thus, it can be claimed that the critiques towards BV are coming from the same intellectuals who advocate for the BV but are influenced by different traditions.

However, the strongest criticisms are the ones concerning the implementation of BV (i.e. one of the biggest detractors of the BV's institutionalization is Acosta, 2015). Particularly, as BV is seen in this context as an appropriated concept of the *Sumak Kawasay/Suma Qamaña* and is argued to be very distant from the principles borrowed by the indigenous peoples, principally with the extractive projects (mining) that have taken place in Ecuador and Bolivia (see Acosta, 2013, 2012; Aylwin, 2013; Huanacuni, 2010; Leon, 2010). For instance, Lalander (2016) claims that there are deep contradictions between the constitutional prescriptions in the BV-oriented Ecuadorian 2008 constitution (see SENPLADES, 2012) and the praxis of law protecting the natural resources.

Other criticisms are concerned with the role of indigenous communities and the idealisation of these groups (Correa, 2007, 2008). Some intellectuals claimed that it is convenient not to fall into an idealised conception of indigenous cultures and the collective imagination that perceives them as non-conflicting and horizontal. The indigenous world was not (and is not) free of problems, conflicts and various forms of domination and asymmetries amongst them. Therefore, as Vanhulst (2015) argued, contemporary discourses of BV are inspired (with greater or lesser strength) of traditional principles reconstructed, reinvented by contemporary social actors (indigenous and non-indigenous) that seek to redefine development trajectories.

Concluding remarks

This chapter has first explored briefly the main development theories, in particular the classic, emergent and transition discourse theories. As explained in the chapter, most of these *development* frameworks have not been developed from indigenous people's struggles and constructed on the basis of indigenous peoples' values and traditions (Acosta, 2013; Huanacuni, 2010; Mignolo, 2001; Quijano, 2011). Second, the authors have revisited the existing literature on the BV theory to understand this as an alternative to development. An in-depth exploration of the conceptualisation of the BV was needed to understand whether such project is an alternative or a neo strategy for *development*. The chapter illustrated few examples that show the advancements of the BV in the LA region as well as present its values and pillars. The authors argue that although there are some criticisms to BV, this theoretical framework can be neither underestimated conceptually nor empirically, as there is evidence of the impacts that the appropriation of BV has generated in some LA countries (see the examples of Bolivia and Ecuador).

Based on the existing BV literature, Diagram 2.2 presents the BV model with its identified values and pillars. As seen in Diagram 2.2, the BV's values echoing indigenous peoples' principles are: community, solidarity and reciprocity and harmony and complementarity. The BV pillars which are meant to be implemented within a *pluriverse* constituted by ecological, spiritual, political, socio-economic, cultural and plural-worldview-oriented dimensions are as follows: decolonisation, plurinational state, economic pluralism, democratisation, rights of nature and community well-being.

Notes

1 See the press release: UN General Assembly's Open Working Group proposes sustainable development goals: https://sustainabledevelopment.un.org/content/documents/4538pressowg13.pdf.

2 Throughout this thesis, the terms Global North (GN) and Global South (GS) will be used to refer to the socio-economic and political division of the globe (Mignolo, 2000), understanding that the GS is compounded of the regions in Africa, Latin America, developing Asia and even the Middle East, and the GN constituted by Western Europe, the United States of America (USA), Canada and the particular case of Japan, Australia and New Zealand (Wallerstein, 1989).

3 The authors refer to post-development as a post-development approach that argues that development was always unjust, never worked and at this point has clearly failed. Although there are different takes on post-development studies, the authors will follow the work on post-development studies (Escobar, 2000; Esteva, 1992; Latouche, 2009; Sachs, 2005) that point out that the models of development are often ethnocentric (in this case Eurocentric), universalist and based on western models of industrialization that are unsustainable in this world of limited resources and ineffective for their ignorance of the local, cultural and historical contexts of the peoples to which they are applied. In essence, the problem post-development theorists see in development and its practice is an imbalance of influence or domination by the west, thus different approaches of development sourced in other epistemologies.

4 At large scale, degrowth is the concept of downscaling production and consumption; it is seen as the contraction of economies arguing that overconsumption lies at the root of long-term environmental issues and social inequalities (Kallis et al., 2012; Schneider et al., 2010). Degrowth is also a

political, economic and social movement based on ecological economic, anti-consumerist and anti-capitalist ideas (see examples in Escobar, 2015; Martinez-Alier, 2002).

5 Development's fatigue is defined by the authors as the fatigue caused by the failure of the development formulas in the continent.

6 Coordinadora de las Organizaciones Indígenas de la Cuenca Amazónica (COICA).

7 In the southern hemisphere, this occurs in June between the 20th and 24th.

8 Genetically modified (GM) is a real issue in countries such as Mexico, Colombia, Chile and Peru. Indigenous peoples cannot grow and trade any food that are not certified by the state. The seeds that are certified are the ones that are claimed to be a GMO seeds (Kloppenburg, 2010).

9 Arnes Naess was a Norwegian philosopher who coined the term 'deep ecology' and was an important intellectual and inspirational figure within the environmental movement of the late twentieth century. Deep ecology argues that the natural world is a subtle balance of complex interrelationships in which the existence of organisms is dependent on the existence of others within ecosystems. Human interference with or destruction of the natural world poses a threat therefore not only to humans but to all organisms constituting the natural order (Naess, 1973).

10 In the socialist/statist approach, BV is understood as the socialism of Sumak Kawsay (Ramírez-Gallegos, 2010, 2011) or the Andean Community Socialism (García-Linera, 2010) in Ecuador and Bolivia, respectively.

11 By representative democracy the authors refer to a type of democracy founded on the principle of elected officials representing a group of people.

12 Pachamamismo is referred to, generally negatively, an indigenous political discourse that only relies on the indigenous peoples' cosmovisión and considered populist as not coherent with the reality of the society (Stefanoni, 2010).

References

Acosta, A. (2012). *El retorno del Estado, Primeros Pasos Postneoliberales, mas no Postcapitalistas*. Quito: FES-ILDIS.

Acosta, A. (2013). *El Buen Vivir: Sumak Kawsay, una oportunidad para imaginar otros mundos*. Icaria Editorial.

Acosta, A. (2015). El Buen Vivir como alternativa al desarrollo. *Revista Política y Sociedad*, *52*(2), 299–330.

Acosta, L. E., Mendoza, D., & García, O. I. (2007). *Hacerlo amanecer: Una Experiencia Participativa del Diálogo de Saberes en la Construcción de Procesos de Etnodesarrollo con Pueblos Indígenas de la Amazonia Colombiana. Etnoecologia y desarrollo sostenible*. Retrieved fromhttps://sinchi.org.co/files/publicaciones/revista/pdf/1/11% 20hacerlo%20amanecer%20una%20experiencia%20participativa%20en%20la%20contruccin%20de%20procesos%20de%20 etnodesarrollo%20con%20pueblos%20indgenas%20en%20la%20amazonia%20colombiana.pdf.

Albó, X. (2009). Suma Qamaña, el Buen Convivir. *Revista OBETS de Ciencias Sociales*, *4*, 25–40.

Amin, S. (1978). *Unequal development: An essay on the social formations of peripheral capitalism*. Translated by Brian Pierce. New York: Monthly Review Press.

Arat, Z. F. (1988). Democracy and economic development: Modernization theory revisited. *Comparative Politics*, *21*(1), 21–36.

Asian Indigenous Peoples Pact Foundation (AIPPF). (2012). *Development aggression as economic growth: A report by the Asian indigenous peoples pact.* AIPP. http://iphrdefenders.net/wp-content/uploads/2015/11/AIPP_Report_4web_final.pdf.

Aya, R. (1978). Norbert Elias and "The Civilizing Process". *Theory and Society*, *5*(2), 219–228.

Aylwin, J. (2013). "Bolivia: Desarrollo o Buen Vivir. El caso del TIPNIS". In J. Aylwin, S. Martí i Puig, C. Wright & N. Yáñez (Eds.), *Entre desarrollo y el Buen Vivir. Recursos naturales y conflictos en los territorios indígenas*. Quito, Ecuador: Catarata.

Baran, P. A. (1952). On the political economy of backwardness. *The Manchester School*, *20*(1), 66–84.

Baran, P. A. (1958). The political-economy of growth. *Economist*, *186*(8), 658–678.

Bernstein, H. (1971). Modernization theory and the sociological study of development. *The Journal of Development Studies*, *7*(2), 141–160.

Bollier, D. (2014). Think like a Commoner: *A short Introduction to the Life of the Commons*. New York: New Society Publishers.

Bollier, D., & Helfrich, S. (2012). *The wealth of the commons: A world beyond market and the state*. New York: Leveller Press.

Bretón, V. (2013). Etnicidad, desarrollo y 'Buen Vivir': Reflexiones críticas en perspectiva histórica. *Revista Europea de Estudios Latinoamericanos y Del Caribe*, *95*, 71–95.

Calvo, S., & Morales, A. (2017). Social and Solidarity Economy: the word's economy with a social face. London: Routledge.

Cardoso, F. H., & Falletto, E. (1979). *Dependency and development in Latin America*. United States: University of California Press.

Caria, S., & Domínguez Martín, R. (2014). *El porvenir de una ilusión: La ideología del Buen Vivir*. Ecuador: procesos, actores e instituciones en 35 años, Vol 67, Páginas 139-163.

Caria, S., & Domínguez, R. (2016). Ecuador's Buen vivir: a new ideology for development. *Latin American Perspectives*, *43*(1), 18–33.

Celiberti, L. (2010). *Feminismo polifónicos, interculturales y dialógicos. El 'Buen Vivir'desde la Mirada de las Mujeres*, 20–28. Buenos Aires, Argentina. https://bdigital.uncu.edu.ar/objetos_digitales/5626/revista-confluencia2012-13-001-damico-pessolano.pdf

Clarke, G. (2001). From ethnocide to ethnodevelopment? Ethnic minorities and indigenous peoples in Southeast Asia. *Third World Quarterly*, 22(3), 413–436.

Cohen, Anthony. P. (1982). *Belonging: Identity and social organization in British rural cultures*. United kingdom: Manchester University Press.

Cohen, Anthony. P. (1985). *The symbolic construction of community*. London; New York: Tavistock.

Coll, J. M., & Ferrás, X. (2017). *Economía de la felicidad*. Plataforma.

Coraggio, J. L. (1994). La Construcción de una Economía Popular: Vía para el Desarrollo Humano. *Revista de Economía y Trabajo, Vol II.*

Coraggio, J. L. (2007). *La Economia Social desde la Periferia: Contribuciones Latinoamericanas*. Altamira.

Coraggio, J. L. (2011). *El Trabajo antes que el Capital*. Ediciones Abya-Yala.

Correa, R. (2007). Discurso del Presidente de la República, Rafael Correa, sobre el levantamiento en Dayuma. *Orellana, 1*, 2007.

Correa, R. (2008). Discurso del Presidente de la República, Rafael Correa, pronunciado en la ceremonia de clausura de la Asamblea Constituyente. *Ciudad Alfaro, 25*, 2008.

Cowen, M., & Shenton, R. (1996). *Doctrines of development*. Taylor & Francis.

Crow, G., & Allan, G. (1994). *Community life: An introduction to local social relations*. Harvester Wheatsheaf.

Cubillo-Guevara, A. P., Hidalgo-Capitán, A. L., & Domínguez-Gómez, J. A. (2014). El pensamiento sobre el Buen Vivir. Entre el indigenismo, el socialismo y el posdesarrollismo. *Revista Del CLAD Reforma y Democracia, 60*.

Dávalos, P. (2011). *Sumak Kawsay (La vida en plenitud). Iberoamerican Journal of Development Studies*, 5(2): 30-57.

De Tocqueville, A. (1994). *Democracy in America*. New York: Fontana Press.

Dos Santos, T. (1968). *La crisis de la teoría del desarrollo y las relaciones de dependencia en América Latina*. Boletin: Universidad de Chile, Centro de Estudios Socioeconómicos.

Dussel, E. (2011). *'Transmodernidad e interculturalidad. Interpretación desde la Filosofía de la Liberación', en Edgardo Lander (Comp.) La colonialidad del saber: Eurocentrismo y ciencias sociales: Perspectivas latinoamericanas* (2nd edición). Ciccus Ediciones.

Escobar, A. (1992). 'Imagining a Post-Development Era? Critical Thought, Development and Social Movements'. *Social Text, 31–32*, 20–56.

Escobar, A. (2000). Beyond the search for a paradigm? Post-development and beyond. *Development, 43*(4), 11–14.

Escobar, A. (2004). Beyond the Third World: Imperial globality, global coloniality and anti-globalization social movements. *Third World Quarterly, 25*(1), 207–230.

Escobar, A. (2010). Latin America at a crossroads: Alternative modernizations, post-liberalism, or post-development? *Cultural Studies, 25*(1), 1–65.

Escobar, A. (2012). *Encountering Development: The making and unmaking of the third world*. Princeton University Press.

Escobar, A. (2015). Degrowth, postdevelopment, and transitions: A preliminary conversation. *Sustainability Science, 10*(3), 451–462.

Esteva, G. (1992). *Development, in the development dictionary. A guide to knowledge as. Power. Edited by Wolfang Sachs, London, ZED Boocks*, 2–26.

Frazer, E. (2000). *The problem of communitarian politics*. Oxford University Press.

Friedman, T. L. (2000). *Understanding globalization: The lexus car and the olive tree*. Foundation for Economic Education. New York, NY: Farrar, Straus, and Giroux https://fee.org/articles/the-lexus-and-the-olive-tree-understanding-globalization/

Fukuyama, F. (2001). Social capital, civil society and development. *Third World Quarterly, 22*(1), 7–20.

García-Linera, Á. (2010). El socialismo comunitario. *Revista de Análisis, 3*(5), 522-534.

Gedicks, A. (2001). *Resource rebels: Native challenges to mining and oil corporations*. South End Press.

Giddings, B., Hopwood, B., & O'brien, G. (2002). Environment, economy and society: Fitting them together into sustainable development. *Sustainable Development, 10*(4), 187–196.

Giovannini, M. (2012). *Social enterprises for development as Buen Vivir*, Journal of Enterprising Communities People and Places in the Global Economy, 6(3), 284–299.

Gow, D., & Jaramillo, D. (2013). *En minga por el Cauca: El Gobierno del Taita Floro Tunubalá (2001-2003)* Universidad del Cauca.

Guandinango Vinueza, Y. A. (2013). *"Del Sumak Kawsay al Allin Kawsay relaciones socioculturales en los sistemas familiars comunitarios una mirada desde las comunidades Kichwas"*. In C. von Barloewen, M. Rivera & K. Töpfer (Eds.), *Desarrollo sostenible en una modernidad plural: Perspectivas latinoamericanas* . Quito, Ecuador: Abya Yala.

Gudynas, E. (2011). 'Buen Vivir: Germinando Alternativas al Desarrollo'. *America Latina en Movimiento, 462.*

Hanh, T. N. (2008). *The world we have: A Buddhist approach to peace and ecology*. Parallax Press.

Harris, N. (1989). *The end of the third world: Newly industrializing countries and the declineof an ideology*. Oxford University Press.

Hettne, B. (1983). The Development of Development Theory. *Acta Sociologica, 26*(3/4), 247–266.

Hidalgo-Capitán, A., & Cubillo-Guevara, A. (2015). La Trinidad Del Buen Vivir En Ecuador. *Política Exterior. Latinoamérica Análisis, 14*(09).

Hidalgo-Capitán, A. L., & Cubillo-Guevara, A. P. (2016). *Transmodernidad y transdesarrollo. El decrecimiento y el buen vivir como dos versiones análogas de un transdesarrollo transmoderno*. Ediciones Bonanza.

Hidalgo-Capitán, Antonio Luis, & Cubillo-Guevara, A. P. (2017). Deconstrucción y genealogía del buen vivir latinoamericano. El (trino) buen vivir y sus diversos manantiales intelectuales. *International Development Policy| Revue Internationale de Politique de Développement, 9*, 9.

Holmes, O. W. (1895). *The poetical works of Oliver Wendell Holmes (Vol. 11)*. Mifflin: Houghton.

Hopkins, R. (2008). *The transition handbook. From oil dependency to local resilience*. Chelsea Green Publishing.

Hopwood, B., Mary, M., & O'Brien, G. (2005). Sustainable Development: Mapping different approaches. *Sustainable Development, 13*(1), 38–52.

Huanacuni, F. (2010). *Buen Vivir/Vivir Bien: Filosofía, Políticas, Estrategias y Experiencias Regionales Andinas*. CAOI Coordinadora Andina de Organizaciones Indígenas.

Instituto Nacional de Estadistica (INE). (2016). *Economia Social Y solidaria.* http://www.ine.gob.bo/default.aspx.

Kallis, G., Kerschner, C., & Martinez-Alier, J. (2012). The economics of degrowth. *Ecological Economics, 84*, 172–180.

Kay, C. (1998). Estructuralismo y teoría de la dependencia en el periodo neoliberal: Una perspectiva latinoamericana. *Nueva Sociedad, 158*, 100–119.

Kloppenburg, J. (2010). Impeding dispossession, enabling repossession: Biological open source and the recovery of seed sovereignty. *Journal of Agrarian Change, 10*(3), 367–388.

Lalander, R. (2016). The Ecuadorian resource dilemma: Sumak Kawsay or development? *Critical Sociology*, *42*(4–5), 623–642.

Lander, E. (2000). *La Colonialidad del Saber: Eurocentrismo y Ciencias Sociales, Perspectivas Latinoamericanas*. CLACSO.

Latouche, S. (2010). *Farewell to growth*. Polity Press, ISBN: 0745646174.

Laurie, N., Robert, A., & Radcliffe, S. (2005). Ethnodevelopment: Social movements, creating experts and professionalising indigenous knowledge in Ecuador. *Antipode*, *37*(3), 470–496.

Lee, D, & Newby, H. (1983). *The problem of sociology: An introduction to the discipline*. Unwin Hyman.

Lee, David, & Newby, H. (1983). *The problem of sociology: An introduction to the discipline*. London: Routledge.

Lemaître, A., & Helmsing, B. (2012). Solidarity economy in Brazil: Movement, discourse and practice. Analysis through a Polanyian understanding of the economy. *Journal of International Development*, *24*(6), 745–762.

Leon, I. (2010). *Sumak Kawsay/ Buen Vivir y Cambios Civilisatorios* (2nd ed.). FEDAEPS.

León-Trujillo, M. (2009). *Cambiar la economía para cambiar la vida. El Buen Vivir. Una Vía Para El Desarrollo*, 63–74.

Lowe, P., Jonathan, M., & Ward, N. (1995). *Networks in rural development: Beyond exogenous and endogenous models*. In J. D. van Der Ploeg & G. van Dijk (Eds.), *Beyond Modernisation: The Impact of Endogenous Rural Development*. Netherlands: Assen, pp. 87–106.

Macas, L. (1991). *"El levantamiento indígena visto por sus protagonistas"*. In I. Almeida (Ed), *Indios: Una reflexión sobre el levantamiento indígena de 1990*. Quito, Ecuador: Abya Yala.

Macey, G. P. (2010). *Response: Cooperative Institutions in Cultural Commons. Cornell Law Review*. *104*(5), 1–30.

Mamani, P. (2006). Territorio y estructuras de accion colectiva: Microgobiernos barriales. *Ephemera*, *6*(3), 276–286.

Martinez-Alier, J. (2002). Environmental justice and economic degrowth: An alliance between two movements. *Capitalism Nature Socialism*, *23*(1), 51–73.

Meléndez, W. L. P. (2005). *Despertar la Amazonia Multicultural y Pluriétnica*. Universidad Libre, Sede Principal, Facultad de Derecho, Centro de Investigaciones Socio-Jurídicas.

Mignolo, W. (2000). *Local Histories/Global Designs: Essays on the Coloniality of Power, Subaltern Knowledges and Border Thinking*. Princeton University Press.

Mignolo, W. (2001). Coloniality of power and subalternity. In I. Rodriguez (Ed.), *The Latin American subaltern studies reader*. Duke University Press.

Mignolo, W. (2010). *El Desprendimiento: Prolegómenos a una Gramática de la Descolonialidad' en* H. y R. Grosfoguel Cairo et al.) *Descolonizar la modernidad, Descolonizar Europa. Un Diálogo Europa-América Latina*. IEPALA. ISBN: 978-84-89743-69-4.

Mignolo, W. (2014a). Pensar como sudaca. Interview with A. Gortázar. *La Diaria*. http://ladiaria.com.uy/articulo/2014/5/pensar-como-sudaca/.

Mignolo, W. (2014b). Spirit out of bounds returns to the East: The closing of the social sciences and the opening of independent thoughts. *Current Sociology*, *62*(4), 584–602.

Mueses, C. (2012). Estado y Movimientos Indígenas en Colombia: Elementos para una Aproximación Histórica. *Revista Ccehs-Multiculturalidad Y Movimientos Indígenas En América Latina*, *10*, 211–244.

Mutuberria, V., & Chiroque, H. (2011). Perspectivas y aportes desde la Economía Comunitaria como alternativa para el desarrollo de "otra economía" en Latinoamérica. *La Revista Del CCC [En Línea]*, *11*.

Naess, A. (1973). The shallow and the deep, long-range ecology movement. A summary. *Inquiry*, *16*(1–4), 95–100.

N'Kaschama, L. (2012). *Ethno-development and Ethnocide in Africa; extracts*. UNESCO. http://unesdoc.unesco.org/images/0005/000508/050868eb.pdf.

Ostrom, E. (1990). *Governing the commons: The evolution of institutions for collective action*. Cambridge University Press.

Oviedo, A. (2011). *Qué es el Sumakawsay*. Quito: Sumak.

Paco, Felix. P. (2004). *Sistema Comunal. Una Propuesta Alternativa al Sistema Liberal*. CEA.

Paco, Felix. P. (2007). *Insurgencia y sumision. Movimientos sociales e indıgenas, segunda edicion ampliada 1983-2007*. Ediciones Yachaywasi.

Partridge, W., Uquillas, J., & Johns, K. (1996). *Including the excluded: Ethnodevelopment in Latin America*. New Society.

Pilataxi Lechón, C. (2014). *Sumak Kawsay organización Comunitaria y Emprendimiento Pro̍ductivo. El Caso de San Pablo Urku, Cayambe*. Abya Yala.

Prebisch, R. (1994). Growth poles. *The elgar companion to radical political economy*, 174, New York:Edward Elgar Pub.

Putnam, R. D. (2001). *Bowling alone: The collapse and revival of American community*. Simon and Schuster.

Quijano, A. (2000). Colonialidad del poder, eurocentrismo y América Latina. *La colonialidad del saber: eurocentrismo y ciencias sociales. Perspectivas Latinoamericanas. Edgardo Lander (comp.) CLACSO, Consejo Latinoamericano de Ciencias Sociales*. http://bibliotecavirtual.clacso.org.ar/ar/libros/lander/quijano.rtf.

Quijano, A. (2011). *'Colonialidad del Poder, Eurocentrismo y América Latina' en Edgardo Lander (Comp.) La Colonialidad del Saber: Eurocentrismo y Ciencias Sociales: Perspectivas Latinoamericanas* (2nd edición). Ciccus Ediciones.

Ramírez-Gallegos, R. (2010). *Socialismo del Sumak Kawsay o biosocialismo republicano*. SENPLADES, Secretaría Nacional de Planificación y Desarrollo.

Ramírez-Gallegos, R. (2011). *La felicidad como medida del buen vivir en Ecuador*. SENPLADES.

Razeto, L. (1984). *Economía de Solidaridad y Mercado Democrático*. Programa de Economía del Trabajo.

Razeto, L. (2000). *Los Caminos de la Economía de Solidaridad*. Rescoop.

Rostow, W. (1952). *The process of economic growth*. W. W. Norton.

Rostow, W. (1960). *The stages of economic growth: A non-communist manifesto*. Cambridge University Press.

Sachs, J. (2005). *The end of poverty: How we can make it happen in our lifetime*. UK: Penguin.

Santos, B. de S. (2003, March 27). *The world social forum: Toward a counter-hegemonic globalisation (PART I)*. XXIV International Congress of the Latin American Studies Association, Dallas.

Santos, B. de S. (2007). *The rise of the global left. The world social forum*. Zed Books.

Santos, B. de S. (2010). Hablamos del socialismo del Buen Vivir. *Camino Socialista*, *9*, 4–7.

Schneider, F., Kallis, G., & Martínez-Alier, J. (2010). Crisis or opportunity? Economic degrowth for social equity and ecological sustainability. *Introduction to This Special Issue. J Clean Prod*, *18*, 511–518.

Schumpeter, J. A. (1961). *The theory of economic development: An inquiry into profits, capital, credit, interest, and the business cycle. Translated by Redvers Opie*. Harvard University Press.

Sen, A. (2000). *Desarrollo y libertad*. Oxford University Press.

Sen, A. (2001). *Development as Freedom*. Oxford University Press.

Sen, A., & Anand, S. (2000). Human development and economic sustainability. *Human Development and Economic Sustainability*, *28*(12), 2029–2049.

SENPLADES. (2009). *Plan Nacional para el Buen Vivir 2009-2013: Construyendo un Estado Plurinacional e Intercultural*. Quito: Talleres Gráficos Calle.

SENPLADES. (2011). Recuperación del Estado para el Buen Vivir, *Revolución Productiva a Través Del Conocimiento y El Talento Humano*. SENPLADES.

SENPLADES. (2012). *Transformación de la matriz productiva. Revolución Productiva a Través Del Conocimiento y El Talento Humano*. SENPLADES.

Shiva, V. (2004). *Monocultures of the mind*. Zed Books.

Shiva, V. (2005). *Earth democracy*. South End Press.

Shiva, V. (2008). *Soil not oil: Environmental justice in an age of climate crisis*. South End Press.

Simbaña, F. (2012). *"El sumak kawsay como proyecto político"*. In M. Lang & D. Mokrani (Eds.), *Más allá del desarrollo* (pp. 219–226). Abya Yala.

Smit, B., & Pilifosova, O. (2003). Adaptation to climate change in the context of sustainable development and equity. *Sustainable Development*, *8*(9), 9.

Springer, S., Birch, K., & MacLeavy, J. (2016). *Handbook of neoliberalism*. Routledge.

Stefanoni, P. (2010). *Indianismo y pachamamismo*. Rebelion. http://www.rebelion.org/noticia.php?id=105233.

Stefanoni, P. (2011). Adónde nos lleva el pachamamismo. *Tabula Rasa*, *15*, 261–264.

Svampa, M. (2011). Extractivismo neodesarrollista y movimientos sociales:¿ Un giro ecoterritorial hacia nuevas alternativas. *Más Allá Del Desarrollo*, *1*, 185–218.

Svampa, M. (2012). *Pensar el desarrollo desde America Latina*. In G Massuh (Ed.), *Renunciar al bien común. Extractivismo y (pos)desarrollo en America Latina*, Buenos Aires: Mardulce, pp. 17–58.

Tauli-Corpuz, V. (1996). *The concept of indigenous peoples' self-determined development or development with identity and culture: Challenges And Trajectories*. Tebtebba Foundation. http://portal.unesco.org/culture/en/files/37745/12197591975Concept_paper_Indigenous_Peoples__Development_with_Identity.pdf/Concept%2Bpaper%2BIndigenous%2BPeoples%2B%2BDevelopment%2Bwith%2BIdentity.pdf.

Temple, D. (2003). la teoría de la reciprocidad, *Tomo I. la reciprocidad y el nacimiento de los valores humanos*. La Paz: Padep-Gtz.

Tödtling, Franz (2010). Endogenous approaches to local and regional development policy, *Handbook of local and regional development*. Routledge. https://doi.org/10.4324/9780203842393.ch28.

Toledo, V. (2009). *Ecología política, sustentabilidad y poder social en Latinoamérica. La Agonía de Un Mito¿ Cómo Reformular El "desarrollo.*

Ulloa, A. (2004). *El Nativo Ecológico. Complejidades, Paradojas y Dilemas de la Relación de los Movimientos Indigenas y el Ambientalismo en Colombia*. Icanh.

Unceta, K. (2014). Desarrollo, postcrecimiento y Buen Vivir. *Debate Constituyente. Quito: Abya-Yala. Recuperado de* Http://Rosalux. Org. Ec/Es/Mediateca/Mediateca-Es-Publicaciones/175-Alternativas-Aldesarrollo/830-Postecrecimientokoldounceta. Html.

Vanhulst, J. (2015). El laberinto de los discursos del Buen vivir: Entre Sumak Kawsay y Socialismo del siglo XXI. *Polis (Santiago)*, *14*(40), 233–261.

Vázquez-Barquero, A. (2003). *Endogenous Development: Networking, Innovation, Institutions, and Cities*. Routledge.

Wallerstein, I. (1974). *The modern world-system (Vol. I)*. Academic Press.

Wallerstein, I. (1989). *The modern world-system (Vol. III)*. Academic Press.

Walsh, C. (2012). 'Other' knowledges, 'other' critiques: Reflections on the politics and practices of philosophy and decoloniality in the 'other' America. *Transmodernity*, *1*(3), 11–27.

Warren, B. (1980). *Imperialism: Pioneer of capitalism*. Verso Books.

Weber, M. (2002). *The protestant ethic and the 'spirit' of capitalism and other writings*. UK: Penguin.

Willmott, P. (1986). *Social networks, informal care and public policy*. Policy Studies Institute.

Willmott, P. (1989). *Community initiatives: Patterns and prospects*. Policy Studies Institute.

Yánez, J. F. T. (2015). Impacto del Plan del Buen Vivir 2013–2017 para el bienestar del pueblo ecuatoriano. *Revista Publicando*, 2(4), 96–110.

Zuñiga, G. (1995). *El Etnodesarrollo: Un Enfoque de Problematización Sobre el Desarrollo Indígena*. Tierra, Territorio y desarrollo indígena IEI-UFRO.

2 Global governance to address local ills

The Universal Periodic Review aiding the creation of a third space in pursuit of land rights that support social innovation, biodiversity and natural capital in Latin America

Louisa Ashley

Introduction

This chapter is based on a study of recommendations and stakeholder submissions made to the government of Colombia during the country's third cycle Universal Periodic Review (UPR) in May 2018. UPR is a United Nations international human rights monitoring mechanism whereby reviewing states address the progress of the state under review against its human rights obligations, making recommendations accordingly. This chapter critically explores two propositions. The first is that UPR is a global governance mechanism for human rights located within an international human right 'regime complex'. A regime complex comprises different entities relevant to a particular field with an overlapping function (Keohane and Victor, 2011, p15–16). The complex accommodates 'an array of partially overlapping and non-hierarchical institutions governing a particular issue-area', where 'the rules in these elemental regimes functionally overlap' (Raustiala and Victor, 2004, p279).

The second proposition is that UPR is uniquely composed and positioned to accommodate a textual and political 'third space', as conceived by Homi Bhabha. In a third space, marginalized identities and muted voices that are central to pioneering and championing social innovation and mobilisation to support social and natural capital have the potential to be present and heard on a global stage. This is due to two fundamental characteristics of UPR. Firstly, UPR takes within its scope recommendations from other mechanisms in the international human rights regime complex that include those made by non-state and civil society actors. Secondly, UPR is a state-to-state peer review mechanism during which state delegations support and thereby commit to human rights promotion, protection and remedy on a global stage. However, premised as it is upon 'peer' review, the process is (unsurprisingly) subject to regionalism and politicization (Terman and Voeten, 2018, pp1–23), with some states using it as a vehicle for 'ideological warfare' (Tomuschat, 2011, p619). Furthermore, UPR provides all states with a platform to instruct on human rights matters, regardless of the position of rights in their own 'backyard' (Human Rights Voices, 2014).

This study specifically considers those recommendations that refer to the right to land, the rights of indigenous peoples and human rights defenders. Action to protect land rights and community interest can create sites of protest within which indigenous peoples, minority communities and human rights defenders come into potentially violent conflict with state and non-state actors. Resistance is often against development projects such as dam building, agri-business and mining that cause the outright loss or degradation of social and natural capital. Repeatedly, it is indigenous peoples and minority communities that are directly affected by the related land dispossession and/or change in land use. Yet the rights holders of these peoples and communities have been historically, and continue to be, subjugated by dominant political and legal state structures. Via UPR the subjects of rights and rights holders that are not addressed in a specific United Nations human rights treaty are given attention.

The realization of these rights is foundational in contributing to the political, cultural, social and institutional conditions necessary to support social innovation by supporting the socially Marginalized and vulnerable to realize their potential to operate as productive economic subjects (Oosterlynck et al., 2013). Analysis of the proportion and content of recommendations that refer to those rights, and the extent to which those recommendations reflect stakeholder submissions and recommendations made by other rights regimes, suggests that UPR does have the potential to accommodate a textual and political third space. The protection of the rights and equality of women is also key to this field and Colombia is a state party to the Convention on the Elimination of Discrimination Against Women, however, despite concerns that there is often 'a significant gap or a "strategic silence"' (Moulaert et al., 2017, p31, citing Bakker, 1994), there is not the scope to specifically include gender here.

In a 'third space', identity is not fixed, it is under negotiation. As such, identity exists in a liminal and hybrid space where new initiatives and identities are created. Although Bhabha's work on liminality and hybridity is focused on postcolonialism in former British colonies, for Céire Broderick it 'resonates with the postcolonial situation in Latin America', where 'already complex identities enter into further negotiation to create new hybrid forms' (Broderick, 2019, p750). For Bhabha:

> ...the importance of hybridity is not to be able to trace the two original moments from which the third emerges, rather hybridity is to me the 'third space' which enables other positions to emerge. This third space displaces the histories that created it, and sets up new structures of authority and political initiatives...
>
> (Rutherford, 1998, p211)

Elsewhere, this author has written in favour of UPR creating 'a uniquely plural space that opens a realm of possibilities not driven solely by one or another international or regional institution, alliance or regime'. Consequentially, 'the pluralism at the heart of UPR creates a broadly conceptualized hybrid space that accommodates similarity and difference, within which the hybrid and the non-hybrid can coexist' (Riches, 2017, p162). Such pluralism supports the proposition of UPR as an ideational third space, albeit one in which political bias and unequal power dynamics mean states 'are less likely to criticize their friends' and 'are more lenient towards their strategic partners in the peer-reviewing process' (Terman and Voeten, 2018, p1). The discursive and iterative process that characterizes UPR has the potential to influence state practice via mimicry and acculturation (Goodman and Jinks, 2013). Conversely, this process can encourage ritualism and institutionalization in which 'ceremonies or formalities that, through repetition, entrench the understandings and the power relationships that they embody' risk an 'embodied performance' that overshadows the significance of a process and its requirements in terms of regulation or governance (Charlesworth and Larking, 2014, p9). The risk is that these factors encourage a one-size-fits-all approach, stifling state ability or inclination to explore alternatives.

Section I briefly identifies some of the key challenges regarding land rights in Colombia and how these are addressed at a national level. Section II outlines why UPR is an apt global governance mechanism for this study, describing UPR's scope and procedure. Section III analyses the nature and the proportion of UPR recommendations to Colombia that relate to the right to land, indigenous peoples and human rights defenders over the course of Colombia's most recent (third cycle) UPR. It considers the thematic nature of those recommendations and the identity of the recommending states. Section IV focuses upon the role of various stakeholders within civil society during UPR and how the contribution of civil society to the recommendation and implementation process can be strengthened. The chapter concludes with some final thoughts on the capacity of UPR to create and accommodate a third space that attends to those issues and identities that exist largely at the margins and periphery of formal state structures.

Colombia: land rights, social and natural capital

Both historically and contemporaneously, land rights, land ownership and land reform in Colombia have been contested (KPMG: Investment in Colombia, 2018 LeGrand Catherine C, 2003). This has played a central role in the destruction and degradation of both social and natural capital. This section provides some context to the national legal mechanisms designed to address land rights in Colombia and the role of the Inter-American Commission on Human Rights (IACHR) and the Inter-American Court of Human Rights (IACtHR) as regional institutions involved in the protection of land rights in Latin America more broadly.

Colombia currently boasts the status of being a 'mega diverse' country, home to 10% of the world's biodiversity. Paradoxically, decades of conflict and civil war appear to have supported the preservation of biodiversity. Despite illegal mining and logging activity at a local level, the virtual absence in conflict-ridden areas of national and international investment to develop the country's extractive and agricultural industries has contributed to the preservation of much of Colombia's biodiversity and natural ecosystems (Salazar et al., 2018; Wheeling, 2019). Yet Colombia is vast and fertile and is enjoying new-found relative peace following the government's signing of the Peace Accords with the FARC (Final Agreement for Ending the Conflict and Building a Stable and Lasting Peace, 24 November 2016, between the government and the Revolutionary Armed Forces of Colombia – People's Army) (FARC-EP) (in Spanish, Fuerzas Armadas Revolucionarias de Colombia – Ejército del Pueblo). This has piqued the interest of overseas business, prompting investors to make significant inroads with potentially adverse implications for both natural and social capital (KPMG: Investment in Colombia, 2018; Smith, 2019).

Struggles in Colombia related to land are entwined in complex narratives of social, cultural and political identity that shape political ecology and, in turn, the methods by which social innovation and natural capital are protected and fostered at local, regional and national levels (Escobar and Paulson, 2005). Displacement from land in Colombia has been primarily through forcible abandonment and coercive legal dispossession (*despojo*) (Peña-Huertas et al., 2017, p1). Legal dispossession of land from smallholders has included sales at an undervalue, with the purchaser subsequently selling the land at up to ten times the price paid (Peña-Huertas et al., 2017, p7). Armed actors and 'powerful civil predators', such as big landowners and agribusiness, took advantage of 'three sources of opportunity to accumulate land' during periods of violence (Peña-Huertas et al., 2017, pp2–3). Firstly, an environment of fear; secondly, opportunities 'to capture or align' state agencies along 'purportedly anti-subversive (legal or illegal) actions'; and thirdly, the weak status of peasant property rights (Peña-Huertas et al., 2017, pp2–3).

Colombia's 'Law 1448', the Victims and Land Restitution Act, was passed in 2011. The objective of the Act, promoted by the then government of President Juan Manuel Santos in direct contrast to what has been described as 'the previous government's policy of denial', is to provide restitution to victims of the conflict (Cortés, 2013). Paula Martínez Cortés identifies a number of factors as to why meeting that objective is problematic. These include the Act being introduced during the conflict; land grabbing; government action to 'dismantle the few legal instruments that defend indigenous, Afro-Colombian and peasant farmers' territories'; and the repression of those attempting to counter the government's approach (Cortés, 2013, p3). There are instances of domestic land tribunals ruling that land be returned to its previous owner but getting to the hearing stage is a long and fraught process, as illustrated by purchases in the Mid-Magdalena River region and rulings in Sabana de Torres – Tribunal de Cúcuta, 09 July 2014 and 25 February 2015 and San Alberto, Tribunal de Cartagena, 1 February 2013 (Peña-Huertas et al., 2017, p763). Whilst the IACHR and the IACtHR have heard cases against Latin American cases involving land rights leading to orders for restitution and reparation, matters before these mechanisms involving Colombia do not currently relate to land (e.g. *Xákmok Kásek Indigenous Community v Paraguay*, Series C No. 214, Judgment of 24 August 2010, IACtHR and *Case of the Mayagna (Sumo) Awas Tingni Community v. Nicaragua. Merits, Reparations and Costs.* Series C No. 79, Judgment of August 31, 2001, IACtHR).

In the 2016 Peace Accord, the government directly addressed issues of land, committing to large-scale land-titling programs, crop substitution, recognition of the displacement and dispossession of land, land restitution and rural reform. All to be underpinned by principles supporting an ethnic-based approach, as detailed in section 3 of the Final Agreement. These commitments are said to hang in the balance. During his election campaign in 2018, the present President, Iván Duque, pledged to dismantle the Peace Accord but has since been hampered by the country's Constitutional Court (Sánchez-Garzoli, 2019). Nonetheless, he is reported to have reduced funding and resources for land related projects as well as truth and justice mechanisms and reintegration programs (Sánchez-Garzoli, 2019).

UPR: an apt global governance mechanism

Taking inspiration from the work of Robert Keohane, David Victor and Kal Raustiala on global governance and 'regime complexes' (Keohane and Victor, 2011; Raustiala and Victor, 2004), this section introduces UPR as a global governance mechanism situated within a regime complex for the governance of international human rights. It then proceeds to explain why UPR presents an apt vehicle via which to promote a human rights based approach to fostering and protecting social innovation for social and natural capital. In doing so, this section outlines key aspects of UPR process and procedure.

A global governance regime

The concepts of governance and global governance are contested. Governance has been described as 'the exercise of control' (Rosenau, 1992, p3), the 'exercise of authority, control, management, power of government' (World Bank, 1992, p3) and as governance in the absence of global government (Ruggie, 2014, p5). There have been attempts to distinguish its forms according to the governance actors involved (non-state and/or state). Global governance *by* government equating to *world* government; global governance *with* government occurring via institutions such as the United Nations; and global governance *without* governments being pursued by transnational actors, such as the International Accounting Standards Board (emphasis added) (Ruggie, 2014, p4). In this study, global governance regimes are taken as those that have been ascribed powers of regulation and authority, and where the principles and norms referred to are not limited to the national borders of individual states, so that 'the ensemble of all forms of regulation... are oriented towards social values and have cross-border effects' (Calliess and Renner, 2007, p22 citing Zürn, 2005, p121 and 127).

The author of this chapter has argued elsewhere that UPR has a central role to play as a human rights global governance mechanism that connects with and reasserts the governance function of other entities within a proposed international human rights regime complex (Ashley, 2018). A regime complex comprises different entities relevant to a particular field, with an overlapping function (Keohane and Victor, 2011, p15–16). Martti Koskenniemi prefers the term 'rule-complex', with a similarly specific focus or form of expertise, such as human rights, trade or the environment, and possesses its own principles and institutions (Koskenniemi, 2006, para 8), whilst Keohane and Victor focus upon governance in the context of climate change. A regime (or rule) complex comprises a collection of related institutions that have developed over time in response to a variety of factors, including political difficulties, a divergence in state interest and/or the dysfunction of current or previous international organization (Keohane and Victor, 2011, p13–15). As noted above, such a complex is characterized by institutions that are non-hierarchical with rules that functionally overlap, 'yet there is no agreed upon hierarchy for resolving conflicts between rules' (Raustiala and Victor, 2004, p279). In this sense, a regime complex thus reflects the disaggregation that, for some, characterizes international law (Raustiala and Victor, 2004, p295).

Whilst there has been no substantial scholarship on the concept and operation of an international human rights regime complex, there has been some passing reference for some time to 'international human rights regimes' and 'human rights regimes' (Shaffer and Ginsburg, 2012, p21 and 25, citing Moravcsik, 2000, p217). Writing in the late 1980s, Bruno Simma and Philip Alston noted that:

> (...) prospects for developing an effective and largely consensual international regime depend significantly on the extent to which those institutions are capable of basing their actions upon a coherent and generally applicable set of human rights norms.
>
> (Simma and Alston, p82–3)

The UPR enjoys a degree of success in this respect. UPR recommendations are seen to replicate, echo or follow the thematic focus of findings and recommendations of other entities within the regime complex, such as treaty bodies, special procedures and civil society (Ashley, 2018). This repetition and reinforcement both assert the legitimacy of the UPR and the authority of the entities within the regime complex.

Institutions within particular regime complexes have generally developed over time due to various factors, including political difficulty, divergence in state interest and/or the dysfunction of current or previous international organisation(s) (Keohane and Victor, 2011, p13–15). The same is true of the international human rights regime complex. It encompasses state and non-state actors and institutions that operate at a domestic, regional and/or global level. This includes, for example, the state and its machinery; international human rights treaties and corresponding committees; the Human Rights Council, including Special Procedures and regular sessions; UPR; regional human rights conventions and corresponding courts; national human rights institutions (NHRIs); civil society; and other treaties that address human rights matters, for example, International Labour Organization (ILO) Convention no. 169 (Indigenous and Tribal Peoples Convention).

UPR origins

UPR is a United Nations Charter mechanism of the Human Rights Council. Its creation was in response to recommendations of a High-level Panel on Threats, Challenges and Change (the Panel) that had been tasked with determining how to adapt the United Nations to meet twenty-first century challenges (UNGA, A/59/569, 2004). The Panel acknowledged the interconnectedness of threats to global security and that 'institutions must overcome their narrow preoccupations and learn to work across the whole range of issues, in a concerted fashion' (UNGA, A/59/569, 2004, vii). Led by the then United Nations Secretary-General

Kofi Annan, the Panel proposed an institution-building package. This package would address the 'legitimacy deficit' of the Commission for Human Rights, which was casting 'a shadow on the reputation of the United Nations system as a whole' (UNGA, A/59/569, 2004, para 182), of which much has been written elsewhere (Freedman, 2013; Oberleitner, 2008; Schrijver, 2007). It would do so by creating a Human Rights Council to include in its remit a UPR 'based on objective and reliable information, of the fulfilment by each State of its human rights obligations and commitments in a manner which ensures universality of coverage and equal treatment with respect to all States' (UNGA A/RES/60/251, para 5(e)). A somewhat challenging objective to meet given the multiplicity of state and non-state actor motivations, including self-interest.

It is a principle of UPR that all stakeholders, including civil society and NHRIs, participate in the review (although the role of civil society is limited, as discussed in section IV below) (UNHRC A/HRC/RES/5/1, para 3(e)). Each United Nations member state is scheduled for review once during each five-year cycle (UNHRC A/HRC/RES/16/21). A state under review receives recommendations during a three and a half hour 'working group session' at the Palais de Nations in Geneva. The state must support or note each recommendation and report on follow-up and implementation of recommendations from the previous UPR cycle at the next review (UNHRC A/HRC/RES/16/21).

UPR commenced in 2008. Fast forward ten years, to the start of the current third UPR cycle in May 2017, when the then High Commissioner for Human Rights asked of the mechanism:

> Has there been real improvement? As we enter the third round of scrutiny, is the UPR deepening in relevance, precision and impact? Is it merely an elaborate performance of mutual diplomatic courtesies, or is it leading to real and powerful changes to anchor peace and development and improve people's lives?
>
> (Hussein and Ra'ad, 2017)

These questions are pertinent, and a body of critical literature on UPR has evolved over the last decade or so (Charlesworth and Larking, 2014; Terman and Voeten, 2018; Tomuschat, 2011). Whilst there are risks, as noted above, of aspects of the UPR process becoming an 'embodied performance' based on ritual and ritualism, certain unifying aspects of ritual such as 'enacting a social consensus' can function to reduce contestation and indicate that 'a way of thinking or being has achieved some degree of permanence and importance' (Charlesworth and Larking, 2014, p9). During the cyclical and iterative UPR process, states are repeatedly encouraged to implement and account for their human rights commitments and challenges, and yet the implementation of recommendations by states remains a concern. Recommending states and civil society are proactive in holding states to account for their follow-up of supported of recommendations, but this is sporadic and in its infancy (Ashley, 2018, sections 5.3.4 and 7.4.2). UPR process has been strengthened by the provision of more specific guidance and support in terms of state preparation and follow-up and the need to consult with civil society and interested parties (Etone, 2017, 264-5). By appropriating aspects of ritual and ritualism, it may be possible that state commitment to UPR processes and principles is developed which in turn leads to normative change.

An apt mechanism

UPR is a unique global governance mechanism within the regime complex for international human rights for two reasons. One, because it has thus far secured universal engagement by United Nations member states, unlike treaty bodies. This fosters UPR legitimacy and authority as well as stakeholder confidence that a state scheduled for review will engage. However, the nature of state engagement varies considerably, with some states advancing UPR legitimacy in a procedural sense only, so that UPR output legitimacy, where state engagement effects actual positive change in rights conditions, is far from guaranteed (Ashley, 2018, 4.4).

Two, UPR has a broad scope that encompasses all legal and voluntary human rights obligations of the state under review. This means UPR is not limited to one right or set of rights, as with the United Nations human rights treaty system. UPR encompasses matters that are not addressed in specific human rights treaties and those included in a treaty that a state is not party to. Colombia was one of 11 states that abstained from voting when the United Nations Declaration on the Rights of Indigenous Peoples (2007) was adopted, but this does not prevent matters relating to the rights of indigenous peoples coming before UPR. Reviewing states can comment and make recommendations in relation to any pertinent human rights matter. This is noteworthy given the intersectionality of indigenous rights with the right to land and rights pertaining to human rights defenders and civil society.

The promotion and protection of human rights is pursued using UPR in a variety of methods. Primarily, this is via a state-to-state peer review during an interactive dialogue whereby reviewing states comment upon the human rights progress of the state under review and make recommendations. The state under review must respond following the working group session to each recommendation by either supporting or noting it. If a recommendation is supported (and the vast majority are), this provides both the recommending state and the civil society grounds upon which to approach the state post review for an update as to follow up and implementation. If noting a recommendation, the state under review is required to explain why that recommendation is not being supported. A new feature of the third cycle is that following the working group session, the OHCHR (Office of the High Commissioner for Human Rights) publishes a matrix of the recommendations made to a particular state, collating them thematically and indicating the status of each (supported/noted). Each recommendation is also aligned to one or more specific sustainable development goals (SDGs), bringing a state's achievements against SDGs into the rights governance arena and emphasizing the link between human rights and development.

Prior to the working group session, the OHCHR summarizes written submissions made by civil society organizations (CSOs) (see section III below) and creates a compilation of recommendations that have been made to the state under review by other regimes in the international human rights regime complex, such as treaty bodies and special procedures. Increasing importance is attributed to the human rights investigations and advocacy of civil society actors, but this comes with a word of warning. As Makau Matua notes, CSOs are largely dominated by Western agencies that are funded by the global north, risking a civilizing mission that echoes imperialism (and potentially validates criticisms levied against the operation of the international human rights framework as a neo-imperialistic vehicle) (Matua, 2016, pviii and 80).

UPR recommendations to Colombia

This section analyses the proportion and content of UPR recommendations to Colombia on the right to land, indigenous peoples and human rights defenders over the last three cycles. Indigenous peoples and human rights defenders play a key role both directly and indirectly in supporting social innovation and the maintenance and restoration of social and natural capital at local and national levels. Across Latin America, those campaigning and advocating to protect community and land rights risk threats and acts of (fatal) violence against them. Activism against the environmental, cultural and health impacts of, for example, the farming of palm oil, geothermal development and illegal logging has been met with violence (Watts, 2018; Agren, 2019; Associated Press in Lima, 2019). Land related tensions and conflicts are variously rooted in the historical legacy of the slave trade and colonialism (Branford and Torres, 2017), global agribusiness (Romano-Armada et al., 2014), legal and illegal logging and extractive industries (McDonald, 2009) and development projects such as hydroelectric power (Branford and Borges, 2019). For Colombia, land grabbing and dispossession connected to decades of civil war and illicit crop farming and trade, as well as 'forms of accumulation [that] are strongly mediated by national institutions', are also significant factors (Borras et al., 2013; Peña-Huertas et al., 2017).

The insecurity and risk faced by community leaders and rights defenders across Colombia is illustrated by the statistics cited in UPR documentation. Ahead of Colombia's third cycle UPR in May 2018, the Ombudsman's Office of Colombia, Colombia's NHRI, reported that '134 social or community leaders and human rights defenders had been killed in Colombia in 2016' and that in the first seven and half months of 2017, there were 58 killings (UNHRC A/HRC/WG.6/30/COL/2, 2018). The Office also stated that 'some 500 cases of threats against social leaders and human rights defenders, 61 of which involved threats against groups, had also been documented' (para 6). In a joint UPR stakeholder submission made by almost 20 NGOs to the OHCHR, it was reported that between 2013 and 2017 there were 'at least 276 killings and 164 attacks' against human rights defenders and social leaders, with many of those killed engaged in defending the right to land in rural areas (UNHRC HRC/WG.6/30/COL/3, para 51).

The data presented in Table 1 for Colombia's first and second cycle UPRs is extracted from a database of UPR recommendations compiled by UPR-Info (UPR-Info). At the time of writing, UPR-Info has yet to publish data on Colombia's third cycle UPR; therefore, the data presented is calculated with reference to the recommendations matrix published by the OHCHR (OHCHR, Matrix). The final column of table 1 contains the 'action-category' ascribed by UPR-Info to each recommendation according to a coding methodology devised by Edward McMahon's (McMahon, 2012). There are five action-categories. Those recommendations that require specific, tangible action are the most demanding of the state under review and often more easily measured in terms of follow-up. These are category five recommendations that commonly request the state to 'conduct, develop, eliminate, establish, investigate' and may contain legal verbs such as 'abolish, accede, adopt, amend, implement, enforce, ratify'. States are being encouraged to make recommendations that are precise and require a higher threshold of action (UPR Info, 2015). Recommendations within category five retain the focus and specificity of category five but err towards the generic, containing verbs such as 'accelerate, address, encourage, engage with, ensure, guarantee, intensify, promote, speed up, strengthen, take action, take measures or steps towards'. Implementation may require little further tangible change on the part of the state. Categories 1–3 require minimal action and are generally simple to evidence in terms of compliance. They contain verbs such as continue, consider, maintain and explore.

Recommendations on the right to land

As Table 1 indicates, only one recommendation to Colombia in the first UPR cycle referred to the right to land. In the second cycle, this rose to 14, amounting to just over 8% of its recommendations, but fell again in the current third cycle to seven (3.3%). These recommendations variously refer to ensuring land restitution and reparation, with nearly half of the second cycle recommendations referring specifically to implementing or enforcing the Victims and Land Restitution Act. This is no doubt in light of criticism of the institutions and processes involved in implementing the Victims and Land Restitution Act (García-Godos and Wiig, 2018). Even so, the proportion of recommendations on the subject of right to land is relatively low. This is surprising given how heavily the issue of land features in the 2016 Peace Accord and in the stakeholder submissions to Colombia's third cycle UPR. The United Nations Western and Other Group (WEOG) made 31% of the total recommendations received by Colombia in its second cycle (statistical data for third cycle recommending groups is not available at the time of writing) (UPR Info, Statistics). This group includes four of the five highest investors of foreign direct investment to Colombia, namely, the UK, US, Spain and Switzerland (Colombia Reports, 2020), and may be a motivation for wanting to see progress in human rights protections in accordance with investment treaties.

Australia, Bolivia and Holy See made recommendations on the right to land in both second and third cycles. The iterative and cyclical nature of UPR reveals the same states making recommendations on a particular rights issue again and again, which have been repeatedly supported by Colombia but have not lead to state action. This reveals the weakness of UPR being absent an enforcement mechanism. This gives a strong foundation upon which those reviewing states, along with civil society (see section IV below), follow-up.

Recommendations on indigenous peoples

The number and proportion of recommendations that refer to the rights of indigenous peoples, and often include Afro-Colombian communities, has risen steadily over the course of Colombia's three UPRs. In the first cycle, there were seven recommendations (6.25%), in the second cycle, there were nine (5.39%) and in third cycle, there were 21 (20%). Those made in the first cycle referred to the Special Rapporteur on the rights and fundamental freedoms of indigenous peoples and The United Nations Declaration on the Rights of Indigenous Peoples (UNDRIP). Second cycle recommendations cited the need for consultation, support for a better quality of life and protection from armed groups. Concerns raised in the third cycle relate to transitional justice, truth and reconciliation, justice and reparation for victims of the violence, access to health, education and protection regarding non-discrimination, and consultation. Bolivia, Brazil, Canada and the UK all made recommendations in the first and third cycles referring to indigenous peoples' rights, and Norway and Senegal in the second and third.

It is surprising to see that only one recommendation (third cycle) refers to the principle of free, prior and informed consent (FPIC). This recommendation was by the Holy See to: Ensure that indigenous and rural communities can express their free and informed consent prior to any measure that may affect their lives and their ancestral land. FPIC is central to development projects and land use. A 'major demand of indigenous peoples facing development projects likely to impact their livelihoods (e.g. mines, dams) is to be able to have a say about whether and how the project should proceed', and FPIC is the vehicle via which having this say is possible, despite it being 'very far short of the ideal' (Hanna and Vanclay, 2013, p146).

Colombia received recommendations on this matter from other human rights regimes within the international human rights regime complex as highlighted within the OHCHR compilation prepared as part of Colombia's UPR and which state missions have access to (UNHRC A/HRC/WG.6/30/COL/2, para 93). Those regimes include the Human Rights Committee for the International Covenant on Civil and Political Rights, the Committee on the Elimination of Racial Discrimination for the Convention on the Elimination of Racial Discrimination and the Committee on the Elimination of Discrimination Against Women for Convention on the Elimination of Discrimination Against Women, each of which monitors Colombia's implementation of commitments as a state party to the respective international human rights treaties.

Recommendations on human rights defenders

During the first cycle UPR, the second highest proportion of recommendations to Colombia referred to human rights defenders, which also includes community and social leaders. This was the seventh highest issue in the second cycle, out of 40 issues cited. In the first cycle, 17 states made recommendations citing themes, such as the need for human rights defenders to be acknowledged and for the state to refrain from linking them, and trade unionists, with illegal guerrilla groups; for their protection to be strengthened and crimes and violations against them, trade unionists and advocacy groups punished; and to ensure that high ranking officials and security forces do not qualify human rights defenders and NGO members as terrorists.

Second cycle recommendations on human rights defenders retained a similar focus. They required Colombia to prevent incidents of violence against all of its people, including community leaders; to strengthen and provide appropriate protection; to recognize the legitimacy of their work; to increase efforts to investigate and prosecute those responsible for threats or violence against human rights defenders, trade unionists, community leaders and journalists; and to ensure judicial authorities carry out thorough and impartial investigations. The protection of human rights defenders has remained consistently high on the agenda with almost a quarter of the third cycle recommendations on this subject, with a continued focus on the need to fight impunity and take measures to prevent killings and attacks against human rights defenders, and social and community leaders.

The majority of these recommendations are category four and five requiring specific action. Hungary made a strong category five recommendation, that Colombia '[e]nact legislation recognizing the legitimate work of human rights defenders and ensuring their life, security and integrity'. By supporting this recommendation, Colombia is ostensibly committing to take action and to reporting to the international community during its fourth cycle review the measures that have or have not been taken. Due to the lack of an UPR enforcement mechanism, state motivation to implement supported recommendations is driven by one or more of a variety of factors including 'politicisation, the "club" mentality, reciprocity, acculturation and being held to account through naming and shaming' (Ashley, 2018, section 5.6). Furthermore, state motivation to implement particular resolutions may be that the recommendations were of a type that 'had been made to all states, they were not biased or targeted by one grouping of states against another, and that made them acceptable' (Ashley, 2018, section 5.6).

Hungary made two recommendations in the previous cycle on the subject of human rights defenders, one asking the government to agree to a visit by the Special Rapporteur on human rights defenders and the other referring to the implementation of the Ministry of the Interior's protection program to defend human rights defenders in the field. Norway and the UK made recommendations on this subject to Colombia during each UPR cycle, Sweden during the first and third cycles and Slovenia during the second and third. The UK and Sweden have also raised this issue via third cycle advance questions. The UK asked whether the government would invite the Special Rapporteur on the situation of human rights defenders to visit Colombia and agree to collaborate on recommendations. Sweden asked for the government to outline its approach 'to ensure that human rights defenders, including those defending social rights and issues regarding land and natural resources, are guaranteed relevant protection' (OHCHR Advance Questions: Colombia Third Cycle).

It is worth noting here that in July 2018, two months after Colombia's third cycle UPR, it was announced that the IACHR was taking matters relating to political violence against members of the Patriotic Union (Union Patriotica – UP) to the Inter-American Court of Human Rights for the government's failure to take action against its recommendations (IACHR Press Release, 2018). These related to investigations of 'successive serious human rights violations perpetrated against more than 6,000 victims who were officials or members of the political party

Patriotic Union in Colombia, for over 20 years starting in 1984' (IACHR Press Release, 2018). The IAHCR's conclusions included violation by the government of the right to a fair trial and to judicial protection, as well as violating the right to humane treatment of victims' families (IACHR Press Release, 2018). There is no explicit reference in UPR recommendations to this particular matter which would have been with the IACHR (rather than the IACtHR) at the time. It would be interesting to see if this would have been different had this announcement been made before Colombia's UPR.

As indicated, a handful of states have made one or more recommendations on one or more of the above rights issues to Colombia in more than one UPR cycle (and there is scope for future research into the motivations for states recommending as they do to Colombia). All of the recommendations have been supported. In supporting a recommendation in a forum such as UPR, a state is (in theory) expressing its political will and commitment to accept relevant human rights norms and principles and to take action accordingly. However, as the renewed focus upon follow-up and implementation at the start of the third UPR cycle illustrates, state action in response to recommendations is often lacking. The diplomatic and political relationship Colombia has with individual recommending states has the capacity to have a positive impact on prospects for compliance with supported recommendations, particularly where the recommending state is a significant aid donor, such as the US, UK and the EU.

UPR and civil society

This section assesses the nature of civil society engagement with UPR in general and Colombia's third cycle in particular (it does not engage in critical debate as to the function and operation of civil society – see Matua, 2016; Oberleitner, 2007; Armstrong et al., 2011). Pursuant to Human Rights Council Resolution 5/1, it is a principle of the UPR that all stakeholders, including NGOs and NHRIs, participate in the review (UNHRC A/HRC/RES/5/1, para 3(e)). In addition, the objectives of the review require 'the sharing of best practice among states and other stakeholders', and under the process and modalities of the review states are 'encouraged to prepare the information through a broad consultation process at the national level with all relevant stakeholders' (UNHRC A/HRC/RES/5/1, paras 4(d) and 15(a)). The investigation and reporting of human rights violations by civil society is an important source of information and data for states in preparing their UPR recommendations. However, two challenges arise for stakeholders, one is the extent to which the subjects of their submissions are translated into UPR recommendations and the other is state implementation and follow-up?

Civil society – third cycle submissions for Colombia

Representations by civil society to reviewing states in the lead up to a state's review are crucial in influencing and shaping recommendations and comments made by peer-reviewing states. NGOs will write their submissions and then draft recommendations to send directly to reviewing states, advocating for that state to and adopt and make that recommendation (Ashley, 2018, section 7.4.2). This advocacy process is strategic and can include lobbying smaller states that might be more open to making a particular recommendation. Post-review, there is scope for CSOs to engage in proactive follow-up with relevant government and public institutions regarding the implementation of relevant recommendations.

Land related rights feature heavily in civil society stakeholder submissions to the third cycle (UNHRC HRC/WG.6/30/COL/3). They are also cited in the compilation of recommendations to the Colombian government made by other United Nations human rights institutions in the international health regulations (IHR) governance regime complex (UNHRC A/HRC/WG.6/30/COL/2). Given the issue of land ownership is a fundamental part of the 2016 Peace Accord, this is to be expected. Yet with only 3.3% of third cycle recommendations relating to land, there is a gap between stakeholder submissions and the recommendations that get made, suggesting that CSO recommendations are not aligned with the reviewing country interests.

Stakeholder submissions refer to land and related rights both generically and specifically. The Ombudsman's Office of Colombia, Amnesty International and Proyecto Nasa (a Colombian NGO that works to protect indigenous peoples and other communities) raised general concerns of limited progress in implementing and providing reparation pursuant to the Victims and Land Restitution Act, noting in particular that the restitution of land and protection of indigenous and Afro-Colombian communities was lacking (UNHRC HRC/WG.6/30/COL/3, paras 7–10, 44 and 101). These issues were the subject of recommendations by six countries in the third cycle, namely, Australia, Bolivia, Haiti, Holy See, El Salvador and France.

In a joint submission by 18 CSOs, it was submitted that the land use planning designations of 'mineral reserve areas', 'rural, economic and social development areas' and 'national strategic interest projects' had been used but without any consultation with local communities and without an environmental impact assessment. A joint submission by over 40 NGOs referred to 'serious social and environmental effects, such as soil contamination, the loss of flora and fauna and severe water pollution' due to drilling for oil and gas and the granting of mining concessions. This submission went on to state that in 2017, '21 departments in Colombia had rivers polluted by mercury from mining activities'

(UNHRC HRC/WG.6/30/COL/3, para 25). Specific reference was made to the Macarena's Special Management Area, an area significantly affected by violent conflict and illicit crop production (Castro-Nunez et al., 2016), as having suffered 'indiscriminate deforestation' and an adverse impact on the ecosystem due to the extraction of hydrocarbons (UNHRC HRC/WG.6/30/COL/3, para 25). No specific reference to these matters was made in the recommendations Colombia received.

Conversely, those CSOs making representations about human rights defenders have had some success with that cause being addressed by 26 states, each making one recommendation (24.76% of the total recommendations made). Stakeholder representations indicated 91 per cent of human rights defenders' deaths remained unpunished and that 51 human rights defenders had been killed from January to June 2017 (UNHRC HRC/WG.6/30/COL/3, para 52). There was a reported increase in violence against and killings of human rights lawyers, with some lawyers abandoning emblematic cases (UNHRC HRC/WG.6/30/COL/3, para 53). Reporters Without Borders referred to the killing of journalists in Colombia whilst World Alliance for Citizen Participation (CIVICUS) and the International Trade Union Confederation (ITUC) noted that the trade unionists were subject to threats and targeted assassinations (UNHRC HRC/WG.6/30/COL/3, para 53). Poverty and the advance of extractive industries had led to changes in the lives of indigenous women who migrated to the cities, where they experienced extreme poverty and labour or sexual exploitation (UNHRC HRC/WG.6/30/COL/3, para 56).

In relation to indigenous rights, it was reported that despite the peace process, 58 indigenous people had been killed (UNHRC HRC/WG.6/30/COL/3, para 97); indigenous and Afro-Colombian peoples 'continued to be victims of the various armed groups' (UNHRC HRC/WG.6/30/COL/3, para 97); and violations continued despite special protection orders of the Constitutional Court (UNHRC HRC/WG.6/30/COL/3, para 97). It was noted by Akabadura that largely due to the armed conflict the nomadic Nukak people 'were at serious risk of physical and cultural extinction', whilst Proyecto Nasa voiced concerns that the indigenous Nasa community 'was at risk of disappearing' (UNHRC HRC/WG.6/30/COL/3, para 98). Further submissions referred to efforts by the government to limit the scope of ILO Convention on Indigenous and Tribal Peoples, 1989 (No. 169) with regard to consultation, with a particular lack of consultation in mining areas. One joint submission from a number of CSOs stated that of the 7.4 million displaced people (and citing this as the highest in the world), 'indigenous and Afro-Colombian populations had been affected disproportionately' (UNHRC HRC/WG.6/30/COL/3, para 106). Whilst 20% (21 recommendations from 20 different states) of third cycle recommendations related to indigenous rights, which is a similarly high proportion as those focusing on human rights defenders,

UPR state recommendations were constructed in general terms, rather than referring to specific communities or instances of violations and concern.

During Colombia's third cycle UPR, the Ombudsman's Office of Colombia welcomed the release of the country's Action Plan on Business and Human Rights. The Action Plan implements the United Nations Guiding Principles on Business and Human Rights, and also takes account of other 'major relevant related standards',[1] and the Sustainable Development Goals. The government appears to pride itself as the first non-European country to have public policy in the field of business and human rights (UNHRC A/HRC/WG.6/30/COL/1, para 141), offering during its review to share good practice (UNHRC A/HRC/39/6, para 118).

However, whilst the Ombudsman's Office welcomed progress on human rights within the framework of international investment agreements, it noted 23% of social protests or demonstrations related to business activity (UNHRC A/HRC/WG.6/30/COL/3, para 4). Further, two CSOs, Consultoría para los Derechos Humanos y el Desplazamiento (CODHES) and Taller de Vida, were concerned that efforts had focused only on the dissemination and adaptation of the Plan, leaving evaluation mechanisms incomplete and capacities at the local level to implement policies in need of strengthening (UNHRC A/HRC/WG.6/30/COL/3, para 4). However, there were only comments welcoming the action of Colombia regarding business and human rights, and there were no recommendations. Nonetheless, the government made a voluntary commitment to implement the second phase of the Action Plan (UNHRC A/HRC/39/6, para 123.4).

Civil society – communities of practice

The stakeholder submissions highlighted above demonstrate UPR being utilized as a third space within which 'communities of practice' can give voice to matters of those communities and concerns in an international forum and demand action. The voices, communities and identities represented are those that are repeatedly marginalized and excluded by dominant legal and political discourse and by the machinery of the state and its institutions. A community of practice is formed by those with a shared interest, practice or pursuit of knowledge (Lave and Wenger, 1991; Wenger-Trayner et al., 2015) and can generate legitimacy for the community and its cause in a social sense (Thomas, 2013, p22).

There are three primary methods by which civil society communities of practices can be facilitated via UPR: one is to form a coalition and make a joint submission, as referred to above. The second is the hosting of a parallel event at the United Nations in Geneva alongside the relevant Working Group of a state under review, and the third is via in-country workshops. Making a written submission to UPR is relatively straightforward. Single submissions should be no more than five pages, joint submissions up to ten and there is no requirement for ECOSOC consultative status (UNHRC A/HRC/DEC/6/102). Consultative status is required to host a parallel event at the United Nations in Geneva at the time of the working group session. Other NGOs and state delegations are invited to attend a side event at which a panel of speakers will speak for a few minutes about matters of concern and the floor will then be opened for questions. In addition, CSOs have the potential to work with the in-country office of the OHCHR to create a democratic space for in-country UPR workshops, engaging relevant state personnel in the process. This process is ad hoc but has met with success in, for example, Cambodia.

The UPR role of civil society at the main event of the working group session is, however, diluted compared to the treaty system of human rights monitoring and protection. An NGO with consultative status can be accredited with observer status and attend the UPR Working Group session of a state under review (Working with ECOSOC, 2011, p18). This is the same for treaty reviews, but in addition there are informal briefings by civil society with members of the committee of experts prior to the formal review. Such close-quartered contact with reviewing state missions prior to a state's UPR is possible only via informal pre-sessions organized by the NGO UPR Info. Furthermore, civil society can submit a report directly to a treaty committee for consideration, which is then provided in full to the state concerned.

Paradoxically, civil society's absence from the Working Group session may prompt state actors to voice the more difficult topics otherwise left to NGOs. During this author's PhD research, one interviewee was asked if states over-rely on civil society. The response was an emphatic yes, particularly in those forums where civil society has a voice:

> (...) within the UN human rights system and the Human Rights Council in particular I think states are very reliant on civil society saying the difficult things. Even countries we would consider like-minded might not say something that is going to impact on their relationship with a particular country if they know an NGO that is further down the speakers' list will say that thing.
>
> (Ashley, 2018, p229)

Therefore, the 'heavy-lifting' where difficult matters are to be addressed sits with the states themselves during UPR. Nonetheless, the role of civil society has been identified as central to securing peace in Colombia (Sánchez-Garzoli, 2016). Success is precarious given threats against the safety and security of human rights defenders and civil society members (Daniels, 2019). However, being represented during UPR via stakeholder submissions and UPR recommendations generates national and global awareness and pressure, with the potential to influence and generate political will to act.

Conclusion – towards a third space?

This chapter has demonstrated how the UPR as a central mechanism in the global governance of human rights is being used as a relational and ideational space in which to raise awareness of pertinent matters regarding the right to land, rights of indigenous peoples and human rights defenders in Colombia. The potential of UPR to operate as a third space nexus, accommodating the interconnectedness of those rights that contribute to stable conditions for the maintenance and restoration of social and natural capital, is to some extent being harnessed. The proportion of recommendations addressing land rights, indigenous peoples and human rights defenders, particularly when aggregated, is significant. In the third cycle, this was approximately 32% (34 out of 105 recommendations). For the second cycle, this was 21% (36 out of 167 recommendations), and for the first cycle, 23% (26 out of 112). These figures are approximate given that one recommendation may overlap with one or more of the other rights issues; however, they suggest an overall increase from the first cycle to the third, with almost a third of UPR recommendations carrying currency for social and natural capital and innovation.

There are no third cycle recommendations that refer specifically to the environment or business and human rights, despite these matters being addressed in stakeholder submissions. Yet the High Commissioner for Human Rights in the annex to her letter to Colombia's Minister of Foreign Affairs, and copied to the Minister of Interior, following the third cycle refers directly to the cross-cutting issues of development, the environment and business and human rights, warning of the need to protect the environment, particularly when exploiting natural resources (High Commissioner for Human Rights, 2018).

Furthermore, by coming together to create communities of practice, civil society is using UPR as a vehicle via which to create and support a textual, literal and metaphorical space akin to Homi Bhabha's concept of a third space. In such a space, 'the historical identity of culture as a unifying force' is challenged by seeing cultural knowledge and cultural performance as a process of translation and negotiation (Bhabha, 2006, 155–175). Forging links and combining interests between different organisations and groups through UPR means civil society can create new, dynamic, hybrid and ideologically open spaces within which difference is shared and new goals, action and initiatives agreed and pursued. By building coalitions, it has been suggested that the UPR recommendations reviewing states make are more relevant and better facilitate follow-up by civil society with the relevant government (OHCHR, 2013).

Communities of practice are those that are subject to the 'power' that claims authority, and by being subject to that power confer upon it its legitimacy (Cotterrell, 2016, p262–268). By engaging with UPR before and after a state's review, those actors that comprise communities of practice legitimize the UPR process; it is worthy of their time and effort. This (social) practice also aligns with the concept of a third space. For Bhabha, the third space is a liminal and hybrid arena where binary distinctions are dissolved in a bid to understand cultural knowledge and cultural performance not as something that is homogeneous, original or pure, but rather as a process of translation and negotiation (Bhabha, 2006, p155–157). In this way, identities resist subjugation by the dominant and restrictive narratives of patriarchal and colonial discourse (Bhabha, 2006). This dynamic process is at the heart of UPR where myriad cultures interact and intersect, negotiating, sharing and disseminating international human rights norms within a particular defined territory. The state delegation receiving UPR recommendations generally consists of high level government ministers with decision-making powers and authority; by supporting the recommendations received, a political commitment to act is being made in a high profile international arena.

Civil society, other stakeholders and recommending states can therefore use these public commitments and the iterative, recursive and cyclical nature of UPR to assist in holding the government and state machinery of Colombia to account. This is particularly so where the same states are making recommendations on the same theme cycle after cycle. In this way, UPR continues to give voice to and maintain focus on those issues and identities that are politically, legally and culturally marginalized yet central to social innovation and the advancement of social and natural capital. Yet, when it falls to reviewing states, CSOs, treaty bodies and others to repeat recommendations on the same theme and issue cycle after cycle, the flaws of UPR are also laid bare. Namely, that UPR is a political mechanism driven by voluntary state engagement, with no formal follow-up and implementation enforcement powers to oversee supported recommendations that lead to positive action and change.

Nonetheless, there is evidence of UPR strengthening the relationship between civil society and the state under review, two examples being Thailand and Colombia. In the second UPR cycle in 2017, joint stakeholder submissions supported by 64 CSOs were made ahead of Thailand's second cycle UPR. Following Thailand's review 'in an unprecedented step, the coalition was invited to present [to the Thai government] their views on the recommendations Thailand received after their second UPR', with the CSO coalition noting 'a clear shift in the way the Government approached them' (UPR Info, 2017, p14). During the first UPR cycle, a recommendation was made by the Czech Republic to Colombia in 2009 'to ensure effective national birth registration, including through programmes of mobile registration units and registration of those without documentation'. The issue of a significant number of unregistered children due to the incomplete process of modernizing and automating the National Register was raised in the summary of stakeholder submissions (by a CSO coalition comprising World Vision, Plan Internacional Colombia, Aldeas SOS Colombia (SOS Children's Villages), Observatorio sobre Infancia de la Universidad Nacional de Colombia (Children's Observatory of the University of Colombia) and Save the Children (UK)). This recommendation has been cited as prompting a partnership between the state and the civil society to assist in the process of registration of over half a million children, ensuring access to education and other services (CSO interview, 2017, transcript on file with the author).

Note

1 Stated as being: The United Nations Principles for Responsible Contracts, the Guidelines of the OECD for Multinational Enterprises, the OECD Due Diligence Guidelines for Responsible Mineral Supply Chains in the Areas of Conflict or High Risk; the Voluntary Principles on Security and Human Rights (VP), the Principles of Global Compact and the ISO 26000 Standard.

References

Agren, David (2019). Mexican activist shot dead before vote on power project he opposed, 20 February, *The Guardian*, https://www.theguardian.com/world/2019/feb/20/mexican-activist-shot-dead-before-vote-on-pipeline-he-opposed.

Al Hussein, & Zeid Ra'ad (2017). Denial of access and lack of cooperation with UN bodies will not diminish scrutiny of a State's human rights record, *Human Rights Council 35th Session*, 06 June, http://www.ohchr.org/EN/NewsEvents/Pages/DisplayNews.aspx?NewsID=21687.

Appiah, Kwame Anthony, & Bhabha, Homi (2018). Cosmopolitanism and convergence. *New Literary History*, 49(2), 171–198.

Armstrong, David, et al. (2011). *Civil Society and International Governance: The Role of Non-state Actors in Global and Regional Regulatory Frameworks*. London: Routledge.

Associated Press in Lima (2019). Unprecedented murder charges for loggers in deaths of indigenous activists, *The Guardian*, 31 October, https://www.theguardian.com/world/2019/oct/31/peru-logging-indigenous-activists-murders.

Ashley, L. J. (2018, November). *A Critical Appraisal of Human Rights Monitoring through the Lens of Global Governance Theory: The Universal Periodic Review in relation to Yemen as a State in Crisis*. Doctoral Thesis, University of Leeds, United Kingdom.

Bakker, I. (ed) (1994). *The Strategic Silence: Gender and Economic Policy*. London: Zed Books.

Bhabha, Homi K. (2006). Cultural diversity and cultural differences. In B. Ashcroft, G. Griffiths, & H. Tiffin (eds), *The Post-Colonial Studies Reader*. New York: Routledge.

Borras, Jr., Saturnino, M., Franco Jennifer, C., & Wang, Chunyu (2013). The challenge of global governance of land grabbing: Changing international agricultural context and competing political views and strategies. *Globalizations*, *10*(1), 161–179.

Branford, Sue, & Borges, Thais (2019). 3 massacres in 12 days: Rural violence escalates in Brazilian Amazon, 08 April, *Mongabay*, https://news.mongabay.com/2019/04/3-massacres-in-12-days-rural-violence-escalates-in-brazilian-amazon/.

Branford, Sue, & Torres, Maurício (2017). 'Quilombolas' community land rights under attack by Brazilian ruralists, *Mongabay*, 25 August, https://news.mongabay.com/2017/08/quilombolas-community-land-rights-under-attack-by-brazilian-ruralists/.

Broderick, Céire (2019). Creating a 'Third Space' through Narration in Mercedes Valdivieso's Maldita yo entre las mujeres'. *Bulletin of Hispanic Studies*, *96*(7), 747–761.

Castro-Nunez, Augusto, Mertz, Ole, & Quintero, Marcela (2016). Propensity of farmers to conserve forest within REDD + projects in areas affected by armed-conflict. *Forest Policy and Economics*, *66*, 22–30.

Cortés, Paula Martínez (2013). The victims and land restitution law in Colombia in context: An analysis of the contradictions between the agrarian model and compensation for the victims, *FDCL TNI*, 3 December, https://www.tni.org/files/download/martinez-victims-law-web.pdf.

Calliess, Gralf-Peter, & Renner, Moritz (2007). From Soft Law to Hard Code: The Juridification of Global Governance, 22 *Ratio Juris 260*, June 2009. Available at SSRN: https://ssrn.com/abstract=1030526.

Charlesworth, Hilary, & Larking, Emma (eds) (2014). *Human Rights and the Universal Periodic Review: Rituals and Ritualism*. Cambridge: Cambridge University Press.

Colombia Reports (2020). Foreign Investments, 09 March, https://colombiareports.com/colombia-fdi-statistics/.

Convention on Biodiversity: Colombia, https://www.cbd.int/countries/profile/?country=cofacts.

De Brabandere, Eric (2018). 'Human Rights and International Investment Law'. In Markus Krajewski & Rhea Hoffmann (eds), *Research Handbook on Foreign Direct Investment*. Cheltenham: Edward Elgar. Grotius Centre Working Paper 2018/75-HRL; Leiden Law School Research Paper. Available at SSRN: https://ssrn.com/abstract=3149387.

Peña-Huertas, del Pilar, Rocío, Ruiz, Parada, Luis Enrique, Mónica, María, Santiago, Zuleta, & Ricardo, Álvarez (2017). Legal dispossession and civil war in Colombia. *Journal of Agrarian Change*, *17*, 759–769.

Cotterrell, Roger (2016). Transnational legal authority: a socio-legal perspective. In Roger Cotterrell & Maksymilian Del Mar (eds), *Authority in Transnational Legal Theory: Theorizing Across Disciplines*. Cheltenham, UK, Northampton, MA, USA: Edward Elgar Publishing.

Daniels, Joe Parkin (2019). Wave of killings threatens civil society work in Colombia, 06 November, Devex, https://www.devex.com/news/wave-of-killings-threatens-civil-society-work-in-colombia-91435.

Escobar, Arturo, & Paulson, Susan (2005). The emergence of collective ethnic identities and alternative political ecologies in the Colombian Pacific rainforest. In Susan Gezon Paulson & L. Lisa (eds), *Political Ecology Across Spaces, Scales, and Social Groups* (pp. 257–278). Rutgers University Press.

Etone, D. (2017). The effectiveness of South Africa's engagement with the Universal Periodic Review (UPR): Potential for ritualism? *South African Journal on Human Rights*, *33*(2), 258.

Final Agreement for Ending the Conflict and Building a Stable and Lasting Peace (2016, 24 November). Between the government and the Fuerzas Armadas Revolucionarias de Colombia—Ejército del Pueblo (Revolutionary Armed Forces of Colombia – People's Army) (FARC-EP), http://especiales.presidencia.gov.co/Documents/20170620-dejacion-armas/acuerdos/acuerdo-final-ingles.pdf.

Freedman, Rosa (2013). *The Human Rights Council: A Critique and Early Assessment*. New York: Routledge.

García-Godos, Jemima, & Wiig, Henrik (2018). Ideals and realities of restitution: the Colombian land restitution programme. *Journal of Human Rights Practice*, *10*(1), 40–57.

Human Rights Voices (2014). UN Rights Council trumpets process of equating Norway with Iran and company, 28 April, http://www.humanrightsvoices.org/site/developments/?d=12139.

Goodman, Ryan, & Jinks, Derek (2013). *Socializing States: Promoting Human Rights Through International Law*. New York: Oxford University Press.

Hanna, Philippe, & Vanclay, Frank (2013). Human rights, indigenous peoples and the concept of free, prior and informed consent. *Impact Assessment and Project Appraisal*, *31*(2), 146–157.

High Commissioner for Human Rights (2018). Letter to the Foreign Minister, 2 November, https://lib.ohchr.org/HRBodies/UPR/Documents/Session30/CO/HC_LetterColombia_30Session_EN.pdf.

IACHR Press Release (2018). IACHR Takes Case Involving Colombia to the Inter-American Court of Human Rights, *Caso Integrantes y Militantes de la Union Patriotica Vs. Colombia*, 25 July, https://www.oas.org/en/iachr/media_center/PReleases/2018/162.asp.

Keohane, Robert O., & Victor, David G. (2011). The regime complex for climate change. *Perspectives on Politics*, *9*, *5*.

Koskenniemi, Martti (2006). Fragmentation of International Law: Difficulties Arising from the Diversification and Expansion of International Law, Report of the Study Group of the International Law Commission' General Assembly, International Law Commission, fifty-eighth session. *A/CN.4/L*, *682*, 13 April.

KPMG: Investment in Colombia (2018). LeGrand Catherine C. (2003) The Colombian Crisis in Historical Perspective, Canadian. *Journal of Latin American and Caribbean Studies*, *28*(55-56), 165–209. 169 10.1080/08263663.2003.10816840.

Lave, Jean, & Wenger, Etienne (1991). *Situated Learning*. Cambridge: Cambridge University Press.

McDonald, Geraldine (2009). Impacts of Extractive Industries in Latin America: Analysis and Guidelines for Future Work, *CIDSE (Coopération Internationale pour le Développement et la Solidarité)*, January, https://www.trocaire.org/sites/default/files/resources/policy/latin-america-extractives.pdf.

McMahon, E. (2012). The Universal Periodic Review: A Work in Progress, An Evaluation of the First Cycle of the New UPR Mechanism of the United Nations Human Rights Council, *in Dialogue on Globalisation Report.* Geneva: Friedrich Ebert Stiftung, September.

Matua, Makau (2016). *Human Rights Standards: Hegemony, Law and Politics.* New York: State University of New York Press.

Moravcsik (2000). The origins of human rights regimes: Democratic dialogue in postwar Europe. *International Organisations*, *54*, 217.

Moulaert Frank, Mehmood Abid, MacCallum Diana, & Leubolt, Bernhard (2017). *Social Innovation as a Trigger for Transformations – The Role of Research.* European Commission.

Oberleitner, Gerd (2007). *Global Human Rights Institutions: Between Remedy and Ritual.* Polity Press.

Oberleitner, Gerd (2008). A decade of mainstreaming human rights in the UN: Achievements, failures, challenges'. *Netherlands Quarterly of Human Rights*, *26*(3), 359–390.

OHCHR (2013). How to Follow Up on United Nations Human Rights Recommendations: A Guide for Civil Society, October, https://www.ohchr.org/Documents/AboutUs/CivilSociety/HowtoFollowUNHRRecommendations.pdf.

OHCHR (2018). Advance Questions: Colombia Third Cycle, https://www.ohchr.org/EN/HRBodies/UPR/Pages/COIndex.aspx.

OHCHR (2018). Matrice of Recommendations produced by the Office of the High Commissioner for Human Rights, https://www.ohchr.org/EN/HRBodies/UPR/Pages/COIndex.aspx.

Oosterlynck, S., Kazepov, Y., Novy, A., Cools, P., Barberis, E., Wukovitsch, F., Sarius, T., & Leubolt, B. (2013). *The butterfly and the elephant: local social innovation, the welfare state and new poverty dynamics,* Working Paper 13.

Raustiala, Kal, & Victor, David G. (2004). The regime complex for plant genetic resources. *International Organization*, *58*, 277–309.

Romano-Armada, Neli, Amoroso, María Julia, & Rajal, Verónica B. (2014). Impacts of agriculture in Latin America: Problems and solutions, *Bioremediation in Latin America: Current Research and Perspectives.* London: Springer.

Rosenau, James (1992). *Governance without Government* (1st ed). Cambridge, United Kingdom: Cambridge University Press.

Riches, Louisa (2017). Legal and normative pluralism, hybridity and human rights: The Universal Periodic Review. In Nicholas Lemay-Hébert & Rosa Freedman (eds), *Hybridity: Law, Culture and Development.* Oxon and New York: Routledge.

Ruggie, John Gerard (2014). Global Governance and "New Governance Theory": Lessons from Business and Human Rights. *Global Governance*, *5*, 1–34.

Rutherford, Jonathan (1998). The Third Space. Interview with Homi Bhabha, *Identity: Community, Culture, Difference.* London: Lawrence & Wishart.

Salazar, A., Sanchez, A., Villegas, J.C., et al. (2018). The ecology of peace: preparing Colombia for new political and planetary climates, *Frontiers in Ecology and the Environment*, 3, https://ore.exeter.ac.uk/repository/bitstream/handle/10871/34420/Salazar_et_al-2018-Frontiers_in_Ecology_and_the_Environment.pdf?sequence=1&isAllowed=y.

Sánchez-Garzoli, Gimena (2016). Civil Society is Colombia's Best Bet for Constructing Peace, *WOLA*, 04 April, https://www.wola.org/analysis/civil-society-is-colombias-best-bet-for-constructing-peace/.

Sánchez-Garzoli, Gimena (2019). The Slow Death of Colombia's Peace Deal, *Foreign Affairs*, 30 October, https://www.foreignaffairs.com/articles/colombia/2019-10-30/slow-death-colombias-peace-deal.

Schrijver, N. (2007). The UN Human Rights Council: A New "Society of the Committed" or Just Old Wine in New Bottles. *Leiden Journal of International Law*, *20*(4), 809–823.

Shaffer, Gregory, & Ginsburg, Tom (2012). The Empirical Turn in International Legal Scholarship. *American Journal of International Law*, *106*, 1–46.

Simma, Bruno, & Alston, Philip (1988). The Sources of Human Rights Law: Custom, Jus Cogens and General Principles. *Australian Yearbook of International Law*, *12*(1989), 82–107.

Smith, Jennie Erin (2019). A group of botanists' fight to save Colombian wax palms, *The Independent*, 14 November, https://www.independent.co.uk/news/long_reads/wax-palms-endangered-tochecito-colombia-botanist-a9185826.html.

Terman, Rochell, & Voeten, Erik (2018). The Relational Politics of Shame: Evidence from the Universal Periodic Review'. *The Review of International Organizations*, *13*, 1–23.

Thomas, C. A. (2013). LSE Legal Studies Working Paper, 12/2013 *The Concept of Legitimacy and International Law*. London: London School of Economics.

Tomuschat, C. (2011). Universal Periodic Review: A New System of International Law with Specific Ground Rules? In Ulrich Fastenrath, et al. (eds), *From Bilateralism to Community Interest: Essays in honour of Bruno Simma*. Oxford University Press, United Kingdom.

UNHRC A/HRC/DEC/6/102 (2007). *Follow-up to Human Rights Council resolution 5/1* (A/HRC/DEC/6/102, 27 September)

UNHRC A/HRC/RES/5/1 (2007). *Institution building of the United Nations Human Rights Council*, 18 June.

UNGA A/RES/60/251 (2006). *Human Rights Council*, 3 April.

UNHRC A/HRC/RES/16/21 (2011). *Review of the work and functioning of the Human Rights Council*, 25 March.

UNHRC A/HRC/WG.6/30/COL/1 (2018). *National report submitted in accordance with paragraph 5 of the annex to Human Rights Council resolution 16/21: Colombia*, 26 February.

UNHRC A/HRC/WG.6/30/COL/2 (2018). *Compilation: Colombia*, 12 March.

UNHRC HRC/WG.6/30/COL/3 (2018). *Summary of Stakeholders' submissions on Colombia: Report of the Office of the United Nations High Commissioner for Human Rights*, 12 March.

UNHRC A/HRC/39/6 (2018). *Report of the Working Group on the Universal Periodic Review: Colombia*, 09 July, 2018.

UNGA A/59/569 (2004). Kofi Annan, 'A More Secure World: Our Shared Responsibility', report of the Secretary-General's High-level Panel on Threats, Challenges and Change, 2 December, http://www.un.org/en/peacebuilding/pdf/historical/hlp_more_secure_world.pdf last accessed 05 March 2018.

UPR Info (2015). A Guide for recommending States at the UPR, https://www.upr-info.org/sites/default/files/general-document/pdf/upr_info_guide_for_recommending_states_2015.pdf.

UPR Info. Database https://www.upr-info.org/database/ and statistics https://www.upr-info.org/database/statistics/.

UPR Info (2017). The Civil Society Compendium: A comprehensive guide for civil society organisations engaging in the Universal Periodic Review, UPR Info, https://www.upr-info.org/sites/default/files/general-document/pdf/upr_info_cso_compendium_en.pdf.

Watts, Jonathan (2018). Murdered land activist adds to rising death toll in Brazil's Amazon, *The Guardian*, 17 April, https://www.theguardian.com/environment/2018/apr/17/murdered-indigenous-land-activist-adds-to-rising-death-toll-in-brazils-amazon.

Wenger-Trayner, E and B. (2015). Communities of Practice: A Brief Introduction 2 (EB), http://wenger-trayner.com/wp-content/uploads/2015/04/07-Brief-introduction-to-communities-of-practice.pdf.

Wheeling, K. (2019). How conflict influenced land use in Colombia, *Eos*, 100, 20 November 2019, https://doi.org/10.1029/2019EO136714.

Working with ECOSOC (2011). An NGO's guide to consultative status, United Nations (New York), http://csonet.org/content/documents/BrochureLite.pdf.

World Bank (1992). *Governance and Development* (World Bank), http://www.gsid.nagoya-u.ac.jp/sotsubo/Governance_and_Development_1992.pdf.

Zürn, Michael (2005). Global governance. In G. F. Schuppert (ed), *Governance-Forschung*. Baden-Baden: Nomos.

Part II

Social Innovation and Natural Capital

3 The environment through the regulation of emissions resulting from the automobile journeys in Peru

José Carlos Soldevila Saavedra

Introduction

GHG mitigation is usually a responsibility and action of government institutions. There are also very particular cases where the private company shows social responsibility and takes environmental sustainability actions that also result in GHG mitigation. However, articulated actions, if any, are not regular and equally not an easy practice to clearly identify as long as there are no elements, strategies or programmes to link them.

Similarly, civil society does not have clear skills or tools to link either with the state or with the private company to generate actions of social responsibility, sustainability and mitigation of GHG in this case, which would obviously come from a knowledge and recognition of the ecological footprint of individuals or collectively at best. That is why it is important to consider the objectives, tools and scopes that each sector has to mitigate GHG emissions. For example, the regulation of motor park's emissions is addressed with different strategies as environmental regulations applied to vehicle builders stand out transit management measures, user awareness, among others.

Regulations aimed at vehicle builders are measures that are unfortunately long term since changing an entire industrial model overnight is virtually "impossible". Transit management measures on their side are short- and medium-term measures which mainly involve making vehicle infrastructure more efficient to reduce the time and distance of people's travel on vehicles whose principal energy matrix is fossil fuels, that is, greenhouse gas emitters. The third mentioned strategy, user awareness, is one with short-, medium- and long-term effects. Raising user's awareness mainly involves making them aware of the effects of their daily transport mode and their responsibility to the environment from this and other daily decisions that may benefit or affect the planet.

What was mentioned does not mean that some strategies need to be taken over others; on the contrary, it is important that they are all taken together through an integrated sustainability plan, where the strategies applied on transport are a priority (considering that the transport industry is the largest emitter of greenhouse gases after construction). Therefore, as well as the three strategies mentioned above, it is also important to integrate three types of actors: private/corporate, public and civil sector.

The approach presented is that the private sector can exercise its social responsibility, with an environmental approach, in public transport, managed and/or regulated by the public sector where civil society converges in its basic need for urban traveling to their workplaces, schools, among others. Under this approach, it is proposed the development of strategies that link the three actors within the basic need of all, daily urban travels, applying strategies on the three fronts mentioned initially: the usage of sustainable vehicles, transit regulations with priority to sustainable transport, and awareness-raising campaigns in vehicles and all public transport-related infrastructure.

The hypothesis is that the environment in which one develops his activities invites a certain type of behaviours. An example would be that if one finds a dirty street, he has few qualms about throwing some residue in a corner where these are accumulated. However, the hypothesis has already been tested in other types of exercises, citing the "Nudge Theory" and the exercise of the "broken window", both demonstrating that a specific environment promotes a certain type of behaviours. Under this concept, it is sought to hold accountable the actors mentioned within the public transport activity, where a large number of people move, which is normally managed and/or regulated by the public sector and in some cases operated by the private sector, but where the private sector can also make investments.

Nowadays, the civil sector, most of it, is not aware of the volume of emissions produced by the transport sector and therefore is not aware of the volume of emissions that occur in the transport system that they choose to move on daily. What is then raised is an awareness programme in all transport modes, so that all users know the volume of GHG produced in each of their journeys according to their transport mode. Regarding the number of people using public transport, and its conditions around sustainability, there is also an emphasis on regulating emissions around their motor park, transit management, and raising awareness of its users.

Under these premises, the objective of this Chapter is to show successful sustainable mobility policies around respect for the environment. A second objective is also to demonstrate the possibilities of generating urban pedagogy within public transport using private resources under social responsibility strategies or similar ones. This urban pedagogy is based on the number of people who could be reached by accounting not only for the number of people exposed to awareness but also the ease and low costs of placing environmental communication on public transport and/or its complementary infrastructure.

That is why the context of the metropolis of Lima and Callao is presented first in terms of mobility and transport and the negative social and environmental impacts that the lack of a culture of sustainable mobility has on the city. This is followed by three strategies from different urban actors with different possibilities and scopes to positively impact society and the environment through mobility strategies that point to the change of awareness of citizens as an engine of change towards an environmentally responsible society oriented through mobility. Finally, the scope of the proposals presented and analysed is set out and how these are grouped as pedagogical proposals that use mobility as a key element to generate social responsibility in different actors for the recovery of social and natural values in urban spaces.

Environmental status of the metropolis

Regarding the vehicle's energy matrix, according to a study carried out by SENAHMI, the projection for 2015 and 2019 shows that diesel accounts for approximately 50% of fuel consumption. This hydrocarbon is responsible for a similar and higher percentage in GHG emissions (CO_2, NO_x, SO_2 and PM_{10}).

The environmental quality of the Lima-Callao metropolis is quite low, positioning it among the worst in the region: the most polluted capital in South America, the 7th most polluted city in South America and the world's 430th most polluted city. In terms of air quality alone, the metropolis is also at very low standards, being within averages this year, among the three cities with the worst air quality in South America.[1]

It is important to mention the environmental conditions in view of the extent that urban travels have an important share and responsibility in air pollution. This activity being one of the largest GHG producer in the metropolis, competing with the construction industry with which it also relates in terms of road infrastructure, example. Similarly, transport is also a powerful emitter of the pollutant particles called $PM_{2.5}$ and PM_{10}, depending on whether they are less than 2.5 microns or 10 microns, respectively. These particles are emitted by vehicles in their combustion processes, with diesel engines emitting the highest percentage of the aforementioned particles. While there is a significant trend of vehicles migrating to vehicular natural gas (GNV), which replaces even liquefied petroleum gas (LPG), which are less polluting, air quality in the metropolis is not experiencing improvements, and energetic matrix change shows not being part of the political portfolio of public management, which we will cite later in this chapter. Regarding the automotive park of vehicles using GNV, it amounted to 251 783 units as of October 2017 and to June this year, it was around 280'000 units. While this amount represents 14.36% of the metropolis's motor park as of 2017, the economic and environmental savings of this energy matrix are important and should be part of stronger policies for changing energy matrix for the capital and the country.

Taking up air quality in Lima-Callao, we first cite the standards set by WHO at the 2005 Global Control Automatization (GCA) u[2]:

> Evidence relating to airborne particulate matter (MP) and its effects on public health coincide with adverse health effects with exposures currently experienced by urban populations, both in countries developed as in development. The range of health effects is wide, but they occur particularly in the respiratory and cardiovascular systems. The entire population is affected, but the susceptibility to contamination can vary with health or age. (…)
> (…) PM10 represents the mass of particles entering the respiratory system, and also includes both coarse particles (between 2.5 and 10o) and fine particles (less than 2.5, PM2.5) that are considered to contribute to the health effects observed in urban environments. The first are basically formed by means of mechanical processes, such as construction works, the resuspension of dust from roads and wind, while the latter come mainly from combustion sources. In most urban environments, both types of particles are present, thick and thin, but the ratio of each of the two types of sizes is likely to vary substantially between cities around the world, depending on the geography, meteorology and specific sources of PM for each location.[3]

Transport in Lima-Callao metropolis

City perspective

The perspective for the metropolis is unfortunately politically disjointed, since there are two different administrative jurisdictions and they do not necessarily handle an articulation in the territory management. On the one hand, we have the municipality of Metropolitan Lima, which manages 43 districts and, on the other hand, the Callao Provincial Municipality that manages another seven districts. In terms of transport, the central theme of this chapter, these administrations have the competence to authorize urban passenger transport routes throughout both territories, making it difficult to organize and to have uniformity of the supply, as well as its balance with respect to the needs of the city. Added to this, there are dynamics of other provinces such as Huarochirí and Cañete that have an increasingly strong relationship with the capital city, also gradually generating a considerable impact within urban transport.

However, on December 26, 2018 with the enactment of Law No. 30900, the Urban Transport Authority for Lima and Callao (ATU) was created, a specialized technical agency attached to the Ministry of Transport and Communications (MTC), with legal personality domestic public law and with administrative, functional, economic and financial autonomy.

Its main objective is to organize, implement and manage the Integrated Transport System of Lima and Callao, merging for this purpose the Urban Transport Management (GTU) of Lima's Metropolitan Municipality, the General Urban Transport Management of Callao's Provincial Municipality, the Autonomous Authority of the Mass Transportation System of Lima and Callao (AATE) and the Metropolitan Transport Institute of Lima (Protransporte).

With the establishment of this new institution, which began active work in November 2019, the recovery of order and life quality around the theme of urban transport is expected to begin. In Lima-Callao, as in many other metropolises, it is evident the need for an articulated, orderly and dignified transport network as basic elements of its operation, and it is also clear that for this it is necessary to have a structure, a network, of transport that responds to the population needs of a city in relation to their dimension. It is then proposed as a need of this new institution, ATU, to focus efforts on collective transport that today in Lima covers even more than 57% of the travels, a figure enviable by any developed city.

Focusing on this aspect is due to the critical figures with which transport reform began in 2015, a reform that by 2019 shows neither great advances nor great results in the chaotic capital transport system, a system that costs millions of human hours. Here are some figures from this critical condition:

- Average length of routes 70.24 km (round trip)
- Total length of all routes of 39 403 km (as of 2012, the city had 1300 km of metropolitan roads)
- Over-position kilometres of the network 1 103 000 km (routes overlap 28 times on average)
- About 25 000 public transport units (combis, custers, buses) involving an over-offer of low-capacity transport
- Average speed in rush hour is at 12 km/h (approx)[4]

Vehicle volume and its characteristics

The metropolis of Lima-Callao is a conurbation that occupies an area of approximately 821 km^2 (within 298.685 hectares of jurisdiction). In this space, there are 10.8 million inhabitants with a low motorization rate, throwing approximately 181 vehicles per 1000 inhabitants away from other metropolis such as Buenos Aires, Argentina with 423 vehicles per 1000 inhabitants.

In this context, it is simplistic but necessary to establish that vehicular traffic, relative to the volume of vehicles, should not be a major problem for Lima-Callao. However, there are other factors that make this "limited" number of vehicles to have highly detrimental effects on the city and its inhabitants. These factors will be addressed to contextualize the mobility situation in Lima-Callao and observe the specific effects on the natural and social environment of the metropolis.

The two main features to address Lima's motor park are its average age and the energy matrix. Regarding the average age, according to the National Strategic Road Safety Plan 2017–2021, the average age of urban passenger transport vehicles (public transport) is 22.5 years, while private vehicles have an average age of 15.5 years in its 2015 base year. The effects of automotive park antiquity are mainly expressed in two problems: environmental pollution and accidentality, two issues with alarming figures in Lima-Callao.

Urban travels and transport systems

Currently, in the metropolis of Lima-Callao, we can identify, as in all cities, private and collective means of transport. An important feature of these in our metropolis is the fact that these two categories give birth to many transport possibilities that range from the particular to the collective, between the public and the private and between formality and informality.

We make specific mention of the collective passenger's transport which currently presents public and private offer (being to some degree mixed). First, we have the public systems, which are the Metro (L1), the BRT (Metropolitano) and high capacity buses called Complementary Corridors (Integrated Transport System – SIT). Then there is the private offer, governed by the free market, marking a competition attitude over the routes with extremely adverse effects related principally to service's quality and to road safety. In addition, there are an oversized number of official taxis, about 120 000, which also have informal taxis in a similar amount adding up to at least 200 000 taxis in the city without counting taxi Apps.

There are also alternative transport offers that also have formal and informal offers from motorbikes, 3 wheels and linear, the so-called "collectives" (private cars that transport different persons in a predefined and unofficial route) and shared vehicle systems that in Lima we can see bicycles and electrical scooters.

As we can see in the figure above, the multiple transport offer finally has greater acceptance or concentration of travels in private collective transport, the one that as mentioned is governed practically by offer and demand (free market). The freedom applied for the implementation of this service makes it an irregular offer for the user since it mostly does not have stations/stops, does not have defined schedules (although certain may be predictable) and do not apply quality standards for vehicles and other physical or administrative components of the service. For workers, the service is also an irregular job offer since it is an affiliative system, where finally the operators of the rolling stock (driver and in some cases a collector) define their profits, their salary, by the number of people that it manages to capture in the service as the savings that achieve from the rental of rolling stock (buses of different capacities/sizes).

Sustainable urban mobility: the environmental challenge for a conscious citizenship

Sustainable mobility campaigns

SAN ISIDRO's district participation in the Sustainable Transport Awards 2018

The reason of presenting this district is because San Isidro's municipality has achieved to transform a car dependent city into an example of sustainable mobility for Peruvian cities. For example, between 2017 and 2018, this municipality presented its work to the Institute for Transportation and Development Policy (ITDP) sustainable transport award by presenting this quote:

San Isidro's public space was invaded by cars, parked in restricted areas even though it has an underused private parking infrastructure. Also, the district experimented a demographic decrease while visitants continue to increase as the car usage does too. As an answer, the municipality actualized its District's Urban Plan with a Transit Oriented Development vision.

As mentioned before, in the metropolitan area, public transport has the biggest share in daily transport selection. According to the data on distribution of transportation modes in San Isidro, in the year 2015, 157 200 (39%) of the 524 000 trips in San Isidro were made by regular public transportation, while 89 080 (17%) were made by taxi. That means that even in a district with a higher motorization (327veh/1000hab) rate than Lima-Callao Metropolis (181veh/1000hab), collective transport still occupies more than 50% of San Isidro's trips, a rate that the 2015–2018 administration proposed to grow against any forecast.

The municipality worked in road safety with urban design interventions. Specifically, it worked with "zone 30" strategies, having implemented the first zone 30 in Peru with great results in sustainable mobility, land value, between others. They also introduced a parking management programme. In public space, parking spaces have been recovered with tactical urbanism. As well, a free rotary public parking system has reduced the unnecessary use of cars as these places can be occupied for two hours top.

In private infrastructure, a reduction of parking requirements was implemented along with new requirements for cyclist's infrastructure. It also allowed a better use of street level for receiving citizens (coffee shops, restaurants, etc.) under a policy of promoting walking habits.

All of this is inscribed in the Neutral Emission Zone (ZEN). This area is being also implemented with urban design which promotes sustainable mobility, environment protection/respect and safety in general. In addition, a local free bus travels the district with new services. One of them access the financial center directly; another one offers children an alternative to go to schools.

And for cyclists, it developed a cyclist's network, with complementary infrastructure and a bicycle-sharing system (unluckily due to political issues, the next administration decided to decline that contract which should have started to operate on January 2019). The transferability of this example to other cities are the policies applied: TOD (transit oriented development). The application of this policy/vision/strategy in the city (district) has shown that metropolitan impact is possible from local policies. Demographic decrease has stopped by offering new housing building possibilities in a district with services and employment, allowing people to reduce unnecessary or long travels. Sustainable mobility consciousness has been increased by different activities in the public space and by intense and accurate communication. In a district with high motorization rate, we've proved that more infrastructure is not the solution to traffic jams and that it is possible to make the existing infrastructure more efficient and equitable for all types of transport.[5]

A milestone for the establishment of TOD strategies was the ordinance 412-MSI which allowed San Isidro to create the first Neutral Emission Zone (as LEZ in other countries) in Lima's CBD,[6] which is an important area of San Isidro's District and for the entire Metropolis. One of this ordinance's strategies is to reduce parking requirements on private buildings in exchange for sustainable conditions such as cycling infrastructure (bicycle parking and dressing rooms, for example), LED illumination, hydric saving equipment and so on. That way, car infrastructure investment was reduced and consequently "car favouritism" as buildings became "green", the opposite of previous administrations which prioritized car usage by negligence.

This ordinance has enabled also a better use of private property's street level. It allows some commercial activities to use the space adjacent to the sidewalk (street level) in order to make more lively streets, where walking is an attractive activity as the streets are vibrant as well. Some conditions are also placed for this opportunity such as architectural integration, where the porosity of the building perimeter (façade) must allow this integration between the private and the public space.

A Mayor's decree project relating to public space was also developed (not yet approved). This project aimed to regulate design and operative conditions in ZEN's public space in order to create sustainable conditions for this area. Again, the first objective is to control emissions from motorized transport principally in this area. This way, motorized transport infrastructure is being reduced as more space is gained for non-motorized transport, principally walking. As the ZEN area hosts Lima-Callao's CBD, a significant number of citizens are commuting, visiting, walking and, in general, living in this area and for enabling a better and liveable public space, it is changing to receive more and wider sidewalks, cycleways, terraces, open-air activities and so on, which are necessary to become a more attractive place to walk, to cycle and to stay. As we can imagine, it aims to be a walking city, where motorized transport is losing territory with an urban design strategy using principally tactical urbanism and Barcelona's superblock strategy.

A superblock pilot was projected to support this decree, a pilot which surrounds an important commercial area where brands and enterprises have their sieges. There, a considerable number of people have been walking and walk in this area, and sidewalks aren't enough for this demand as the average width is 1.20 m whereas over 3.00 m is needed. Following that need, part of the superblock was implemented with strategies to discourage cars to enter this area and by allowing only residents or users to enter in its first pilot stage. In this stage, pass-through transit is the one being discouraged principally and walking and cycling habits are being promoted.

San Isidro's Municipality, by their sustainable development vision, has been elaborating and developing land management policies aiming for the accomplishment of the district's strategic objectives. Following this direction, the municipality has actualized the District's Urban Plan considering sustainable urban development objectives established by the UN, San Isidro's Local Development Concerted Plan and National and Metropolitan normative dispositions for urban plan's development and actualization where the Neutral Emission Zone (ZEN) is determined and delimited.

Another milestone of TOD and land management policies was the approval of the 437-MSI San Isidro's Municipality Ordinance which compiles and consolidates all normative referred to urban development, applying sustainable mobility and development concepts and modifying parking requirements between other strategies.

This ordinance established guidelines to promote "municipal retirement's"[7] use, a space previously not used, underused or used incorrectly. This device established modifications as more commercial types allowed, aligned with the street level establishments.

The mobility zone known as "Neutral Emission Zone", where this ordinance is applied, is essentially the CBD, where the priority will be the creation of attractive streets for pedestrian and private business merge with public space. In this zone, the actual situation is recognized for high parking requirements for any project, without considering that the district's commerce zones, visitor's trips into commerce and business are made principally on foot or taxi, resulting uncoherent the requirement of parking which won't be used. The urban sustainable development concept that the administration implemented aimed as principle to discourage the use of low occupancy vehicles, especially private cars, as it looked to contribute to enhance the environmental quality from the reduction on GHG and the optimization of natural resources.

This regulation aimed also to incentivize, promote and preserve residential use through planning towards a sustainable and resilient district, which allows to safely cope with the district's evolution. This flexibility is possible only through a healthy and complementary land's occupation where an adequate diversity of land use promoted allows, in the case of the Financial Center and its surrounding areas (ZEN), to have offices, shops, equipment and services complemented by housing.

San Isidro is one of the most important centralities since it hosts the city's financial center; it is home to many work centers and most workers are professionals with a high education level. In this way, there is a great potential of professional people working in the Financial Center who might be interested in having a home near their work center. While the land value is high, it turns out to be an attractive area given the offer of services, connectivity and equipment. Similarly, parking has been regulated considering the accessibility to public transport, as well as its services and equipment.

The Municipality has also raised the possibility that building projects, in the Financial Center, which have metropolitan trade zoning (CM), may have higher building level than allowed, provided that the owner of the property is withdrawn at the level floor to leave public space. This application is aimed at improving the provision of public spaces in the district, because if the designer finds advantages in height and densification, he/she would be willing to allow part of the property to be intended for public use, without it being possible to modify its settings after the project is approved.

In another proposed system, with funding through the Public–Private Partnership, bicycles would have been rented for short trips within the district. This is expected to reduce CO_2 emissions and motivate the use of non-motorized transport. The shared bicycle system was strategic for the district as its sustainable urban mobility plan identified in daily trips with distances below 7 km.

Public space management strategies were also in the project portfolio. The superblocks development proposed eight superblock pilots that were designed with tactical urbanism strategies in order to modify street sections in favour of pedestrians and cyclists. The concept of these superblocks is to group blocks into another virtual and bigger block (superblock) that concentrates motorized transport in its perimeter. This allows the interior of a superblock to develop their streets with preference for non-motorized transport, which will reduce transit accidents and greenhouse gas emissions (GGE). One superblock and previous and punctual interventions for another seven have already been placed with excellent results in perception and statistics; interventions like parking space recycling, wider sidewalks, parklets, between others.

"Urban Interventions" was the given name by the administration of physical interventions on public space where urban design is the tool for promoting sustainable transport with emphasis on non-motorized transport. Following that premise, defending the pedestrian has been their priority as they are the most vulnerable street's users. Observations and studies have been held in order to sustain these interventions which in some cases have blocked street accesses completely. In some cases, they have eliminated surface parking from the whole extension of a street. So, the interventions aim to stop subsidizing the usage of private motorized vehicles with citizen's taxes and compromising public space. These interventions have been also tactical for urbanism.

A similar and complementary strategy was the "urban activations". In order to enhance tactical urbanism design, different kinds of activities have been placed in these interventions to "activate" the street's usage, to correct the misconception that public space is only parks and squares. The objective of most of these urban activations is to recover public space for the persons, to stop car invasion of the streets and acknowledge them as public space and consequently use it vibrantly. Paint workshops, concerts, gardening and other activities have been placed under the "+Ciudad" brand (in Spanish, more city); that promotes a better city, a better life quality and better citizens; conscious of the environment and the consequences of their transport options.

As for parking policies, which are an important game changer within the TOD strategies, San Isidro's administration had three principal policies for surface parking in public space. Parking slots reduction, as a specific policy, had a basis on reducing car dependency as pedestrian urban characteristics were enhanced. Parking slots then were transformed into non-motorized transport area such as wider sidewalks, bicycle parking, tress and benches, among other uses of the street which complemented and agreeable experience in public space. The first sector to have these policies implemented was again the "ZEN" as this area has different public transport services within walking distance, and being so, all public space projects weren't having in consideration public parking slots for automobiles, with the only exception of RMP (reduced mobility person). Also, this area had been a victim of car-favouritism normative from the first half of the 20th century; from that crime is possible to identify 115 079 parking slots where 21 927 were on the street; evidence that the streets don't need more cars parked in.

"The street isn't a garage" was another programme that applied urban normative innovation which allowed the district to implement district transit sanctions and the usage of car cranes and an impound lot. Previously, districts weren't allowed to implement this kind of service and the metropolitan government wasn't able to oversee the whole urban territory. This service has been a strong deterrent for car drivers who often parked irregularly on the street as infringement wasn't given and so the punishment for this "misbehaviour" didn't exist.

Also, a "rotary parking system" was established. Once again, the district municipality competences are limited and they're not allowed to intervene independently on public parking; the main problem is that the district is not allowed to change the rates, the most important element on parking management. Why this was important? Because public parking slots are limited in the district and even more those which the municipality was able to charge users (there are metropolitan conditions in order to allow charging). The problem? Some users, office workers usually, used these parking slots for their working periods (10 hours on average) and by so denying the proper use of public parking slots: short visits which allow different drivers, commerce and others to benefit fairly.

So, again innovation was present on urban management and the "rotary parking system" was implemented. It consisted simply of allowing only 2 hours of parking in each public slot and if this time was exceeded, the vehicle would be transported to the impound with its proper ticket. This new deterrent allowed 1173 parking slots on the street being multiplied until nine times depending on the place where the strategy was applied. This new use of parking slots had positive effects on small commerce which could receive new sporadic clients.

Bicycle promotion had been also a very important tool for promoting sustainable mobility. According to a JICA report (Japan International Cooperation Agency), between 2005 and 2015, the number of trips made by bicycle increased from 517 to 4716 travels daily (Lima Cómo Vamos), meaning that the use of bicycles had shown an annually increase of 24.7% in 11 years.

By the year 2016, with the new mobility policies, the use of bicycles began to exponentially grow, surpassing the natural trend of previous years, and setting up a 56.5% difference from 2015, by going from 4716 to 7381 trips. The same behaviour can be seen from the data of 2017, showing that more than 11 550 trips are now made by bicycle, representing 2.2% of the 524 000 trips made in San Isidro each day.

This growth in bicycle use has been complemented with pro-cycling campaigns, as set in the 7th Program of San Isidro's Sustainable Urban Mobility Plan (PMUS). It also includes the "Sustainable Urban Mobility Pact" as a strategy in which more than 50 enterprises with 13 825 employees got involved in an agreement with the local government to encourage sustainable commuting among their employees. Since the arrangement was established, it has brought up more than 450 new bike commuters to San Isidro, which represent an increment from 0.9% to 3.26% between 2015 and 2017.

One of the most active companies in promoting bicycle use, and involved in the agreement, is R.S. An interesting fact is that the rate of bike commuting among R.S. employees grew from 2% to 7% since they committed to the "Sustainable Urban Mobility Pact". That proves that a positive trend concerning bicycle use among companies can be created when the right stimulus system is put into practice.

Also, cycling and bus routes/stations are integrated in different layers. For cycling, there are numerous parking places for regular bicycles (more than 400) and before the end of 2018, there will be 50 stations of shared bicycle system with 900 bicycle slots. These bicycle places/systems are integrated with the public transport system and "MiBus" system, where both kinds of bicycle slots are placed near bus stations in order to serve as feeders or as last mile travel alternative.

Another mobility strategy, or system in this case, is the MiBus system implemented by the San Isidro's municipality, an exclusive service for the district commuters which approach and connect them with five sectors. These sectors include intermodal connectivity with the whereabouts of the Interconnected Metropolitan Transportation System: Metropolitano, Corredor Complementario Azul (Arequipa Avenue), Corredor Complementario Rojo (Javier Prado Avenue), Cycle-lane stops in the district of San Isidro and out of it, that communicate to Line 1's LIMA's METRO stations. Between May 2017 and May 2018, MiBus has provided, on average, 170 daily trips within the district with more than 83 740 passengers.

Thanks to the strategies presented before, the TOD impact and replicability were easy to recognize. The regulations implemented had clear impacts on their first years, even though they should be analysed at least after 10 years. Some of their results are listed below:

i. "Municipal retirement" use for commercial activities Operating License: 23
ii. Exceptional standards for areas with special urban characteristics (ZEN): Operating licenses for parking reduction: nine (seven parking reduction in buildings and two parking lots)
iii. Provisions to promote sustainability in residential areas: 737 housing units (increasing by 82%), 540 parking lots (decreasing the requirement in one-third) and 91 bicycle parking lots (previously not proposed in projects)

    From 2012 to 2016, in the application area 15 licenses were issued, and from the regulation's publication until March 2018, nine licenses were issued (increased 60%).
iv. Public space generation: one approved preliminary project, generating approximately 833.66 m^2 of public space. A total of 41

(32 L.F + 9 L.E) licenses were granted between operating and building licenses.

San Isidro's municipality has implemented these land management policies following the standards established by the Metropolitan Municipality of Lima by the Ordinance on Urban Mobility and the national standard approved by DS. No. 022-2016-MVCS, where the regulations on territorial conditioning and sustainable urban development are approved. Similarly, the adjoining districts such as San Borja, Miraflores and Surquillo have been implementing mobility plans with a network of cycleways that allow intermodal connection points for public transport and the non-motorized transport (pedestrian and cyclist slings).

Finally, we have observed the rise of car-sharing modes in the metropolis and of course in San Isidro's district. As the district policy was to reduce the private car dependency by reducing car's infrastructure, with emphasis on surface car parking, people had chosen to share rides with friends and family and also by Apps (Uber pool) and informal "collective" services we call "colectivos". Colectivos is a Spanish word for "collectives" which are drivers that offer transport services in regular private cars. This last option does not represent a solution, but it is an improvement.

A better placement on cycling and public transport infrastructure has also done its job as we see how in the last years non-motorized transport and public transport share have been increasing in the district despite the district's continuous motorization rate growth as well as in Lima-Callao Metropolis.

Proposals for stakeholder integration: participatory innovation in awareness and change of habits

The tools of the 21st century, such as Information and Communications Technology (ICT) and the capabilities that offer users to access information and exchange experiences between them, allow in the same way the link between different actors, allowing their integration. What is proposed is that stakeholders can have a common objective which should be to raise awareness of the environmental social value of the city and in it. Having identified the basic problem that is the "lack of citizenship" and the "lack of knowledge" about sustainability, resilience and similar/associated terms that should be part of people's daily lives, we then believe in the need of pedagogical processes for the "change of habits" of the inhabitants of the metropolis, which is generally a polluting/non-concerned/uninformed society.

This section then proposes two platforms/programmes that link different stakeholders to raise awareness of the intrinsic and social value of nature using mobility and urban space as a driver and pedagogical canvas.

Play-City: live on play mode

Play-City is an urban programme (or activation) that uses open space (public space) as a playfield and aims to make "journeys/urban travels" a valuable, amusing activity. By introducing game, this programme aims to enhance the quality of different kinds of transport modes and make them become a pedagogical platform as well.

The first idea to improve mobility (without innovation yet) is to motivate walking as the main complement to the rest of the means of transport (public, automobile). Campaigns to promote walking have been implemented in cities such as Paris (2012) by the "INPES", being a local and national programme to promote physical activity with a very simple principle: "moving thirty (30) minutes a day is easy". However, it is found that this is not sufficient for us under the context where average citizens are always in a hurry and/or tired. That is why we are looking to make a proposal that makes urban travels in general an activity with an added value, something motivating, something fun.

The idea evolves then to make the displacements "a game" evoking the concept of "Homo Ludens". Homo Ludens, "The Player Man", is a book written in 1938 by Dutch historian, cultural theorist and professor Johan Huizinga. His work deals with the importance of games for society and for culture. Huizinga uses the term "Game Theory" in the book to define the conceptual space where the game takes place. Huizinga suggests that the game is first and a necessary (not enough thought) condition of the generation of culture.

To introduce the game, Huizinga identifies five features that the game must have:

I. Playing is free, it's actually freedom.
II. Playing is not "ordinary" or "real" life.
III. The game is different from the "ordinary" life, equally for where and for duration.
IV. Playing creates order, it's order. Play demands absolute and supreme order.
V. Playing is linked to no material interest and cannot obtain any benefit from it.

These statements are conditioned in relation to urban mobility:

I. Mobility is a right, the right to move freely (free is possible only to a certain level such as walking and some non-motorized modes).

II. Mobility or travel is a daily activity (with the game it is proposed that the activity comes out of the ordinary).
III. Mobility, rather travels, takes a place in time and territory specifically (again, the space/time combination is sought to be removed from the ordinary).
IV. Mobility proposes order (a mobility policy in relation to development plans – Development of Transversal Skills (DOTS)).
V. Mobility has no material interests (directly); however, one benefits from a good travel policy.

Then, by raising the city as a playground, Homo Ludens will find itself in its territory and continue its evolution. The moment when travel, mobility, becomes a game, we will have a different complementary activity that will be far from being a nuisance or lost time. The concept for improving urban mobility is then called “Play-City”.

Imagine, for example, that in our travel we can collect urban “items”, and we collect elements that we will find only in a specific urban space. For example, during a subject’s daily walk, he will find games. If we stick to the idea of collecting urban elements, this person will be aware on his journey until reaching his destination. The walk becomes in that context part of the game in which you need to scroll, awareness, to find those elements. The collection of such elements may be carried out in different ways according to specific urban, social and technological contexts.

As an example, it is proposed the collection of elements of urban art, quoting the artist “SPACE INVADER”, thus being able to “collect” his pieces as the elements of the game in different cities of the world (http://www.space-invaders.com/home/).

The graffiti labeller “Space Invader”, which is an urban symbol of Paris and Parisians, allows with his work to enhance the proposal of “Play-City”. Its work theme also comes from a video game and this allows the positioning of the “Play-City” image more easily.

The player in this case would aim to collect the “space invaders” that are on the streets of Paris (and other cities). This activity has even long formed specific tourist walks, and so the proposal would be to popularize such activity and structure it as a game. The player on his or her journey, on foot, for example, will identify the “space invaders” and mark their position. In a first stage, this identification can be personal and shared orally with other “players” (citizens). It is projected that players will take photos and in time share them in different digital/social media. The popularity of the game and of the “space invaders” impulse the development of applications (Apps) that allow to capture the mentioned urban art. This step is part of a trend of games on real terrain and/or with augmented reality using urban space as a playground that can geolocate any activity (as PokemonGo or Ingress). This clearly allows a different recognition of the cities, thus being able to promote certain places. This practice we recognize would be done through "game" and a physical activity such as walking or, in any case, during the activity of urban traveling.

"Urban games" have already been implemented, however, never in the domain of mobility. For example, "the fun theory" with the project "Piano stairs" aims to make people take the regular stairs instead of the automatic stairs, being able to register in the framework of "moving is healthy", "physical activity". If such devices are implemented by enrolling them in the context of mobility, it could be mentioned that the "Play-City" would be composed of a network of urban games.

One element for the promotion of "Play-City" would also be the development of Android/IOS applications. The basic idea is also to generate a "role playing game" (RPG) where any individual can locate the games on a virtual database (on a real territory) that changes according to the mobility demands (the presence of a traffic jam on the territory would direct players to another route/place, for example).

Finally, the concept of mobility around "Play-City" is to include an activity, a game, in the daily commutes so that they become entertained destination. These activities should also be changing so that the city can also reinvent itself through such games. An example that is not distant is the urban art that makes the city a great canvas. The urban game of "Play-City" must also be changing like urban (as well as free) artistic expressions so that everyday commuting goes out of the ordinary. The changing location of these games will also contribute to the creation of an urban order that influences mobility while being able to direct urban flows, displacements by positioning the games. For example, motivating motorists to intermodality through interactive routes that make travelling easier for everyone and, secondly, animation and certain productivity according to the game is proposed (TED /Jane McGonigal: gaming can make a better world – http://www.youtube.com/watch?v=dE1DuBesGYM).

To build the "Play-City", we propose that it be the institutions of public/urban management (e.g. municipalities) that set the rules of the games, the rules for establishing the games, and that these be manufactured by those with initiatives such as entrepreneurs, citizen awareness societies and so on. If the city encourages citizens to live it, to use it and to travel daily "playing", it will become more social, allow more encounters and interactions democratize.

PLAN B: rediscover the city without haste

PLAN B is a platform that offers everyday life alternatives consistent with the needs of the environment. Through a virtual space, PLAN B offers life's alternatives in the city, in the public space, with routes that allow to visit respectful stakeholders regarding nature (sustainable traders). It is through kinder routes/journeys that we live a pedagogical process replicable by all and living the city without haste, under the same activity of moving, we are sustainable, and we are an example of resilience.

The identified problem to be addressed is that the inhabitants of Lima do not know the impact of their decisions on the city and on the environment. There is no easy, accessible and fast-consumption information that allows Lima's untamed inhabitants to be aware of the effects of their daily life on their economy and their own living environment.

The basic goods do not communicate the ecological footprint generated by their production and consumption. This footprint falls on the city, society and the environment, among others. There is little access to this information on an up-to-date basis and it is not available to everyone, making it difficult for people to be aware of the consequences of their habits. Accessing information would allow us to start changing habits or at least to learn about the direct effect of them.

The proposed idea is to create an urban life network on a local scale through a georeferenced and multipurpose App that invites the community and its visitors (neighbours from other districts or tourists) to consume responsibly and make use of spaces in a safe and pleasant way; so urban space and virtual space complement each other as educational elements in sustainable living. The App seeks to group different synergies starting with a network of local and/or responsible companies that integrate a virtual and physical path through tours.

Between the objectives of the platform is to generate citizen awareness, recognizing rules of coexistence to know/rediscover and adopt the district, thus achieving the respect and integration of the public space. People consume territory responsibly. The current fleeting journey is one of the main causes of the inappropriate use of spaces and the little respect for their care and preservation. The lack of pause gives rise to ignorance and makes the territory a "nobody's space" producing an unrespectful behaviour to the city. We seek to reduce the perception of speed (being able to go slower or faster) generating a route and proposing the conception of "living travel" regardless of the transport mode. Thus, transport stops being just a way of reaching a destination and becomes an attractive activity in itself. The route must be pedagogical through its inhabitants, the traders who operate there and the public space itself aligned with the sustainable message of the municipality. This is how we all make a sustainable district (or another jurisdiction/territory), with the possibility of implementing behaviours that may be replicable.

The projection aims to have a district where trade, culture and gastronomy emerge. Miraflores as a pilot district in the metropolis is a versatile district par excellence where couples, bohemians, tourists, families, large companies and small producers come, where surfing is practiced and where you dress in high heels and tie. Everyone is invited.

Miraflores is also the fusion of all urban networks: the cultural galleries are linked to the cafes where visitors gather before going to a play. The local stores have reserved products for local restaurants that need fresh items immediately. A book fair is on the most common pedestrian route of people leaving work in direction to the public transport hubs. This route is also a network of people and companies consistent with the environment, and that is where the municipality will be the connection between the individuals and the network. In this way, the municipality will assess the relevance of the offer of services when they prove to be responsible and consistent with the environment. At that time, your product will be exposed to the neighbour and the visiting neighbour through the municipal network, the public space and the virtual network.

The proposal also looks out to link with public objectives as the Sustainable Development Goals (SDGs). The direct related ones are:

3 Health and welfare: healthy products and services
4 Quality education: environmental responsibility

7 Affordable and non-polluting energy: non-motorized transport
8 Decent work and economic growth: product and service platform

11 Sustainable cities and communities: compact, sustainable and intelligent city model
12 Responsible production and consumption: network of producers and consumers
13 Climate action: project raises sustainability

17 Partnerships to achieve the objectives: different actors converge on the platform

The project impacts too on climate change mitigation and adaptation directly on the user, the person. Through the proposal, we seek to raise awareness of the effects of their daily activities on the environment. We also understand that the practice of sustainable living is not necessarily attractive to all, and so we seek through the platform to generate benefits to those who have resilient and environmentally friendly practices. This is achieved by linking actors who offer services and can grant discounts (among other activities) or other attractive elements to citizens.

The proposal seeks to intervene the streets to be an activity in itself: the public space is interactive, playful and pleasant. This results in the adoption of the space by residents and visitors. This appropriation of the city will create a bond, which leads people to come to love it as their own, as an extension of their living space.

The creation of axes of life is also an important part of the approach, the alternative of a journey is in itself communication and awareness about the needs of the environment. It is a Route B Plan, avoiding congested and contaminated routes and taking a path where feeling safe is the priority.

This axes would allow activating local commerce as a shop network is not only physically integrated in the district, but also within the Communication App offering sales, promotions and strategic alliances (download an App to get a discount), as a pretext for provide information on the benefits of sustainable and environmentally responsible products.

It's necessary also to group brands of responsible private companies that generate a sustainable trade that is identifiable by passers-by and by all the people who pass in front of them. This group as a district "Brand" is a recognition that allows to bring together the responsible entities with the environment not only in the virtual space (through the App), but also in the same public space through a plate designated by the "Brand".

The proposal then allows too to raise people's sustainability as, by recognizing an alternative ride, they will understand through it in an interactive and communicative way sustainable living choices such as the meaning of bicycle use compared to a car, among several other everyday examples.

It's mapped also the need of creating an App as an interactive and communicative mean to achieve the activation and recognition of sustainable local commerce. ICTs then are really necessary to recognize and use properly according to the needs of the proposal.

What this proposal offers that allows to differentiate it from similar programmes is a direct link between key players in the city making sustainability a collective and participatory practice. A platform/App that links the private sector, public institutions and citizens offering services and information linked on the web and in the public space. The platform offers services related to municipal interventions/events, thus being a synergy for the benefit of the citizen by offering alternatives of services and sustainable products, all under a framework of citizen pedagogy on the environment.

The greatest risk is that the platform does not find the network of stakeholders needed to position itself in the everyday consumer market. We aim to make it an application/technological necessity once the pedagogical process has been well landed. Another risk is also not to find the stakeholder who catalyses the pedagogical process thinking of local governments today. Nevertheless, this risk is very low as local municipalities, between others, wouldn't reject a non-cost project which has the same sustainable development objectives.

Economic sustainability for the project is important in order to lower the risk. Revenue from the "PlanB" platform comes mainly from advertising and its sponsors. As it is the creation of a stakeholder's network responsible for the environment, it is stipulated that there is sponsorship by companies and producers that benefit from being part of that "PlanB" network. Likewise, since it is a project/entrepreneurship for the purpose of environmental conservation and promotion of sustainable life, it is also stipulated that financing can be captured by institutions such as Inter-American Development Bank (IDB), Corporacion Andina de Fomento (CAF), and the Agence Française de Development (AFD), among others.

The targeted market is residents and visitors of the district who own a smartphone. In this way, we target around 330 000 (80 000 residents and 250 000 visitors in the Miraflores case), people who can purchase the App, join the platform and/or be part of the "PlanB" network. This population should be considered a potential for daily consumers.

Measuring the IMPACT of this proposal is also important; therefore, different strategies are adopted too. In the public space, within the route "PlanB" counts are made; in shops/services, income counting is made, and cash flow is also requested. To users, surveys are conducted to evaluate the knowledge and practice of daily sustainability. For institutional indicators, tons of recycled waste, water consumption and electricity consumption should be properly measured.

This project/idea has already a first recognition of the proposal in the course/contest "Sustainable Cities" 2017 organized by the OEA in Miraflores district in collaboration with Southern Scientific University (UCSUR).

Conclusions

Lima-Callao Metropolis has a very complex and poor context in terms of mobility and sustainability. Contradictions such as a motorization rate of 181veh/1000 habitants and being one of the most polluted and congested cities in the region and in the world make part of this complexity where it's important to have detailed analysis of the urban context, the society and all the indicators that influence mobility.

The metropolis has also interesting advantages such as 57% of the travels are in collective modes, which is an excellent ratio. Nevertheless, it's also important to realize that from the 25 000 vehicles that the passenger transport has, almost 40% are more than 10 years old, almost 85% run by diesel full (cancer alert) and more than 30% of the vehicles have a capacity of 12 persons (combis). ATU, which was established to be a game changer in Lima-Callao's urban mobility, by July 2020 hasn't yet started a "full operation" as the institutions it was supposed to absorb still wait for proper legal approval.

San Isidro's Municipality with its 11 km^2 jurisdiction, for example, has proven that measured local strategies can have metropolitan positive impacts. The 2015–2018 administration approach, or urban sustainability mobility, a city for people, transport-oriented development, within a 21st century vision for the district and for the metropolis showed that jurisdiction is abstract and that everybody in the city is a neighbour. An important San Isidro's achievement is the 362% increase of bicycle commuters in the first 2 years of administration in a district where the motorization rate almost doubles the metropolis average.

As nudge theory implied, San Isidro's environment under TOD policies promoted sustainable behaviours that have been confirmed in different ratios as the raise of sustainable buildings projects, raise of sustainable transport (cyclists and public transport commuters) and walking habits, space. Street renewals have raised the presence of people, outdoor activities and business, which have had other positive impacts on the city. For example, based on surveys, more than 79% of the citizens surveyed say that interventions in public spaces allow them to enjoy the district.[8]

What is most important from this survey, as mentioned previously, is that the motorization rate on the district, residents and visitors, is the highest among all Lima-Callao's districts, underlining the importance and impact of these kinds of strategies on transport. It is important too to mention that all these strategies are based on environmental issues as the district logo for this administration was "San Isidro_sustainable city". TOD strategies have been proposed and landed for environmental/natural value towards citizens awareness, which can be implied too as raising "social value" again from an environmental perspective.

The "Play-City" programme presents the idea to make the city a playground, where mobility becomes the "dice", the opportunities are vast, and we can give accurate examples (as given already) on how stakeholders could invest in this kind of project and how it can be pedagogical in restoring natural and social value in urban contexts.

For example, transport stations/stops are excellent places to advertise and ergo publicity becomes an investor on urban transport equipment: the station is implemented (illumination, benches, etc.) in exchange for a quantity of advertising square meters. If this equipment is part of the game, and the advertising square meters are also information canvases, we can have a pedagogical gaming field where advertising can gain exposition and sustainability can gain adepts by sensibilization.

As gaming, playing is also a strategy for learning process, the subject can be natural and social value. As also said before, journeys/transport is kind of a "dead-activity" in itself as we acknowledge the phrase "time loss in transport". Then gaming can change the image of this activity and make it fun, useful, and a learning process in sustainability for this specific context. Then transport become an educational process, an awareness raising process for society and a benefit for the individuals as transport becomes a profitable activity in different ways thanks to the Play-City programme.

On "PlanB", as presented, there are also low budget possibilities to integrate different actors in order to raise awareness on natural/social value through a commercial network which would auto-finance itself. The principal idea of this project is to raise awareness in general sustainability but directed into regular daily habits. The project also aims intelligently to make sustainability "profitable" from the benefits that the platform proposes directly and indirectly. Mobility in this platform is essential as the main daily activity which is addressed is daily travels and how the transport mode choice affects the collective environment and the personal economy. Through mobility, different subjects are addressed in the travel network and by the involved actors. As an example, a renewed street gives priority to non-motorized transport, and so people are eager to walk and by trough this way. In this street, you can find veggie burgers which communicate the impact of the meat industry on the nature and on our own health. At the end of the street, urban design leaves a space like a plaza where constant activations take place and the subject would be always sustainability and for attracting daily commuters, discounts on responsible commerce would be given in exchange of participating for a few minutes in the pedagogical proposal (which would be a game, a pep-talk, or others).

The presented projects/ideas with urban intervention possibilities mixing public and private space as public and private actors wants to address the opportunity cost of non-intelligent urban administrations. By non-intelligent we mean that opportunities are lost when we do not use urban potential to address environmental issues.

Nowadays nature doesn't fit the urban imaginary; when we think of cities, we think of grey concrete. The projects/ideas mentioned before, by raising awareness in all urban stakeholders, aim also to recover the place for nature in urban environments, and recovering nature not only for economic or environmental issues but also for social ones.

Nature is the greatest benefit and objective as well for human societies. Nature give us resources and give us a home to live. Urban environments should not be different, but our 20th century cities have the opposite idea: living here and resources away from here. From that point of view, cities are the problem, but from our 21st century point of view, cities are the solution. Cities concentrate the human potential, potential to make considerable changes, and they must come as natural as everyday habits. So, the projects presented, having the nudge theory as a base, playing as an order, and economic benefits as an attractor, present cities as our best weapon against global warning and nature depreciation.

Mobility and open space in this term is the selected best strategy as daily journeys). As people are obliged to move, to travel, to their workplaces and

Illustration 3.1 Wiñaywayna, quechua settlement which merge with its environment.

to their study centers (principally), the transport mode they choose and the route they take are the key to make behavioural changes as is the best way/place to communicate/influence citizens. If urban administrations can "nudge" citizens into sustainability and they can benefit from it, mixing different actors would be easy in open (public mostly) space, where all of them get connected. The objective then is not to create or enhance natural value, but to recover it from daily opportunities in urban environments, exactly where it is most needed (Figure 3.1).

Notes

1 https://www.airvisual.com/world-air-quality-ranking.
2 This guide states that the permissible maximum limits for PM_{10} levels are 20 g/m^3 on average per year and 50 g/m^3 on average per day (24 h); while y for $PM_{2.5}$ levels is 10 g/m^3 on average per year and 25 g/m^3 on average daily (24 h). Lima's average air quality is far away from those standards.
3 OMS (2006). Guías de calidad del aire de la OMS relativas al material particulado, el ozono, el dióxido de nitrógeno y el dióxido de azufre.
4 An hour lost on traffic congestion represents a yearly personal loss of S/. 1 062, which equals a city loss of S/. 5 310 212 400 (PEA = 5 M, 2015). Considering an hour income of S/3,54 (minimal legal income) and an average daily trip over 2 hours, the daily personal social investmen is S/ 7,08 or S/212,4 monthly – Willard Manrique- 2017 / La República.
5 http://msi.gob.pe/portal/sostenibilidad/movilidad-urbana/.
6 Central Business District.
7 "Municipal retirement" is a part of the private property which is next to the street. Depending on the property location, this space has specific length where normally it is forbidden to build or place any commercial activity.
8 Maguiña (2018). Servicio De Consultoría Para La Elaboración De Reporte De Impacto Del Programa + Ciudad.

References

Thaler, & Sunstein (2008). *Nudge: Improving Decisions About Health, Wealth, and Happiness*. New York: Penguin Book.

Kelling, George, & Coles, Catherine (1997). Fixing Broken Windows: Restoring Order and Reducing Crime in Our Communities. https://www.airvisual.com/world-air-quality-ranking.

OMS (2006). *Guías de calidad del aire de la OMS relativas al material particulado, el ozono, el dióxido de nitrógeno y el dióxido de azufre*.

Manrique, Willard (2017). La República Journal, http://msi.gob.pe/portal/sostenibilidad/movilidad-urbana/.

Jacobs, J. (1961). *The Death and Life of Great American Cities*. Nueva York: Random House.

Miraflores, Municipailidad de (2016). *Plan Urbano Distrital 2016-2026*. Lima: Municipalidad de Miraflores.

Muromachi, Y. (2015). Symbiosis of Vehicles, People and Nature. In K. Ohta, *Transport Policy in Perspective: 2015* (pp. 41–53). Tokyo: Japan Research Center for Transport Policy.

Orfeuil, J. (2008). *Une approche laïque de la mobilité*. París: Éditions Descartes & Cie.

APOMIPE (2011). Manual para la Articulación de Redes Empresariales, *Programa de Apoyo a la Micro y Pequeña Empresa en el Perú (APOMIPE)*. Lima: Cosude.

4 The Purepechas of Cheran

Community solidarity, public security and environmental conservation in Mexico

Karol Gil-Vasquez

Introduction

Political turmoil, social instability, environmental degradation, and violence have increased around the globe. In the foreword of *The Great Transformation: The Political and Economic Origins of Our Times,* Stiglitz (2001 [1957]) states that Karl Polanyi's analysis of the XVII century is of great relevance for instituting a paradigm inspired in the Global South. A region that is experiencing *Great Transformations* of its own. He writes, "we recognize that the extended periods of unemployment, the persistent high levels of inequality, poverty and squalor in much of Latin America [L.A.], has had a disastrous effect on social cohesion, and been a contributing force to the high and rising levels of violence" (ibid: x).

Mexico illustrates such scenario as the nation undergoes a Great Transformation after implementing the North American Free Trade Agreement (NAFTA) in 1994 (Cordera, 2015). After more than three decades, Mexico's regions of disparity spread across its territory, which is populated by decaying urban centers and rural towns where environmental degradation, economic marginalization, political instability, and violence immerse themselves into the societal fabric. By 2016, Mexico, after Syria, became the second most deadly conflict zone in the world, surpassing Iraq and Afghanistan in the number of human casualties, the majority registered in states that became the battlegrounds of U.S.-Mexico's War on Drugs in 2006. Since the beginning of the conflict, approximately 105,000 people have lost their lives in a plethora of dispersed battles, where offensive and defensive trenches are not identified, as impunity and corruption blur the line between enemies and allies (IISS, 2017).[1]

The phenomenon of violence and criminality in Mexico cannot be decontextualized. Polanyi (2001 [1957]) shows that human despair becomes the norm under the auspices of modernization. As indicated by Harvey (2013, 2014), a main feature of global capitalism is its accumulating capacity through dispossessing. The latter is perceived as an unintended consequence of human progress. Thus, it should not be surprising to find the level of economic exhaustion and environmental deterioration after years of empowering neoliberalism in a region where accumulation patterns have not historically receded, and inequality accentuates via structural adjustment programs.

According to the 2014 Global Wealth Report, 64.4% of the country's wealth is concentrated in the hands of Mexico's wealthiest 10%. The rate at which their capital gains accumulates grow is unprecedented – whereas in 1996 their fortunes averaged $25,000 million, after 2008, the average has increased to $142,900 million. Esquivel-Hernández (2016) calculates the power concentrated in these few hands and concludes that if the wealthiest Mexicans were to generate minimum-wage jobs by spending their investment returns, a total of 3 million workers would find employment. Even then, the poverty issue is far from resolved, as the minimum wage is not a living wage, averaging approximately $3.75 per day. To compensate for the income shortage, the pool of the working poor, the underemployed, or sub-employed join the informal economy, which supplies 60% of the jobs in the country.

In 2015, *The Economist* stated that Mexico is a country divided into: *El Mexico Imaginario*, which milks from the global economy, and El *Mexico Profundo*, which survives with less than two dollars a day. Accordingly, "Mexico has failed to bridge the gap between a globalized minority and a majority that lives [...] in 'backwardness and poverty.' When México joined [NAFTA], income per head has grown by an annual average of barely 1%. About half of the population remains stuck in poverty; another quarter risk slipping back into penury" (1). The Mexico's two comparisons indicate the impact of an economic policy that fragments a social fabric by widening the gap between the 'haves' and 'haves not' through privatizing, deregulating, financializing, and placing adjustments upon poor families (Cordera, 2015).

According to 2016 National Council for the Evaluation of Social Development (CONEVAL)'s data, 43.6% of the Mexican population live in poverty, a total of 53 million people. Those living in extreme poverty amount to 9.4 million people. From the entire population, the most affected are the *pueblos originarios* or the indigenous population[2] who tend to be clustered in statistics of destitution. Estimates indicate that 10% of the Mexican population is indigenous, approximately 12 million people, out of which around 71.9% live in poverty. Five of the states that concentrate most of the *pueblos originarios*' population surpass the average national poverty rate (43.6%). In Oaxaca and Chiapas, 77.1% and 71.3% of the indigenous population, respectively, report earning the minimum wage or less. In addition to material deprivation, completing elementary levels of education is an important issue to overcome as 19.8% of the population (ages of 30 and 64) are illiterate. Furthermore, 30% of the indigenous population show deficiencies in food access, almost 80% do not have access to any social welfare program, while 56.3% do not have basic shelter services.

The growing abysm between NAFTA's 'winners' and 'losers' makes it difficult for *El Mexico Imaginario* to have contact with *El Mexico Profundo*. The two notions of Mexico are anthropologically elaborated in *Mexico Profundo: Reclaiming a Civilization*. In his work, Bonfil Batalla (2009[1996]) argues that Mexico is a political construction that rests upon two divergent nations. One nation *el Mexico Imaginario* is encompassed by the circles of power that connect with a Westernized vision of progress, centered on modernization, industrialization, and the global economy. Accordingly, "[these] ruling groups of the country, who make or impose the most important decisions affecting all of Mexico's society, have never admitted that to advance might imply liberating and encouraging the cultural capacities that really exist in the majority of the population". *El Mexico Profundo* has historically resisted the various attempts of transformation, providing a potent cultural capacity by rooting itself in the cosmovision of the *pueblos originarios*.

With the rise of Mexico's laissez faire capitalism, NAFTA's mechanisms enhance uneven distribution of benefits among regions. The neoliberal process, driven primarily by a global economy that rips the country's social fabric apart, divides the population into income brackets as well as favored versus unfavored ethnic categories (Blanco, 2017; Krozer, 2019). Regional marginalization and income inequality among the population function as instruments of a structural violence that materializes into criminal activity. To this phenomenon, it must be added a deteriorating environment with increasing levels of pollution and extraction of natural resources. Mexico's decaying social, political, environmental, and economic scenario continues to accentuate the lack of credibility on their political institutions. Over the last years, Mexico's streets are continuously filled with massive demonstrations that ventilate the discontent accumulated through years of implementing a policy of 'accumulation' through 'dispossession' that threatens the livelihood of millions.

The most radical and effective responses to neoliberalism stem from marginalized communities. NAFTA's inauguration contested by the Zapatista Army of National Liberation (EZLN acronym) in 1994 resonates almost three decades later at the practical level. Inspired by more than 500 years of indigenous resistance to colonialism, the Zapatistas, with their 3000–5000 soldiers, stand against the policies that would undermine working class as well as rural farmers and indigenous communities. Recently, Mexico witnesses the first national proposal emerging from the *pueblo originarios*: the National Indigenous Council (CNI in Spanish acronym).

The CNI is a grassroots organization that unites communities, towns, and neighborhoods with the indigenous of Mexico and provides a space of unity, reflection, and organization by promoting the internal reconstitutions of the *pueblos originarios* and the construction of a society in which all the cultures, all the colors, and all the towns are incorporated into the political composition of the country (CNI, 2017). Established in 1998 and formed by 153 delegates, representing Mexico's *pueblos originarios*, the CNI represents the first political instrument that presents proposals that emerge from grassroots indigenous organizations to Mexican society. According to Nirmal and Rocheleau (2019), the CNI "[becomes] a point of encounter, co-thinking, mutual support and leverage for indigenous peoples in Mexico, who faced a rising wave of territorial assaults on land, water, and autonomy".

In 2017, the CNI nominates its spokeswoman and first presidential candidate Maria de Jesus Patricio Gonzalez, a respected Nahua woman leader and herbalist (Baschet, 2017; Dangl, 2017). During her presidential campaign, Mrs. Patricio-Gonzalez knits a critique to neoliberalism, a perspective that links Mexico's rising criminality with the structural violence that stems from *Mexico Imaginario's* neoliberal policies. To this, she states: "we have to tear up the roots of what's hurting Mexico[...] This country needs healing[...] The political class only sees the earth and our natural resources as means of making money, not things that benefit the community and need protecting". The latter only demonstrates that *Mexico Profundo*'s marginalized communities remain conscious and take measures to resolve their daily struggles and reconstruct political institutions by empowering the bases. "The threats, insecurity, and violence against the communities in recent decades have required many to form community police to rid themselves of the scourge of narco capitalism and complicity police and military, and regain control of their streets, fields, forest, homes, water, and small businesses" (McDonnell, 2017).

According to Esteva (2014), the ultimate objective of this type of initiative "consists of restoring worlds through re-commoning land, water, forests, and governing structures. They are pruning connections with growth-economies and re-rooting within and between place(s) through rhizomatic networks of freely circulating people, goods, services, ideas, and practices" (478). In this regard, the Purepechas grassroots initiatives implemented in Cherán gain relevance. Based on the International Labor Organization (ILO)'s Convention 169, Cherán demonstrates the impact of measures—driven by solidarity, community, and direct representation—on reinstalling the rule of law in an environment threatened by widespread public and economic marginalization.

The present study represents an institutional ethnography that belongs to the Great Transition Initiative (GTI). The latter is constituted by a discursive revolution,[3] involving a shift from a modern understanding of the world into a fresh and innovative conceptualization that goes beyond dualistic and reductionist practices. Its methodology requires unpacking and acknowledging the works of ancient institutions, "to train ourselves to see what culturally we have been thought to overlook, namely, the participation of [ancient] institutional practices in the construction of the world practices" (Escobar, 1998, p. 113). The following section accounts for the agency of indigenous peoples' cultural legacy in moving forward to effectively confront contemporary issues in Mexico.

Resistance and reconstruction: the historical agency of the *Pueblos Originarios* in Mexico

The *pueblos originarios*' agency has remained in motion throughout Mexican history. In 2018, President Andres Manuel Lopez Obrador, following the official inauguration, celebrated a pre-dawn indigenous ceremony to consecrate the *baston de mando*—a wooden staff symbolizing government—that representatives from Mexico's 68 ethnic groups would present to him. For the first time in Mexican contemporary history, the *pueblos originarios* place on a nationally elected President their trust, demanding their rights and interests to be safeguarded. In the predawn ceremony, symbolically, they requested respect for their perspectives, including their paradigm of development, a cosmovision that marries prioritizing Mother Nature with a holistic vision of progress (Carlsen, 2018; Oestreich, 2019).

Contrasting Mexico's indigenous vision, the 1951 United Nation's Department of Social and Economic Affairs speaks to the destructive assumption embedded in modern programs, which considers that ancient visions must be "strapped; old social institutions have to disintegrate [...] and large numbers of persons who cannot keep up with [this idea of] progress have to have their expectations of a comfortable life frustrated". Throughout these years, nevertheless, those who tend to represent the 'clients of development' are far from simply assimilating these foreign ideas of progress. Furthermore, they are not passive when confronting the daily issues brought about the development discourse.

In this case, the *pueblos originarios* of Mexico mobilize to address a variety of issues, as the 1994 EZLN uprising against global capitalism demonstrates. Throughout this work, the underlying argument reiterates that the agency of Mexico's indigenous population must be accounted in the making of institutions needed to face the challenges of a post-neoliberal era. Hence, they must be made visible by resisting any methodologies that measure them against Westernized conceptualizations. As accurately described by Bonfil-Batallas (2007 [1996]), "[t]here were no 'Indians,' nor a concept that described uniformly all the population of the continent [...] That great internal diversity was annihilated at the very moment in which the process of conquest [took place]: Pre-Hispanic peoples were going to see their specific history masked. They were converted, within the new colonial context, into a plural and uniform being: the Indian, the Indians" (p. 4).

Overriding the historical attempts—colonization, nationalization, and globalization—to homogenize and dilute the meaningful existence of L.A.'s pre-Hispanic population, Rodriguez (2001) indicates that "the Indian stands in the same relationship to modernity as did to Spain –willing to marry, to breed, to disappear in order to ensure her inclusion in time, refuting to absent herself from the future" (p. 418). Concerning effective resilience, Scott (1985) argues that so-called indigenous peoples have, at their disposal, weapons that ensure their survival throughout colonial and postcolonial encounters. Such mechanism of defense is encompassed by tactics of passive resistance, which ensure the reproduction of their institutions. In this process, those who are disempowered tend to miscegenate with dominant forms. In L.A., in a way of resistive adaptation, to survive, the indigenous crawl; to win, the indigenous breed. In other words, the indigenous continue to live, interact, and exist, at least, under a subordinate position.

Grace Miller (2004) sustains that indigenous people not just have overcome attempts of nation building by resisting cultural homogeneous discourses of miscegenation. For the Mexican case, Rodriguez (2001) argues that in fact the Indian has taken over the Spanish other at the ideological level.[4] Passive acts of resistance demand reconsidering the hegemony of false consciousness. Passivity and inevitability are practices rarely observed in the daily behavior of subordinate classes. People tend to be more radical at the ideological level, and oppressive institutional structures do not necessarily impede them from materializing their thoughts—be it armed revolution, ideological decolonization, or addressing a public concern. Pragmatic initiatives often rest on an antithesis that rolls back to 'pre-modern' principles of community, direct representation, and solidarity (Scott, 1985). In other words, methods of resistance historically shelter the subaltern's interests, while defying social, political, and cultural norms.

Degrees of coercion rearticulate with emerging institutions, which redefine power laden relationships that either widen or limit the space of maneuver. Marginalized classes utilize symbolic tools that penetrate, neutralize, and negate the coercive practices of hegemonic institutions in the everyday living. Such paradigm branches out to analyzing Mexico's contemporary issues—NAFTA's negative social, economic, and political implications—and the *pueblos originarios*' response to this broader context. It recognizes a level of interaction that is inseparable from local cultural practices, which tend to accommodate or resist political agendas and, to a certain degree, bring under their control negative outcomes. This critical framework reminds us of Stavenhagen (1963, 1970), who argues that 'dual societies' do not necessarily illustrate a dichotomy (Lewis 1954, 1955; Fei and Rania, 1964; Jorgenson, 1961; Rostow, 1960).

Linking the concept of 'dual societies' with Bonfil-Batallas (2007 [1996])'s work, *El Mexico Imaginario* and *El Mexico Profundo* resemble the modern and traditional units, respectively, both interrelated given that both processes originate in a historical moment. This means that both sectors perform specific roles simultaneously generating notions of 'backwardness' and 'modernization.' Therefore, I argue that the practices of the *Mexico Profundo* have instrumental value in transformative processes as their traditions conveniently incorporate themselves in reforming economic and political institutions. Ancient practices, habits of thought, and culture continue to shape the contemporary reality, functioning as lubricating mechanisms that smooth complex transitions. That is, the 'Indian' continues to play a role in Mexico's historical dialectics, particularly in troubled times that demand innovation.

In neoliberal Mexico, the resistance of *pueblos originarios* is translated into grassroots movements that resolve a variety of issues, from extreme poverty, malnutrition, and unemployment to public education and public security. Their initiatives are based on non-market principles that flourish in the invisible spheres of Mexican market society to be part of the social fabric by restoring cultural, social, and political practices. In turn, this process is anchored in the adjusting framework of global governance. For instance, a measure to address unemployment and extreme poverty was implemented by the Totonaca[5] community of Espinal in 2010. The Espinal is a rural municipality of Veracruz with a population of approximately 25,000 peoples. In response to an initiative created by students and professors from the Intercultural University of Veracruz, the community issues *tumines*, a social currency. The bills, adorned with images of Diego Rivera and Emiliano Zapata, represent an alternative monetary system rooted in fair trade, an alternative vision of consumption and production (Lucas-Dos Santos, 2018), which together comprise a form of resistance to market fundamentalism. In doing so, the Totanacas set the ground for a solidarity economy that has the potential of expanding its non-market driven practices, as *tumines* now circulate in 16 states of the Mexican Republic (Russian Television, 2017).

In addressing issues of public safety, the Mixtecos[6] of Ayutla fulfill the vacuum left by a failed local government and re-institute a legal system. Reacting to Guerrero's troubled environment, one of the most marginalized and violent in the country, the Mixteco community has set the example of a grassroots initiative that directly confronts rampant levels of criminality by establishing the Union of Peoples and Organization of Guerrero (UPOC in Spanish acronym), a communal police force. UPOC proves to be capable of restoring peace and stability in a rural town that is surrounded by the powerful presence of transnational drug trafficking organizations (TDTOs). Organizations that fight for land to harvest poppies for heroine production. UPOC recreates a system of justice that rests upon the principles of internal normative systems (*usos y costumbres*). Under its legal umbrella, suspects of crime face civil trials where sentences and punishments are determined by communal authorities.

The trials are open to the public and community assemblies witness judicial procedures.

In the same token, the Purepechas of Cherán establish their own government to guarantee their living and safety under an environment shaped by increasing levels of violence. In Michoacán, compared to other states in the country, TDTOs penetrate and control several realms of economic activity. Operating under widespread corruption and impunity, TDTOs augment their participation in sectors that directly interact with the global economy, including the extraction of natural resources (logging) and the agricultural sector (avocado production), increasing productivity and the rate of environmental degradation. Hence, by re-establishing the rule of law in 2011, the Purepechas not only ensure public security to Cherán, but also reinstall the non-market principles of internal normative systems respected by the Mexican Constitution and re-appropriate, or as stated by Esteva (2014), 're-common' natural resources.

The effective resistance that originates from small rural municipalities where Mexico's *pueblos originarios* reside finds support in global legal structures that paradoxically came along with the rise of market fundamentalism. Such international conventions open the opportunity for indigenous peoples to access a country's legal framework to achieve autonomy and cultural dignification. Through a mechanism of direct democracy, the *Totonacas*, the *Mixtecos*, and the Purepechas are protected by ILO's 169 Convention, the umbrella that shields traditions and internal normative systems around the globe (Najar, 2012a, 2012b).

According to ILO 169 Convention's preamble, the developing situation of indigenous and tribal peoples makes it suitable to "adopt new international standards [...] with a view to removing the assimilationist orientation of the earlier standards, and recognizing the aspirations of these peoples to exercise control over their own institutions" (International Labor Organization, 2009). In 1990, the Mexican government ratified the 169 Convention, and the endorsement was followed by an amendment to Mexican Constitution's Article 4 that recognizes Mexico's pluri-ethnic composition. Following the EZLN's uprising, the Mexican government negotiated the San Andres Peace Accords in 1996. The agreement establishes the state's commitment to respect their right for self-determination while guaranteeing access to justice and recognizing their internal normative systems. The respect to internal normative systems functions as the mechanism that protects a vision of life encompassed by traditions, usages, and costumes that do not necessarily marry with the notion of modernity embraced by the development discourse.

In Mexico, internal normative systems resemble a social fabric that emerges to aid those who feel disfranchised from the Mexico *Imaginario*. Based on modernization's premises, it is incessantly argued that peasants and indigenous peoples along their practices will continue to be pushed out and transformed as the market captures all spheres of social interactions. However, how the present study shows, the nuclei of traditions and culture are not diluted into abstract elements, and contest as opposed to articulate, Western values of individuality and commodification.

Michoacán: Intersecting Neoliberal Policies, Organized Crime, and Indigenous Resistance and Mobilization

The name Michoacán originates from the Nahuatl: Michhuhcan, which means 'place of the fishermen,' whereas Purepechas mean people who are considered late 'newcomers.' Michoacán's origins date back to the XII century when Tariacuri gathered communities around the Lake Patzcuaro into one strong state by naming his sons Hiripan and Tangaxoan as lords of Ihuatzio and Tzintzuntzan, respectively, and himself the ruler of Patzcuari City. The story marks the establishment of the Purepechas (Tarascan)[7] Empire, the only one able to maintain its independence from the overreaching Triple Alliance (Aztec Empire)'s dominance. A variety of theories exist regarding the origins of the founders of Michoacán. Mälmstrom (1995) argues that the Purepechas added a new dimension to the debate about human origins in the western hemisphere. According to the *Lienzo de Jucutacato*, the 'newcomers' journeyed for many moons from a homeland far to the south (South America) to reach the Rio Balsas' mount.

According to the indigenous people of Zacatula, their forefathers tell them that from time to time people had come to that coast from certain islands on the south in large dugout canoes, bringing excellent things to trade and taking other things from the land (Warren, 1985). The historical memory is a testimony of the presumed existence of navigation in South America, which propelled patterns of migration and exchange within Mesoamerica and the South American region (Wolf, 2010[1982]). Based on this assumption, the migrants enter the Rio Balsas and established their first settlements near the lakes where climate allowed for inhabitation. The pattern of migration coincides with the Purepechas legacy that comprises knowledge of metallurgy and Quechua.

Michoacán is home to a rich environment. The state is crossed by two important mountain chains, the Sierra Madre del Sur and the Trans-Mexican Volcanic Belt, as well as a waterway that includes parts of Mexico's two largest rivers, namely, Rio Balsas and Rio Lerma. Its ecosystems vary by altitude, and still 60% of the state is covered by forests, with the most important of these producing lumber and raisin. With approximately 4 million people, the state's economy is based on agriculture, livestock, fishing, and the production of forest products and crafts. In the political arena, the state stands up for being the birthplace of Lazaro Cardenas, the Mexican President who decided to expropriate the oil industry from U.S. corporations in 1932 and reinstated one of the major programs of redistribution of land. Both policies were inspired by the nationalist legacy of the 1910 Mexican Revolution.

According to the Better Life Initiative report of the Organization for Economic Cooperation and Development (OECD) (2017), inequality exists throughout Michoacán's regions. Morelia, the state's capital, presents the highest level of well-being, and the southern state regions isolated by mountain chains present the lowest index. Located in the northcentral part, the P'urhépecha region is subdivided traditionally into four regions: Japondarhu (Place of a Lake), Eraxamani (Canyon of Eleven Towns), Juatarisi (Meseta), La Cienega de Zacapu, and the ancient region of Jurhio (Place of Hot lands). In today's Michoacán, Purepechas amount to a population of approximately 16,000 people, concentrated in the P'urhépecha region, known as the Meseta P'urhépecha, and the cities of Uruapan and Patzcuaro (Instituto National of the Pueblos Indigenas, 2019).

In the NAFTA era, Michoacán's economic activity is concentrated in the industry for export. Most of the job creation concentrates in the agricultural, mining, and commercial sectors. The entity is the largest producer of avocados in the world, nationally, the second largest producer of coke, and the third largest producer of iron, the latter is essential to Mexico's steel industry. Nevertheless, Michoacán's industry supplies only 1.64% of the steel consumed in the country (Instituto Nacional para el Federalismo y el Desarrollo Municipal, 2009).

Throughout the NAFTA era, Michoacán maintains strong ties with the United States (U.S.)'s economy. The entity demonstrates to be one of the states with the highest share of Mexican migrants working in the U.S. Remittances sent by these workers have represented for several years a major source of income, particularly in Michoacán's rural communities (Vega and Urrieta, 2006). The remaining labor force is absorbed by the industries for export or the informal economy. The connection established between Michoacán and the U.S. is of relevancy as the present-day issues faced by the *Michoacán Profundo* have to do with dynamics of the international markets. The social pressure—propelled by massive migration, dependence on U.S. economy, and increasing poverty—erupted when Michoacán became the first battleground for the U.S.-Mexican's War on Drugs that began in 2006. The arrival of conservative President Felipe Calderon symbolizes the first pledge launched by the federal government to put an end to TDTOs' profitable activities, financially auspicated by the U.S. government via the Merida Initiative.

The U.S.-Mexican War on Drugs brings to the surface the complex dynamics of a shadow economy that has been operating in the North American region for decades. The buoyant drug trafficking industry is well entrenched in Mexico, a country that sustains the comparative advantage of producing for the world's largest consumer of illicit drugs. However, in Michoacán, as in other states of Mexico, TDTOs' influence surpasses the sphere of the informal economy. Two of Mexico's major TDTOs—*La Familia Michoacán* and *Los Caballeros Templarios*—operate in Michoacán and produce most of the methamphetamine for export to the United States (Herrera and Aguirre, 2013). Nevertheless, given the political and economic vacuum left by a decentralized government and NAFTA's laissez faire economy, Michoacán's local authorities are in *de facto* substituted by TDTOs' social, political, and economic influence. Henceforth, the political and economic structure of Michoacán begins to operate under the siege of factual powers that gradually penetrated the formal market, changing supply chains, increasing productivity and efficiency, and bringing under their control natural resources.

A drastic instance of this phenomenon as it connects to the global market is the avocado industry, which now provides 45% of the world supply. Michoacan's avocado industry currently operates under a fractured political environment and the rising TDTOs' influence, which impose on some regions a form of taxation/tributary system that directly impacts production, communities, and the environment. The system only increases productivity by the TDTOs ability to expand their activities into exploiting resources for the benefit of multinational corporations (Larmer, 2018; Linthicum, 2019; Rainsford, 2019; Marcial-Pérez, 2019).

Between 2012 and 2013, Michoacán captures the national and international attention when several towns organize self-defense forces that held as main objective recuperating the control of their communities from the *narco* state (Asfura-Heim and Espach, 2013). At the same time, rural communities implement grassroot mechanisms to regain control over their lives. That is, the *pueblos originarios* find themselves at the front of this struggle. Resembling case scenarios in Mexico and Latin America alike (Global Witness, 2017), the *pueblos originarios* of Michoacán are at the barricades of protecting the land. The *Michoacán Profundo* effectively confronts the variety of issues brought about by neoliberalism by taking measures to acquire autonomy, regain sovereignty over natural resources, and reinstall the rule of law. This study is discussed in the following section.

Cherán: Women Stepping Up for Public Security

Cherán is one of the 22 municipalities where the P'urhépecha population lives.[8] Located in the Meseta, Cherán is surrounded by one of the state's most important forest reserves. Due to its political and economic instability, as well as the abundance of lumber in its forest, the community becomes TDTOs target for several years. When TDTOs deforesting Cherán is about to reach one of its natural springs, the locals become concerned about contamination of their water supply, and when realizing that the local authorities are not on their side, they decide to organize for change (Zabludovsky, 2012).

The Purepechas' struggles for survival date back to the Revolutionary times. They participated in most Mexico's social processes as their resistance against labor exploitation, land deprivation, and exploitation of natural resources remains vivid through the 1900s. For instance, their incursion into the 1910 Revolution is in direct response to Aristeo Mercado's government, which promoted privatization of land, favoring the interests of foreign investors that brutally exploited the *campesinado* and the forest. During the Porfirio Diaz's era, the policy of favoring foreign investors is also maintained so the dispossession of land, water, and forest. Consequently, the revolutionary bursts that take place in the Meseta P'urhépecha are strongly associated with the issue of lodging exploitation, particularly the one carried out by the *Industria de Michoacan S.A.' s Company*, at the time directed by the U.S. citizen Santiago Slade Junior (Méndez-Jacob, 2010).

Resembling the neoliberal era, the policy of accumulation through dispossession exercised by foreign companies was legalized and endorsed by federal and state authorities at the beginning of the XX century. Ever since, the forest's leasing agreements were abusive and predatory. Setting the historical example, Cherán underwent an upheaval that caused the assassination of Federico Hernandez Tapia, who stood against the contract established between state authorities and the *Industria de Michoacán S.A.' Company*. Related to indiscriminate logging, several leaders emerged in the Meseta to revendicate the interest of their communities, including Nieves Cardiel, who worked in Cherán along Atziruin and Felix C. Ramirez in the defense of the Paracho forest. In addition, a notorious P'urhépecha leader from Cherán was Casimiro Lopez Lexo, who commanded a total of 150 men with the ultimate purpose of evicting the *Industria de Michoacán, S.A.'s Company* in order to prevent the arbitrary exploitation of the Meseta forest (*ibid*).

The post-revolutionary Purepechas resistance was re-wired and auspicated by Lazaro Cardenas' *indigenismo*, a national policy oriented towards building the mestizo discourse by placing cultural value to the legacy inherited by pre-Hispanic societies. *Michoacan Profundo's* institutions were further supported by several amendments to the Mexican Constitution, ignited by the EZLN uprising and the ILO's 169 Convention's ratification, which permitted under its legal umbrella political autonomy and the operation of institutions based on internal normative systems to effectively address issues brought about by a growing market economy.

Consequently, the 2011 Cherán's experience of establishing self-governance and self-defense appears as a direct implication of decades of resistance. Resembling previous events, at the beginning of the 2000s, Cherán experiences a rising tide of violence as unwelcome visitors appeared in town to explicitly predate the forest. At the time, Cherán was made up of 27,000 hectares of forest, which were mostly destroyed. In other words, illegal logging razed 20,000 hectares to the ground, affecting the fauna, flora, and ecosystems, severely impacting the community's self-sustainability. The community's state is worsened by being curtailed from the only economic activity available to already impoverished families: logging (Zabludovsky, 2012).

The first signs of rebellion were initially expressed by a group of courageous women, who took matters into their own hands. On April 15, 2011, they blockaded the loggers' pick-up trucks and took some of them hostage. The women armed themselves and set off fireworks, establishing the *Ronda Comunitaria*, a local militia, to protect the town from intruders. They gathered the townspeople, who came together and demanded the cartels, police, and politicians to be exiled. After a tense stand-off, police and local politicians were driven out of the town.

Based on interviews from the documentary titled 'Cherán: Tierra para Soñar,' one woman describes:

> When we set out it was dawn and still dark, around 6:30 in the morning. The church bells were ringing calling people to mass [...] I never really thought this would go far [...] We were just five women from here, from this neighborhood, a bunch of older women, there were no men, maybe a few men but mostly women [...] We chased after the cars throwing stones, one woman even got hit and scraped all the skin off her knee when a car backed into her.
>
> (Labaronne, 2014)

After the scene, the neighbors, and later the community, impressed by the women's movement, implemented a neighborhood watch system with groups patrolling both the town and the mountain forest. People met around bonfires to forge pacts and ensure that nobody outside the community interfered in its administration.

The official transition to political autonomy followed the resistance in the streets. In 2011, Mexico's Electoral Tribunal of the Federal Judiciary cancelled municipal elections in Cherán, which opened the door to autonomous consultation within the community. The tribunal decision resulted in establishing the *K'eris* Council (a council of elders) to practice self-governance based on a normative system that specifically pertains to Purepechas internal rules and conventions, without recourse to elections. In 2014, Mexico's Supreme Court recognized the community of Cherán's right to consultation, each time legislative or administrative changes are proposed, which might have an impact on the community and its way of life, in accordance with the ILO's 169 Convention.

In 2015, a group submitted a petition to the electoral authority in Michoacán in which they requested the traditional system of political parties be restored. The electoral authority reached a consensus in favor of the communal government, acknowledging the people of Cherán's right to determine their own future. Given the vacuum left in Cherán by the absence of all layers of government, alternative ways of governing are perceived as credible and sustainable within the current context. Cherán still receives federal and state funding, but with its recognized autonomy as a P'urhépecha community, it has been able to confirm its right to not participate in local, state or federal elections (El Enemigo Comun, 2018).

Conclusions

Given their historical placement, indigenous peoples around the world are at the barricades of the struggle to defend natural resources and their ways of lives. Their historical relocation—relegated to rural areas, disconnected from the areas of 'development' and job creation, and closer to ecological or 'protected' environmental reserves—makes them increasingly vulnerable in a neoliberal era that pushes for privatizing the commons. Although the deplorable living standards of indigenous peoples are undeniable, the GTI pushes for analyzing beyond the development discourse by embracing innovate alternatives that rely on non-market notions to envision a world beyond neoliberalism. Alternatives are clearly proposed by the indigenous peoples' pragmatic methods to resolve first-hand issues related to public and economic insecurity.

Resilience represents a parallel transition to the conventional notion of sustainable development. This change requires seeding communities with institutional diversity by increasing reliance on social and economic self-organizations. As demonstrated by Cherán, the legal framework developed by the ILO is primordial to restoring a social fabric based on principles of solidarity, direct democracy, and the 'commons.' Standing against the 'tragedy of the commons' (Hardin, 2008), within the context of a failed state, the idea of thinking the public space and the commons (the forest) as a shared responsibility assists in reinstalling the rule of law in a small rural community, guaranteeing the security of citizens. As stated by Esteva (2014), the social commons do not represent resources, they are also not defined by ownership, instead "the idea is to ensure equitable access to them for all commoners, a democratic and transparent administration and appropriate, equitable distribution of the benefits" (p. 155).

The present analysis sheds light on the crossroads where contemporary Mexico finds itself, as potentially many L.A. countries. Mexico is at a breaking point, a result of an accelerating expansion into a modern era primarily determined by NAFTA's dynamics. The crossroads implies joining one of the following worldviews: evolutionary, catastrophic, and transformational (Escobar, 2012). Anchoring in the ancient institutions of Mexico's *pueblos originarios*, the transformational worldview promises lasting solutions to contemporary challenges, but it requires fundamental changes in values as well as novel socioeconomic and institutional arrangements. Consequently, I suggest beginning this transformative process by first engaging in the analysis and discussion of the peoples most affected by neoliberal policies. Accounting for their responses, placing their agency in the center of analysis, while identifying the strengths, limitations, and capabilities of their initiatives as they influence this fast-paced world.

Notes

1 As of June 2017, Mexico breaks its own record of assassinations, the highest in 20 years. The first semester of 2017 is particularly violent. It amounts to a total of 12 155 investigation on homicides, a 30 percent increase from 2016. The states of Guerrero and Mexico are considered the most violent this year, the former with the greatest amount of forced disappeared cases (Guthrie, 2018).

2 According to Navarrete-Linares (2008), the term indigenous means someone who originates from a specific country or territory. Indigenous and/or *pueblos originarios* (original peoples) are the concepts employed in Mexico's official institutions and laws to refer to a sector of the population that identify themselves as such, usually based on the spoken language. The terms are preferred to 'Indian' that is often seen as derogatory, since it is unfortunately associated with the one given by the Spaniard 'conquerors' of the XVI century. Throughout this text, I utilize both terms to stay away from categories that place this sector of the Mexican population in an inferior status.

3 According to Escobar (1995), transitional discourses represent an emergent scholarship domain, which is based on hybrid cultural and institutional transformation.

4 "Mexico is littered with the shells and skulls of Spain, cathedrals, poems, and the limbs of orange trees. But everywhere you look is this great museum of Spain you see living Indians. Where are the conquistadores? Postcolonial Europe expresses pity or guild behind its sleeve, pities the Indian the loss of her gods or her tongue. But let the Indian speak for herself. Spanish is now an Indian language. Mexico has captured Spanish" (ibid, p. 23-24).

5 The Totonacas reside in the eastern states of Veracruz, Puebla, and Hidalgo. They are one of the possible builders of the pre-Columbian city of El Tajin. Until the mid-19th century, they were the world's main producers of vanilla. In 1519, major Totonaca centers were Papantla, with an estimated population of 60,000, Xalapa (around 120,000), and Cempoala (around 80,000). Today, approximately 90,000 Totonac speakers reside in Mexico (Sandstrom and Garcia-Valencia, 2005).

6 The *Mixtecos* inhabit the region known as the *Mixteca*, which comprises the states of Oaxaca, Puebla, and Guerrero. The major Mixtec Polity was Tututepec, which rose to prominence in the 11th century. Pre-Columbian *Mixtecos* numbered around 1.5 million. Today, there are approximately 800,000 *Mixteco* people in Mexico. There is also a large population in the United States. As of 2011, an estimated 150,00 Mixtec people were living in California and 25,000 to 30,000 in New York City (Torrens, 2011).

7 "Although the area and the peoples are known as Tarascan, the name represents a misnomer that perpetuates a misuse by the Spaniards. On the

demand of their conquerors, the hapless natives proffered their daughters to the Spaniards with the word tarhaskua (father-in-law) to legitimize the relationship. However, when the Spaniards at best insensitively and at words derisively used the word to identify the natives, they quickly came to regard it as a term of derogation" (Mälmstrom, 1995, p. 2).

8 Th P'urhépecha are distributed in 95 of the 113 municipalities of Michoacan. They are mostly concentrated in the following municipalities: Coeneo, Charapan, Chilchota, Erongaricuaro, Los Reyes, Nahuatzen, Nuevo Prag Parangaricutiri, Paracho, Patzcuaro, Periban, Quiroga, Tancitaro, Tangamandapio, Tangancicuaro, Tingambato, Tinguindin, Tocumbo, Tizintzuntzan, Uruapan, Zacapu, and Ziracuaretiro (National Institute of Indigenous Peoples, 2019).

References

Aguirre, J., & Herrera, H. A. (2013). Institutional weakness and organized crime in Mexico: the case of Michoacán. *Trends in Organized Crime*, *16*, 221–238.

Asfura-Heim, P., & Espach, R. H. (2013). The rise of México's self-defense forces. *Foreign Affairs*, 92(4), 143–150.

Baschet, J. (2017). *Podemos gobernarnos nosotros mismos: La autonomía, una política sin el estado*. Edition Cideci-Unitierra Chiapas: San Cristóbal de las Casas, México. https://radiozapatista.org/wpcontent/uploads/2018/JeromeBaschet_Autonomia.pdf.

Blanco, E. (2017, July 19). ¿Cuándo inciden el origen social y el color de la piel en la desigualdad educativa? *Nexos*. Retrieved from: https://educacion.nexos.com.mx/?p=605.

Bonfil-Batallas, G. (1996). In A. Phillip trans., *Mexico profundo: Reclaiming a civilization*. Dennis. Austin: University of Texas Press.

Cardenas, L. (2016, December 5). Life without politicians: A Mexican indigenous community finds its own way. *Truthout*. Retrieved from: https://truthout.org/articles/life-without-politicians-a-mexican-indigenous-community-finds-its-own-way/.

Carlsen, L. (2018, December 4). AMLO's inauguration and the future of México. *NACLA Reporting on the Americas Since 1967*. Retrieved from: https://nacla.org/news/2018/12/04/amlo%E2%80%99s-inauguration-and-future-mexico.

CNI (Congreso Nacional Indígena). (2017). What is the CNI? Retrieved from: https://www.congresonacionalindigena.org/what-is-the-cni/.

Cordera, R. (2015). The 'great transformation' of the Mexican miracle. 20 years after NAFTA: From adoption to adaptation. *Problemas de Desarrollo*, *46*, 180–211.

Correa, E. (2014). Institutional changes in financial crises: Lessons from Latin America. *Journal of Economic Issues*, *158*(201), 323–329.

Credit Suisse. (2014). Global wealth report 2014. Retrieved from: https://economics.uwo.ca/people/davies_docs/credit-suisse-global-wealth-report-2014.pdf.

Dangl, B. (2017). Dismantling power: The Zapatista indigenous presidential candidate's vision to transform Mexico from below. *Common Dreams*. July 8.

https://www.commondrams.org/views/2017/07/08/dismantling-power-zapatista-indigenous-presidential-candidates-vision-transform.
El Enemigo Comun. (2018, August 15). Celebrating seven years of self-governance in Cherán, Michoacán: Purepecha municipality names third council of elders to their communal government. *IC Magazine*. Retrieved from: https://intercontinentalcry.org/category/world-news/.
Elakbawy, S. (2018, August 22). How women changed the fate of Cherán. *More than a magazine, a movement. Ms. More than a Magazine, a Movement*. Retrieved from: https://msmagazine.com/2018/08/22/women-changed-fate-cheran/.
Escobar, A. (1995). *Encountering development: The making and unmaking of the third world*. Princeton and Oxford: Princeton University Press.
Escobar, A. (1998). Power and visibility: Development and the invention and management of the third world. *Cultural Anthropology*, *3*(4), 428–443.
Escobar, A. (2012). *"Preface to the 2012 edition" in Encountering development: The making and unmaking of the third world, Escobar, Arturo*. Princeton and Oxford: Stanford University Press.
Esquivel-Hernández, G. (2016). *Desigualdad extrema en México: Concentración del poder económico y político*. Oxfam-México. https://www.oxfammexico.org/sites/default/files/desigualdadextrema_informe.pdf.
Esteva, G. (2014). Commoning in the new society. *Community Development Journal*, *49*(S1 January), 144–159.
Fei, J., & Rania, Gustavo (1964). *Development of the labour surplus economy: Theory and policy*. Homewood, Illinois: Richard A. Irwin, Inc.
Global Witness. (2017). Defenders of the earth. *Global Witness*. Retrieved from: https://www.globalwitness.org/en/campaigns/environmental-activists/defenders-earth/.
Grace-Miller, M. (2004). *Rise and fall of the cosmic race: The cult of mestizaje in Latin America*. Austin, Texas: University of Texas Press.
Guthrie, A. (2018, July 30). Mexico had more homicides in 2017 than previously thought. *Associated Press*. Retrieved from: https://web.archive.org/web/20180731014410/https://abcnews.go.com/International/wireStory/mexico-homicides-2017-previously-thought-56923297.
Hardin, G. (2008). Tragedy of the commons. In D. R. Henderson (ed.), *Concise encyclopedia of economics*. Indianapolis: Library of Economics and Liberty.
Harvey, D. (2003). *The new imperialism*. Oxford: Oxford University Press.
Harvey, D. (2004). The 'new' imperialism: accumulation by dispossession. *Socialist Register*, *40*, 63–87.
Instituto Nacional de los Pueblos Indígenas. (2019). *Atlas de los pueblos indígenas de México: P'urhépechas – etnografía*, México D.F: Instituto Nacional de los Pueblos Indígenas. http://atlas.inpi.gob.mx/?page_id=5178.
Instituto Nacional de los Pueblos Indígenas. (2017). Indicadores socioeconómicos de los pueblos indígenas de México, 2015. Retrieved from: https://www.gob.mx/inpi/documentos/indicadores-socioeconomicos-de-los-pueblos-indigenas-de-mexico-2015.
Instituto Nacional para el Federalismo y el Desarrollo Municipal. (2009). *Enciclopedia de los municipios de México, Michoacán*. México: Instituto Nacional para el Federalismo y el Desarrollo Municipal. http://www.inafed.gob.mx/work/enciclopedia/EMM16michoacan/index.html.

International Institute o for Strategic Studies (IISS). (2017). The armed conflict survey. *International Institute for Strategic Studies*. Retrieved from: https://www.iiss.org/search?query=Mexico%20IISS%20Report%202017.

International Labor Organization. (2009). Indigenous and tribal people's rights in practice—A guide to ILO Convention No. 169. *International Labor Standards*. http://www.ilo.org/wcmsp5/groups/public/ed/norm/norms/documents/publication/wcms/106474.pdf.

Jorgenson, D. W. (1961). The development of a dual economy. *Economic Journal*, *71*, 309–334.

Krozer, A. (2019, March 7). Elites y racismo: el privilegio de ser blanco en México, o como un rico reconoce a otro rico. *Nexos*. Retrieved from: https://economia.nexos.com.mx/?p=2153.

Larmer, B. (2018, March 27). *How the avocado became the fruit of global trade. The New York Times Magazine*. Retrieved from: https://www.nytimes.com/2018/03/27/magazine/the-fruit-of-global-trade-in-one-fruit-the-avocado.html.

Labaronne, S. (2014). Cheran, tierra para soñar. *RumboSur Cine*. Retrieved from: https://www.youtube.com/watch?v=DnV_T4c_lKI.

Lewis, A. W. (1954). Economic development with unlimited supplies of labour. *The Manchester School*, *22*(2), 139–191.

Lewis, A. W. (1955). *The theory of economic growth*. Homewood, Illinois: Richard D. Irwin.

Linthicum, K. (2019, November 21). Inside the bloody cartel war for Mexico's multibillion-dollar avocado industry. *Los Angeles Times*. Retrieved from: https://www.latimes.com/world-nation/story/2019-11-20/mexico-cartel-violence-avocados.

Lucas-Dos Santos, L. (2018). Under the flyover: Homeless people, power of choice and the practice of autonomy through an exchange fair. *Conjunctions, Transdisciplinary Journal for Cultural Participation*, *5*(1), 3–22.

Mälmstrom, V. H. (1995). Geographical origins of the Tarascans. *Geographic Review*, 85 (1). https://www.dartmouth.edu/~izapa/M-28.pdf.

Marcial-Pérez, D. (2019, February 11). The curse of the Mexican avocado. *El País*. Retrieved from: https://elpais.com/elpais/2019/02/06/inenglish/1549467945_461680.html.

Méndez-Jacob, E. (2010). *Los P'urhepechas en la Revolución 1910-1917*. México: Master Thesis, Universidad Michoacana de San Nicolas de Hidalgo, Morelia, Michoacán.

Monroy, L. S. and Gómez, F. (2017, June 20). ¿Importa el color de la piel en México? *Nexos*. Retrieved from: https://economia.nexos.com.mx/?p=397.

McDonnell, P. J. (2017, July 10). One Mexican town revolts against violence and corruption. Six years in, its experiment is working. *Los Angeles Times*. Retrieved from: https://www.latimes.com/world/mexico-americas/la-fg-mexico-cheran-20170710-htmlstory.html.

Navarrete-Linares, F. (2008). Los pueblos indígenas de México: Pueblos indígenas del México contemporáneo. *México, D.F: CDI*. http://www.cdi.gob.mx/dmdocuments/monografia_nacional_pueblos_indigenas_mexico.pdf.

Najar, A. (2012, January 25). El pueblo mexicano que se gobierna a sí mismo. *British Broadcasting Corporation*. Retrieved from: https://www.bbc.com/mundo/noticias/2012/01/120125_cheran_michoacan_indigenas_an.

Najar, A. (2012b, January 26). El pueblo que invento sus billetes. *British Broadcasting Corporation*. Retrieved from: https://www.bbc.com/mundo/noticias/2012/01/120126_tumin_dinero_mexico_an.

Nirmal, P., & Rocheleau, D. (2019). Decolonizing degrowth in the post-development convergence: Questions, experiences, and proposals from two indigenous territories. *Nature and Space*, *2*(3), 465–492.

Organization for Economic Cooperation and Development. (2017). *Better life index: Mexico*. Retrieved from: https://www.oecd.org/statistics/Better-Life-Initiative-country-note-Mexico.pdf.

Oestreich, C. (2019, February 11). Mexico's new president incorporated indigenous ceremonies in his inauguration. *Pow Wows.Com*. Retrieved from: https://www.powwows.com/mexicos-new-president-incorporated-indigenous-ceremonies-in-his-inauguration/.

Polanyi, K. (2001 [1957]). *The great transformation: The political and economic origins of our times*. Boston: Beacon Press.

Rainsford, C. (2019, September 30). 4 of Mexico's cartels are fighting for control of the avocado business. *InSight Crime*. Retrieved from: https://www.businessinsider.com/mexican-cartels-are-fighting-for-control-of-theavocado-business-2019-9.

Raskin, P., et. al. (2002). *The great transition: The promise and lure of the time ahead. A report of the global scenario group*. Boston: Stockholm Environment Institute.

Reis, J., & Ranis, G. (1964). *Development of the labour surplus economy: Theory and policy*. Homewood, Illinois: Richard A. Irwin, Inc.

Rodriguez, R. (2001). Days of obligation: An argument with my Mexican Father. In Ileana Rodriguez (ed.), *The Latin American subaltern studies reader*. Durham and London: Duke University Press.

Rostow, W. W. (1960). *The stages of economic growth: A non-communist manifesto*. Cambridge: Cambridge University Press.

Russian Television. (2017, March 26). "Chip solidario": El irresistible éxito del túmin en plena escasez de dinero en México. *Russian Television*. Retrieved from: https://actualidad.rt.com/actualidad/239516-chip-solidario-moneda-alternativa-tumin-mexico.

Sandstrom, A. R. & Garcia-Valencia, H. (Eds). (2005). *Native peoples of the Gulf coast of Mexico*. Tucson: The University of Arizona Press.

Scott, J. (1985). *Weapons of the weak: Everyday forms of peasant resistance*. Bethany, Connecticut: Brevis Press.

Smith, A. (1999 [1776]). *The wealth of nations, books I-III*. London: Penguin Group.

Stabb, M. (1959). Indigenism and racism in Mexican thought: 1857-1911. *Journal of Inter-American Studies*, *1*(4), 405–423.

Stavenhagen, R. (1963). Clases, colonialismo y aculturación en América Latina. *Rtro Latinoamericano de Investigaciones en Ciencias Sociales*, *6*(4 (Outubro-dezembre)), 63–104.

Stavenhagen, R. (1970). *Agrarian problems and peasant movements in Latin America*. Garden City, New York: Anchor Books.

Stiglitz, J. (2001 [1957]). Preface in Polanyi, K. (2001 [1957]), *The great transformation: The political and economic origins of our times*. Boston: Beacon Press.

Terraciano, K. (2001). *The Mixtecs of colonial Oaxaca: Nudzahui history, sixteen through eighteen centuries*. Stanford: Stanford University Press.

Torrens, C. (2011, September, 28). Some NY immigrants cite lack of Spanish as barrier. USanDiego.com. Retrieved from: https://www.sandiegouniontribune.com/sdut-some-ny-immigrants-cite-lack-of-spanish-as-barrier-2011may28-story.html.

The Economist. (2015a, September 19). *Development in Mexico: Of cars and carts. The Economist*. Retrieved from: https://www.economist.com/briefing/2015/09/19/of-cars-and-carts.

The Economist. (2015b, September 19). *Development: the two Mexicos*. Retrieved from: https://www.economist.com/leaders/2015/09/19/the-two-mexicos.

U.N. Department of Economic and Social Affairs. (1951). *Measures for the economic development of the underdeveloped countries*. New York: United Nations.

Vega, J., & Urrieta, L. (2006). The immigration debate in the United States: Historical trends, migration, and educational issues. *Cimexus: Revista Nicolaita de Politicas Publicas,*, *1*(1). https://www.cimexus.umich.mx/index.php/cim1/article/view/15/13.

Villalobos, J. (2014, September 1). El infierno al sur de México. *Nexos*. Retrieved from: http://www.nexos.com.mx/?p=22331.

Warren, J. B. (1985). *The conquest of Michoacán: The Spanish domination of the Tarascan kingdom is western Mexico* (pp. 1521–1530). Norman: University of Oklahoma Press.

Wolf, E. (2010 [1982]). *Europe and the people without history. Berkeley and Los Angeles*. University of California Press.

Zabludovsky, K. (2012, August 2). Reclaiming the forest and the right to feel safe. *The New York Times*, Retrieved from: https://www.nytimes.com/2012/08/03/world/americas/in-mexico-reclaiming-the-forests-and-the-right-to-feel-safe.html.

5 The sustainable innovation of Salinerito in Ecuador

Fabián Vargas and Mario Cadena López

Introduction

This chapter refers to the case of Salinas de Guaranda in Ecuador, a process characterized by developing sustainable innovation with identity within the framework of cooperativism and the social and solidarity economy based on characteristic elements of Andean culture such as sharing, solidarity and reciprocity combined with elements of the Social Doctrine of the Church. The processing of the saline waters that arise from the ground has been a central activity to elaborate salt in this territory since pre-Columbian times. This continued in times of the Spanish colony and later also as a republic of Ecuador until the seventies of the XX century, but in conditions of exploitation and precariousness for people and families, both indigenous and mestizo, directly linked to work with salt depending on the estate. "Thus, aware of the limitations and sins that accompany every human adventure, we dare to define the 'salinera utopia' as Christianly inspired, without being confessional, open to the new, without leaving the best of the old, attentive to culture, without falling into sterile simplifications, aware of the importance of politics, without falling into its known deviations, centered on the person and the organization, but taking seriously the economy, their sources and forms of accounting and administrative control, flexible in applications, faithful to the principles..." (Polo, 2015: 10–11). In this chapter, some of the main achievements of this process are cited, as well as the challenges to continue facing and it closes with several conclusions.

Context and starting point of the Salinas innovation process

Since 1884, Salinas has been a rural civil parish of the Guaranda canton, Bolivar province, Ecuador. Located in the foothills of the Western "Cordillera de los Andes", it occupies 465,3 km^2, descending from 4400 to 500 m above sea level (masl), with a population of 7262 inhabitants[1] in 30 communities plus the parish center, located at 3550 masl and 30 km northeast of Guaranda, provincial capital.

It owes its name to the salty waters that emerge in its territory. Members of the Tomabela chiefdom, belonging to the Chimbos ethnic group, processed and marketed the salt and continued during the time of Incas domination. With the Spanish presence, in 1548 the crown of Castile took into account the territory of the "Community" of Salinas, granting it lands of the moor; at the same time, it gave the landowners the best land and the salt control (Cantero et al., 2012: 59).

In 1758, the church of Guaranda received lands from the Royal Ensign and Alderman of Riobamba, General Anselmo Villavicencio and Torres, who donated the Matiaví farm; in 1815, Captain Jose Barragan and Estrada donated the Pilcopitic property to the Vicariate of San Jose de Chimbo (Gavilanes, 1995: 238–239).

In 1861, during the Republican era, Domingo Cordovez bought the lands of Talahua, Mondonguera and Sinde from General Juan Jose Flores (first president of Ecuador). During the first decades of the twentieth century, the Cordovez family consolidated their estates.

The salt works were organized at the level of poor indigenous and mestizo families, with a prominent role of women as responsible for the management of the farms, which in Salinas were family units of non-agricultural production and comprised the entire processing unit of the salt. Older men and boys were also asked to perform agricultural tasks, repair fences and carry out other tasks (Pomeroy, 1986: 18–19). The same author points out that the extraction of salt required a large investment of family labor force and forest resources in relation to the amount of product obtained.

Fritz W. Up de Graff,[2] who during 1896 was a partner of the Cordovez family, marked an interesting but fugacious milestone in the life of Salinas by promoting the semi-industrial process of salt through cauldrons, but above all for paying cash "Sucre" 10 cents per labor wage, with the consequent disagreement of Domingo Cordovez, who "was so persuaded that it was silly to pay so much money when the promise was enough..." (Up de Graff, 1996: 41–42-43).

That the 1950s salt workers produced as they produced (that is, in a very rudimentary and uncertain way with absolute dependence on the landowners, especially if they have become their "debtors" for supposed or actually received loans) is confirmed by their indigent economic situation. The Cordovez family, owner of the Cachipamba farm and some adjacent farms, imposed a 30% tax on the obtained salt and established the system of employing debtors as laborers to pay what they owed with their work, which was difficult to avoid (Up de Graff, 1996: 23–25; Pomeroy, 1986: 18).

During 1960–1970, local and national events generated an environment conducive to changes and the first Salinas population's reactions:

Monsignor Candido Rada, first Bishop of Guaranda (Gavilanes, 1995: 231–233), became interested in vulnerable rural families by promoting the "Land Redistribution Program" of the church.[3] In 1962, there was a failed attempt by the Community of Salinas to control what, at that time, was the main source of sustenance, the salt mines (Cantero et al., 2012: 61). In 1967, promoted by Monsignor Raza, local salt workers leaders tried to create a savings and credit cooperative to endow themselves with an instrument that would allow them to become detached from the control of the Cordovez (Cantero et al., 2012: 61).

In 1970, at the request of Bishop Rada, the Mato Grosso Operation Salesian organization (MGO) arrived in the province of Bolivar. This action began in Simiatug and then went on to Salinas and Facundo Vela (Gavilanes, 1995: 260–261). The MGO volunteers (eight including Father Antonio Polo...) appeared on foot in July 1971 on the hill that dominated from the west the town of Salinas (Polo, 2015: 27). In 1976, Alfredo Cordovez died, and the process of intra-family litigation began, and this caused the transfer of land to new owners.

Poverty levels were high: in 1970, child mortality was 45% of live births[4] and illiteracy about 85%. There was no permanent road, and they did not have basic services such as drinking water, electricity, telephones; the houses were humble huts of earth and straw (Naranjo, 2009: 120). The population in the absence of work migrated temporarily to the subtropics and coastal cities (Babahoyo, Ventanas, Quevedo) or definitively to Quito and Guayaquil (Bebbington et al., 1992: 53). The MGO and Father Antonio Polo found this reality, with initial signs of local reactions, which Vaugdana (2012: 37) refers to as "a world that was already fermenting".

The innovation process

Immediate responses

Father Antonio Polo describes: "The reception has been cheerful and cordial... in the almost only block house... that houses us for months... Construction... gives us the opportunity to start right away with something concrete, to know and make ourselves known: it is about finishing the communal house" (Polo, 2015: 28). A new MGO volunteer who arrives in December 1971 is dedicated to organizing the Cooperative (Savings and Credit suggested by Monsignor Candido Rada) and the first works (road, piped water, block houses...) the question was floating in the air ...What can we do? And the answer came from them, clear and invariable: "a little school, Father, help us build a little school." The first schools arise one after the other, of earth and straw, of blocks and zinc, of wood of the mountain (in the subtropics where new settlements were also forming). There are the Mass, the meeting, the "Minga",[5] the three strength points that build not only the school, but together with the community (Polo, 2015: 42–43).

Although it is true that solidarity characterized Salinas, it was evident that it was an "emergency solidarity": the people joined spontaneously in the face of a misfortune, a sick person... The "emergency solidarity" had to be transformed into a capable structure to give a change to all this... effectively... and quickly... because the young people could no longer bear it... many of them had already taken the uncertain path of migration to the city. The organizational instrument suggested by Monsignor Rada has been the Savings and Credit Cooperative (Polo, 2015: 30).

This Cooperative was established in 1972 to gain community access to salt mines, and thus the first stone of the salt framework was achieved.[6] "The great achievement was to verify that together you can do things that nobody had dreamed of" (P. Polo). This conquest was so much more encouraging that the Cordovez gave up controlling the salt flats... that withdrawal was seen as a collective triumph (Cantero et al., 2012: 61). The Cooperative initiated the extraction of salt as a community work that was unsuccessful, since soon the price of salt fell due to the commercialization of sea salt (Naranjo: 2009: 121). However, the valuable thing about the salt mine fight was that the Cooperative recovered for itself the community character of the old farmers' economy (Bebbington et al., 1992: 33).

Beyond all, the Cooperative played an important role in the progressive deconcentration of the lands and in the investment plans in community works (Noorth, L. in Chiriboga et al., 1999). After this first achievement, the process was launched. What characterized it was that double aspect of internal empowerment and external intervention. An example was the construction of communal houses at the end of 1973 along with the beginning of the reforestation and the beginning of the roads... that interwove the existing communities... In 1974, two more links were launched: the creation of the cheese makers and the texal craft center-first productive continued activity of the Cooperative[7] (today with its own legal status as Texal Salinas Craft Development Association) and which also had the interest of being completely in the hands of women (Cantero et al., 2012: 61–62).

The birth of the Texal on the basis of "trial and error" marks the path of adding value to their raw materials, creating a high-quality and artisanal product that characterizes Salinas innovation. Father Antonio Polo recounts: since the area had sheep, the "wool collection warehouse was organized, we bought at a good price and people brought it in quantity; when we sold... the price was no longer good... we lost. But we understood the lesson: we must first transform the natural product... washing, drying, spinning by hand... looms for (making) ponchos and blankets ... for tapestries and scarves, the first sweaters... the Texal is born... from the determined will of some women of Salinas" (Polo, 2015: 36).

The second link was the first community cheese plant (imitating the "hacienda") that closed early due to transport, commercialization and profit margin problems (Naranjo, 2009: 121). It will be until the arrival in 1978[8] of Jose Dubach that we would learn a true lesson from all that it means to give "added value" to a natural resource: with him we learned not only to make good cheese, but to organize a coherent process, from the raw material production improvement, a correct and varied elaboration of the products and their effective distribution for sale (Polo, 2015: 37). Dubach was able to hear the problems that the community had with its first experience and presented concrete alternatives. He proposed the farmers not only to join agro-industrial activities, but also to learn to market their products in better conditions... they would have risks and benefits at all steps: raw materials production, milk processing and cheese marketing[9] (Cadena et al., 1998: 37–38). The "Salinerito" cheese brand is born.

The emergence of the current Salinas needed a process for its affirmation. Processes of struggle, of learning in which failure, conflicts and discouragements were not missing. A long-term process in which there was always a double aspect, that of the external visionaries and those who believed from within, but also those who inside or outside were discouraged and faltered (Cantero et al., 2012: 61).

Organizational structuring and strengthening

Understanding the Salinas organizational ecosystem requires opening the mind and understanding the structural needs to discover instances that support and promote social and solidary economy processes.

Salinas organization is justified as a historical and human path (the path is made by walking). In 1972, the Saving and Credit Cooperative Salinas Ltd. was born. Its legal organization was based on "Principles of Cooperativism", but in practice, the words "Savings and Credit" would be the engine to promote a culture of community organization. This would allow to undertake initiatives that strengthen the integral community process through different ways to add value to raw material, but above all to generate a new social network fair, equitable, inclusive, participatory and supportive.

The empathy between the Italian volunteers of the MGO led by Father Antonio Polo and the Salinas population was the link that led them towards the path of good living, a process of constant struggle, faith, learning, reciprocity, challenges and responsibility, with different phases that in these 50 years of history makes visible utopias that have become a reality of common well-being.

The first step was to get together as organizations in meetings and long days to exchange ideas, to present needs and possible solutions, with the "minga" as an effective and efficient tool for priority works: schools, communal houses, piped water systems, neighborhood roads and so on. At the same time, training in simple and fundamental issues that helped identify leaders who subsequently assumed roles as social promoters.

Obtaining the organizations legal status was a process of learning and maturity, it required to specify socio-economic objectives, to have human talent and material resources to consolidate instances that respond to the challenges. The elements that shored up local development were: valuing the Salinas reality, motivated and committed partners, empowered and trained managers, meetings, "mingas", savings and credit, simple administrative systems and large assemblies for accountability.

The associative-cooperative organization process of the Salinas social economy and solidary differs from others in the following aspects:

- The Salinas community organization has always been an organic structure and non-union or political-partisan.
- The leadership functions harmoniously in direct relation to decisions of the assemblies (top authorities) supported in complying with relevant regulations and laws.
- The business name of productive organizations is linked to adding value to the local raw material, articulated with social and financial sustainability.
- The second and third grade entities have been umbrellas to articulate the various grassroots organizations in common objectives, training, production, value addition and commercialization.
- Diversifying the organization action areas has allowed greater inclusion of actors and development themes, consolidating them as stable and sustainable social and solidary economy entities.

The road traveled opened the door to formalize and consolidate a complex, but effective formal organizational, productive, commercial, financial and services system, which integrates its inhabitants under a new paradigm not only for social justice. The emphasis on an attitude of Entrepreneurship and innovation in various areas of the community organization has had an impact on Family Popular Economic Units.

According to Albuquerque (2004: 2–84), the economic development depends essentially on the capacity to introduce innovations within the productive base and the business network of a territory and it is necessary to underline that the development strategy has its importance in terms of employment and territory, based on economic, social, cultural and territorial factors.

It is in this context and with the conviction in a decentralized scheme that Salinas promoted organizations in its 30 communities responding to their realities and needs, and then they were formalized accompanied first by the Salesian Mission and then by second and third degree organizations:

FUNORSAL, FUNCONQUERUCOM,[10] GRUPPO SALINAS Development Corporation. Social organizations and production units formed by members of the community were formed as partners, producers, workers and/or marketers, generating a sense of belonging, co-responsibility and their visualization as local actors that build the Salinas territorial development.

Local development seeks to increase the possibilities of a society taking advantage of the potential of the subjects as initiators of innovative ideas that cause economic and social impact through entrepreneurship, enabling progressive growth not only in employment but also at productive, economic and social levels in the communities (Duarte and Ruiz, 2009: 326–331); in this sense, the growth in several areas motivated the formation of the Gruppo Salinas Development Corporation in 2006, as an integrating instance of the organizational processes and solidary social enterprises, becoming a referent of the philosophy of community work that protects the identity, principles and values of the Salinas Solidary Economy.

The "Salinerito" community farmer brand, a key element of parish identity, brings together as a commercial image community products and services of the process; as such the Gruppo Salinas Development Corporation protects it from its legal representation and commercial and political management.

This brand implies co-responsibility of its actors and compliance with norms and policies in organizational, productive, health and safety processes, as well as commercial ones to show the market and the consumer that its products and services represent quality, competitiveness, craftsmanship, equity, variety, innovation, inclusion, fair prices and respect for nature; that is, a way of life and a farmer's vision – small producers – organized, capable of building a recognized position in the Ecuadorian market and international presence, especially in the Fair Trade of Italy, Germany, Spain, Switzerland, Japan and the USA.

Territorially, the Ecuadorian State is organized in regions, provinces, cantons and urban and rural parishes.

- To plan, together with other public sector institutions and society actors, the parish development and its corresponding territorial planning, in coordination with the cantonal and provincial government within the framework of inter-culturality and multinationality and respect for diversity.
- To plan, build and maintain the physical infrastructure, facilities and public spaces of the parish, contained in the development plans and included in the annual participatory budgets.
- To encourage the development of community productive activities, the preservation of biodiversity and the protection of the environment

GADs (Decentralized Autonomous Governments) generate their financial resources and participate in state revenues in accordance with the principles of subsidiarity, solidarity and equity. In 2018, the Salinas Rural Parish GAD administered a budget of US $ 345,000[11] to fulfill their competencies throughout the territory. The investment per family for physical infrastructure in communities represented 127 US dollars and 100 in the parish center.

Strengthening – diversification of work sources

The Salinas development of these 50 years has encouraged activities close to the experience of the population, its human and territorial potentialities; with the appropriate external support, it has generated several local sources of work linked to markets for goods and services where Salinas is present, eliminating the participation of intermediaries in almost all activities, complemented by the permanent tourist affluence[12] to learn about the experience of Salinas development and the parish natural environment.

Several products are processed by social and solidary companies: cheese, butter, meat sausages, chocolates, nougat, aromatic herbs, dehydrated fruits and mushrooms, jams, essential oils, soap, shampoo, soy products, sheep's wool yarn and alpaca fiber, varied crafts and so on; also, several services are offered related to marketing, community tourism, training – technical and socio-organizational assistance in management issues of Salinas organizations. On the other hand, there is the production of the Family Popular Economic Units: handicrafts, balls, artisanal liquors, meat sausages, aromatic herbs and dehydrated mushrooms, cosmetology products, chocolates, nougat, cheese, artisanal production of raw cane sugar and alcohol, trout farm, as well as the services offered to tourists, such as hotels, experiential tourism, restaurants, cafes, Sami Yaku ecolodge permaculture. Table 5.1 shows the organizations and actors that coexist in the Salinas process, energized from a community approach and with spaces for Family Popular Economic Units that together allow Salinas to show up effectively against current challenges.

It is clear that around 70% of inhabitants of the parish capital and the 30 communities that are part of Salinas parish are included directly or indirectly in the process of social and solidarity economy through the different organizations or social companies that generate products or services, either from the community type (cooperatives, associations) or familiar (productive economic units) that have been created as part of this process. Such inclusion may be as partners, producers, suppliers, workers or leaders. The permanent workers in the parish are 498 (82.1%) and 108 (17.9%) who work for services, which amounts to 606 (100%); on the other hand, of the total, 56.1% work in community

Table 5.1 Organizational ecosystem of Salinas Parish, Guaranda Canton

Type of actors: public, social, community	*Entity/organization*	*Beneficiary/partners Producers/students*	*Workers*	
			Fixed	*By services*
a. PARISH CENTER				
a.1. Public sector entities	• Decentralized Autonomous Government – Salinas Rural Parish (Salinas GAD)	7262	12	-
	• Political Deputy Office	7262	2	-
	• Salinas Intercultural Millennium Educational Unit	718	42	-
	• Public Health Center	400	7	-
	• Child Care Center	38	7	-
	• Senior Care Center	32	5	-
	• Technical Office (Ministry of Agriculture and Livestock)	400	2	-
Subtotal of Public Sector Entities Parish center		-	77	-
a 2. Civil Society Entities				
Communal Organizations	• Matiavi Salinas Community	7262	6	-
	• Water Management Board	350	3	-
	• Community Tourism Center	350	3	7[13]
Organizations of Gruppo Salinas CGS Corporation	• Salinas Salesian Family Foundation – FFSS (Evangelization, Pastoral: Educational, Social, Health and Environmental, Community Enterprises	800	53	-
	• Youth Residence			
	• 13 Community Enterprises			

• 3 Commercialization Centers			
• 1 Community Radio			
• Living Nature Society			
• Salinas Yuyay – MUSAYU Museum			
• Experimental workshops for new products (based on soy, noodles and others)			
• Salinas Rural Organizations Foundation – FUNORSAL (attention to communities, training – technical assistance)	3000	28	-
• 2 youth community enterprises and 3 farming productive initiatives			
• Youth Group Foundation – FGJS	120	4	-
• Mushrooms and fruits dehydrator			
• El Refugio Hotel			
• Savings and Credit Cooperative Salinas Ltd. COACSAL (Popular and Solidary Finances)	3900	21	-
• Headquarter in parish center and 2 agencies in communities			

(Continued)

Table 5.1 *(continued)*

Type of actors: public, social, community	*Entity/organization*	*Beneficiary/partners Producers/students*	*Workers*	
			Fixed	*By services*
	• "El Salinerito" Production Cooperative PRODUCOOP (Cheese makers and other dairy derivatives; 2 farmer productive initiatives	200	14	
	• TEXAL Women Artisanal Association • (Craft making: sheep wool, alpaca fiber)	101	3	101[20]
	• Community Rural Cheese Makers Consortium Foundation FUNCONQUERUCOM (Farmer products commercialization, training and ttechnical assistance)	1200	37	–
	• 3 Local "Salinerito"-Bolivar Cheese Stores in Quito			
Subtotal of organizations of the Community and CGS organizations in the Parish center			172	108
Family Popular Economic Units	• 18 tourism services entrepreneurships	18	33	–
	• 21 *productive entrepreneurships*	21	40	–
Subtotal of the Civil Society Entities in the Parish center		39	73	–
Subtotal of the Parish Center		–	322	108
b. 30 COMMUNITIES IN THE PARISH				
b. 1 Entities of the public sector	• 2 Medical Centers			
	• 8 Child Care Centers	600 172	7 16	
	• 15 Educational Centers (13 basic education, 2 high school)	399	18	

(Continued)

	• 2 Native Forest Reserves in the Subtropic (Peña Blanca, Tigreurco)	200	-	-
	• 4 Moor communities, 4200 mosl (Pachancho, Yurac Ucsha, Natahua and Rincon de los Andes) are part of the Fauna Production Reserve of Chimborazo	594	–	–
Subtotal of Public Sector Entities of the parish communities		–	41	–
b. 2 Civil Society Entities				
Community Organizations	• 24 Community Cheese Makers[21] (4 Cooperatives, 20 Associations)	680	30	–
	• 4 Community enterprises (meat sausages factories, micro-sugar mill, balanced food factory and woodwork)	80	10	–
	• 2 Savings and Credit Pre-Cooperatives	200	2	–
	• 6 Savings and Credit Banks	100	6	–
	• 1 Foundation	12	2	–
	• 8 Community Tourism Entrepreneurships	25	10	–
Subtotal of Communal Organizations of the parish communities			60	
Family Popular Economic Units	• 50 family entrepreneurships	–	75	
Subtotal of Popular Economic Units of the parish communities		–	75	–
Subtotal of the parish communities		–	176	–
SALINAS PARISH TOTAL			498	108
		Grand Total	606	

Sources: Annual Report, FUNORSAL Cheese Technic Report, Documents of the Salinas Community Tourism Center Own elaboration.

organizations, 24.4% in Family Popular Economic Units and 19.5% in public sector entities. There is greater concentration in the parish center (82.1%) than in the communities (17.9%).

Of 167 productive and service initiatives in the parish, 78 are community businesses and 89 Family Popular Economic Units. It is important to note that even though the Salinas people work in social and solidary economy organizations and other local sources of work, they do not neglect agricultural work, as mentioned by Borja and Polo (2005: 19). 68% of the Salinas population obtains an agricultural family income in a range of 200–400 US dollars per month, mainly for raw materials generated, and 32% of public, private and productive entrepreneurship jobs, with 450–1200 US dollars per month.

From cooperativism to social and solidary economy

According to the International Cooperative Alliance (ACI),[13] the cooperative is an autonomous association of people voluntarily united to meet their common economic, social and cultural needs and aspirations through a jointly and democratically controlled company. They are based on values of mutual aid, responsibility, democracy, equality, equity and solidarity. Following the tradition of its founders, its members believe in ethical values of honesty, transparency, social responsibility and concern for others.

Since 1962 the Salinas population dabble in cooperativism with diverse results, reiterating in cooperativism and other forms of community-associative organization. According to F. Antonio Polo, "a fundamental foundation of the Salinas road has been the organization of the Cooperative… Salinas has received a lot from some of its strengths… they have been the 'first tool' that we had in hand and that still maintain its effectiveness…" (Polo, 2015: 30.31). In Ecuador, in the 1970s, pastoral agents, nationals and foreigners became great promoters of popular organizations and in particular of cooperatives (Miño, 2013: 65). In Salinas, a series of activities organized in the form of cooperatives began, aimed at overcoming obstacles to development, in giving value to local human and material resources, improving living conditions, regaining confidence, commitment and participation (Vaudagna, 2012: 52).

Values such as Andean community solidarity, the principle of free work for the common good, reciprocity and parity of benefits constituted local bases for the formation of Salinas cooperatives (Vaudagna: 2012: 47). It has been decisive that the rigid cooperative scheme has been adapted by the Salesian Mission to the local needs and cultural characteristics of the population, transforming them into community cooperatives that display activities dictated by circumstances, rather than by rigid programming. In this sense, there is no static "image-objective" of planning, but a permanent process of strengthening society with the creation of a productive, commercial and of services infrastructure dictated by the search for collective interest and social action… creating the appropriate environment to "forge development with a community approach" (Bebbington et al., 1992: 44). From 1978, the road of the cheese makers was strengthened by identifying with that of the cooperatives, and the cooperatives were strengthened by finding (in the cheese makers) an efficient and simple instrument of production, a safe source of self-management (Polo 2015: 38).

Some cultural demonstrations embodied in goods, products and services can generate a feeling of belonging to a group, territory and community (sense of identity) and also foster a vision of development of the territory that implies the quality of life improvement of its population (Molano, 2007: 83). Moreover, a process of historical construction of a society, from its own actors, leads to the empowerment and settlement of its identity with the territory, not as the physical space but as the result of cohesion that could serve as the basis for local development (Ortega, 2018: 33).

That is precisely the case of Salinas but, in addition, it is an example of what Berdegue & Schejtman (cited by Ortega, 2018: 32), in the sense that the territory is not only the physical space but all the processes that in it are given, the historical, its geography, social structures, institutions and actors that differentiate it from others. However, in the group of actors that may enter into conflict (active or latent), there may be innovative groups that promote successful dynamics that ultimately achieve institutional productive transformations, especially in rural territories aimed at reducing poverty and inequality.

Among the reasons that drive innovation and entrepreneurship with local resources to generate development of the population of Salinas is the need to have economic resources to improve the quality of life, to be recognized as a community and entrepreneurial population. It highlights the objective of social welfare and solidary economy of the ventures of this population, which has led it to become an emporium of companies. These results coincide with Petit (cited by Barragán and Ayauri, 2017: 76) where innovation and entrepreneurship constitute mechanisms that boost resources, capabilities and skills for the generation of knowledge that is reflected in strategies to exploit new opportunities that economically generate value.

According to Barragan (2017: 76–77), in Salinas, Guaranda only 3.2% of the surveyed population considers innovation as important. It also points out that this can be explained through field observation and interviews conducted as he was able to verify that the concept of innovation is not clear and is very easily confused with entrepreneurship and continuous process improvement. The same author points out that aspects of community organization, solidary economy, leadership and entrepreneurial culture are considered key factors of success in Salinas ventures.

The Organic Law of Popular and Solidary Economy rules and gathers the nature and function of community sectors, associations, cooperatives and popular economic units; its purpose is to develop the constitutional norms that determine that the Ecuadorian economic system is social and solidary,[14] forcing the State to make visible, encourage, promote and control organizations in this sector, structured and self-managed by their own partners (Miño, 2013: 111). Salinas evidences what Richard (2019: 10) says, the Solidary Economy, or expressed more broadly, the Solidary Social Economy, is a theory under construction which is contributed to by various socio-political disciplines and perspectives such as cooperativism, socialism, grassroots Christianity, ecology, fair trade and responsible consumption, popular education, food sovereignty, among others.

"The main thing about its success is that Salinas has been very open and has taken advantage of that opening. We have not taken refuge in the passive claims like other communities that claim the worldview and identity neglecting the present. I think it is good to recognize your own identity and deepen into the worldview and history but we cannot take refuge in it. Many politicians live on it. They hold on to these proposals without a vision of the future and, meanwhile, they have good salaries and enjoy privileges that their people do not have. Here we have overcome that. I believe in Salinas because we are realistic. Idealistic and realistic" (Fabián Vargas, cited by Cantero et al., 2012: 31): Salinas is defined as People with Social and Solidary Economy.

Achievements

Some aspects can be considered as achievements in the Salinas process:

- The process of recreation and empowerment of Salinas identity, achieving a new form of community-cooperative-associative organization, with social cohesion making it possible to innovate and diversify economic activities that generate income of community property, but also of Popular Family Economic Units.
- Advances in developing organizational capacity of social and solidarity economic structures (cooperatives, associations, foundations, corporations) in a process that by its very nature requires permanent evaluation and adjustments, since it implies advances, setbacks or deviations as Cantero et al. (2012: 61) argues, "in Salinas there have been strong crises that, if they sometimes jeopardized the trajectory, allowed rethinking that, in the long run, reinforced the process".
- To go from a town dependent on the farm to be an organized, agro-industrial town, generator of quality products and services. In this regard, a parish icon is the "Salinerito" community farmer brand, with recognition and positioning in the national market as well as abroad; although it started as a cheese brand, it progressively

incorporated the new Salinas community products and services. There are also the specific brands of some community companies with products for certain market niches, but the biggest part of its production is marketed as "Salinerito" in larger markets; besides there are the brands of the Family Popular Economic Units. This is how, together, the economy of the Salinas parish has been energized.

- In 2018 (Table 5.2), the community social enterprises billed 13,795,317 US dollars. The data must be understood not only as a monetary indicator, it matters – and much – its distribution in the links of the social economy and solidary economy circuit; for example: a 1 kg "Andino" cheese: 70.1% of the retail price; PSP remains in the links of the social and solidary circuit of "Salinerito" production-transformation-marketing (63.6% of the PSP goes directly to milk producers and the cheese makers), the remaining 29.9% leaves the system towards other commercial actors. It is interesting to take care of the fixed income of small producers, workers, administrators, marketers, transporters, tourist guides, artisans of social and solidary companies.

Recreation and identity enhancement boosted the improvement of Salinas population living conditions and development seeking true development under a new paradigm and with shared values, that is, the step for each and everyone, from less human living conditions to more human conditions, as pointed out by the Populorum Progressio Encyclical.[15]

- Illiteracy decreased from 85% in 1970 to 19% in 2015;[16] it is also important to point out the education levels of Salinas population[17]: Primary 47%, secondary 25%, superior 8% and fourth level 1%.
- An incontrovertible fact of recent years is the impressive change at the level of formal education, to the point of reversing the situation: either at secondary level or at higher level; Salinas female students by far outnumber men, in number and performance (Polo, 2015: 187).
- Unlike many regions of Ecuador where migration is the option to find a better standard of living, in Salinas its inhabitants remain working in their place of origin and, moreover, there is a concurrence of people from nearby areas who come to work in the place (Ortega, 2018: 107).
- In Salinas, there has been an intergenerational transmission with a takeover in the organization management. Several actors testify their experiences of childhood, adolescence and early years of youth linked to community action and to the Salinas organizations to which they related early.
- Although the Salinas process has had a contribution from the Salesian Mission - MGO and other actors, the villagers have appropriated its process and constitute the pillars that support it.

Table 5.2 Consolidated billing of Salinas community companies in 2018

Production	*USD*	%	
25 Community Cheese Makers Including PRODUCOOP	2.385.048	47,36	
FFSS	1.279.421	25,41	
FUNORSAL	1.179.460	23,42	
FUGUS	75.374	1,50	
TEXAL	116.254	2,31	
SUBTOTAL	**5.035.557**	**100,00**	**36,50**
Commercialization	*USD*	%	
Export Center	2.022.336	26,10	
CONA	1.107.543	14,29	
PRODUCHEESE	713.803	9,21	
FUNORSAL Collection Center	349.982	4,52	
FUNCONQUERUCOM[24]	3.554.804	45,88	
SUBTOTAL	**7.748.468**	**100,00**	**56,17**
SERVICES	*USD*	%	
COACSAL	929.222	91,88	
FUNORSAL (Credit-info)	61.258	6,06	
FFSS RADIO	20.812	2,06	
SUBTOTAL	**1.011.292**	**100,00**	**7,33**
TOTAL	**13.795.317**	–	**100,00**

Source: Salinas Gruppo Corporation, 2018.

- When the presence of institutions and external people ends in Salinas, some less important activities will be extinguished, but the fundamentals will remain in place, which boosts the economy and organizations: the entrepreneurial spirit, the ability to sacrifice and save, community work, the desire for change and justice, union and solidarity. These are the bases that give life to farmer community businesses and everything that is being done (Beatriz Chamorro, Judith Chamorro and Jaime Aldaz, cited by Vaudagna, 2012: 223–224).

Challenges

In these five decades the Salinas population faced the difficulties with decision, being a living laboratory of open doors, with permanent revision. Among the aspects to pay attention, we have:

1. To maintain and strengthen the essence, values and principles: Salinas identity as People of Social and Solidary Economy. It can contribute to specify the desired Salinas instance for systematic and permanent training in Social and Solidary Economy which, in turn, is the center of accompaniment and innovation of products and services for organizations.

2. To promote greater training and specialization of Salinas young women and men in various subjects. Likewise, to stimulate their inclusion in organizations management levels and reinforce intergenerational takeover.
3. In a participatory manner, to fine-tune management and articulation strategies of the Salinas organizations that: a.- strengthen organizations in relation to their bases and their empowerment, reinforce their functioning and achievements according to their objectives; b.- they influence the integrating instances of Salinas aiming to optimize the mobilization of resources and efforts, energize issues of common interest around the "Salinerito" brand and other local brands; local reinvestment of surpluses; closeness with partners of organizations, with customers and consumers; avoid the operation of proposals through parallel channels.
4. To identify appropriate strategies to motivate and facilitate the relationship and integration of Family Popular Economic Units in a comprehensive Salinas perspective.
5. To promote without a partisan political flag, from the fourth cooperative principle (autonomy and independence) synergies with local and national "State political organizations",[18] according to point 17 of the SDGs (Alliances to achieve the objectives) in a sustained process of territorial development so that the State assumes its fields of action in an adequate manner in favor of the population and community organization.
6. To strengthen the equity between the parish center and the communities, mainly with those located in the moor.
7. To increase the protected areas of the moor and subtropics, the replacement of plant mass (forestation - reforestation) with native species, the replacement of plastic in our products by natural, non-polluting products.
8. To visualize the Salinas experience, the actions and advances related to the Millennium Development Goals, SDG.

Conclusions

Salinas process demonstrates that peasant communities are characterized by marginalization and abandonment by the State, they live in general conditions of high precariousness. They can achieve positive changes in their way of life, strengthening their identity based on the principles, values and methods of work, born from their own experiences of solidarity, combined and enriched with the practice of cooperativism, more specific, of the social and solidarity economy, having as outstanding elements of this identity path, the peasant effort and its openness towards innovation. The innovation is an outstanding component of Salinas identity evidenced in the community organizations and in family initiatives better known as Productive Economic Units.

In NGOs the action of the Catholic Church stands out as a key factor because they initiated a structural change in the parish, with agrarian reform actions on the lands they owned.

Salinas road has not obeyed a previous feasibility study and strict medium/long-term planning for parish development. What has been applied is a combination of concrete projects and the practice of "trial and error", with high community participation. Rather, in these days most of Salinas organizations, including the Parish Board, carry out their strategic planning for formality or for their own need.

The synergy has constituted a fundamental pillar of the socio-organizational and productive sustainability of Salinas, in which the application of elementary management criteria has been added because organizations are achieving a corporate dimension without losing the principles and values that motivated them since their beginning. Finally, it should be considered in mind that this continues to be a process in constant construction and improvement to face the risks and new challenges presented by the reality of the country.

Notes

1 Data from the 2015 parish GAD technical team: 20.5% in the parish center and 79.5% in communities; the 2010 National Population Census indicated 5821 inhabitants.

2 Fritz W. Up de Graff (1873–1927), American, friend of a son of Domingo Cordovez, whom he calls The Count and who he met in the United States (when he was studying Civil Engineering). He arrived in Ecuador in December 1894 invited by The Count to implement associated companies.

3 Thus, the church of Guaranda was the first to make agrarian reform in Ecuador. In Riobamba, Monsignor Leonidas Proaño would be somewhat before giving free land to indigenous people (Gavilanes, 1995: 242).

4 Mortality in the first month of life and before the age of 5 is the result of several social, economic and health circumstances in which boys and girls develop. Therefore, they not only refer, among its various conditioning, to access to health care but to their poverty situation, their availability of drinking water and environmental sanitation and to the educational levels of their mother. Social Observatory of Ecuador (2018: 64).

5 In the salt experience, the minga is understood as a collective work of the members of the community or organization that is carried out in a free and motivated way. It is about participating in essential topics for the coexistence of families in the community or organization, such as obtaining water, opening neighborhood roads, afforestation-reforestation, agricultural crops, construction of communal school-houses or small production units. The planning of the minga is carried out based on what is established in community policies or after debates and consensus in large assemblies, where the leaders make the call and lead both its organization and its execution. At the end of the minga, among all the participants they share the food that each of them has brought.

6 The Salinas experience on cooperativism: 1st Interclassism (Interetnicism)... each person is equal in front of the group and is entitled to the same vote,

without social class considerations... The principle was automatically applied to ethnical belonging. From the beginning, indigenous and mestizos found themselves in the same organization. 2nd. community production 3rd. the decision of individual non-distribution of surpluses "kind of social rebalancing, the fate of the surpluses preferably favors the poorest: social assistance, cover disease expenses..." (Polo, 2015: 33, 39).

7 February 27, 1978: "Agreement between the Government of the Republic of Ecuador and the Swiss Federal Council, concerning... A Cheese Production Project in Ecuador" through which they agree: Creation of Cheese Production Centers in Bolívar (Cadena, et al. 1998: 26).

8 A month after installing the first Cheese factory in Salinas, a store was opened for the storage and sale of cheese in Quito: "Cheese makers Bolivar Store", which evolved into the Community Rural Cheese Makers Consortium Foundation, FUNCONQUERUCOM, formed as such in 1999.

9 Salinas Farmer Organizations Foundation, second grade entity, whose objective is the support to the socio-organizational development of the communities of Salinas, formed in 1982 as UNORSAL and in 1987 as FUNORSAL.

10 Community Rural Cheese Maker Consortium Foundation, second grade entity; its objective is to contribute to improving the quality of life of small and medium producers of dairy, meat and related products, strengthening their organizations, improving the productive chain and the development of training services, technical advice and commercialization of primary and processed products of agricultural origin.

11 Salinas parish GAD and Ministerial Agreement 0115, September 27, 2018, Ministry of Economy and Finances.

12 Community Tourism Center Register: in 2018, 20,000 tourists visited Salinas, national and foreigners, groups of community organizations, families, students and backpackers.

13 Community Tourist Guides certified by the Ministry of Tourism.

14 It started in 1984 with young people (Carpentry Workshop); since 1988, it works with young people who, by agreement between organizations, study at Salinas school and complement their training with internships in community companies. 450 men and 100 women from 9 provinces and different nationalities ethnicities/places have participated: Bolívar (mestizo), Imbabura (Otavalo), Cotopaxi (Angamarca), Tungurahua (Pilahuin, Salasaca), Loja (Saraguro), Esmeraldas (Chachi), Los Ríos (montubio), Pastaza (Shuar).

15 Chocolate, Nougat, Jam Essential Oil factories, etc.

16 FFSS-FUNORSAL Salinas Parish Board Alliance to manage compost production with organic waste from the Parish Head.

17 Meat Sausage Factory, Intercommunal Spinning; pig farm, 2 community farms (cattle, camelids, sheep and afforestation).

18 PRODUCOOP has international certification of Food Manufacturing Good Practices (BPM).

References

Albuquerque, F. (2004). El Enfoque del Desarrollo Económico Local (The Local Economic Development Approach). *International Labor Organization*, ISBN: 92-2-316549-0 *1*, 2–84.

Barragán, M. y Ayauri, V. (2017). Innovación y Emprendimiento y su relación con el Desarrollo Local del Pueblo de Salinas de Guaranda, Provincia Bolivar,

Ecuador, Información tecnológica, 28, 6, pp. 71–80, ESPOCH, http://dspace.espoch.edu.ec/bitstream/123456789/9051/6/20T01179.pdf

Bebbington, A., et al. (1992). *Actores de una Década Ganada (Tribus, Comunidades y Campesinos en la Modernidad) ((Actors of a Won Decade (Tribes, Communities and Farmers in Modernity))*. Quito: Comunidec.

Cadena, M., et al. (1998). *Las Queserías Rurales del Ecuador, Trabajo de Don José y otros soñadores del Desarrollo Rural (The Rural Cheese Makers, Work of Don Jose and other Dreamers of Rural Development)*. Quito: Cosude/FEPP Press.

Cantero, P., et al. (2012). *Salinas, Guaranda, Horizonte de Economía Solidaria (Solidary Economy Horizon)*. Quito: Abya Yala Editorial.

Carroll, T., Editor. (2002). *Construyendo capacidades colectivas (Building Collective Capacities)*. Quito: Rispergraf Press.

Organic Code of Territorial Organization, Autonomy and Decentralization (COOTAD) (2015). Official Register 303, October 19, 2010, modified in January 16

Constitution of the Republic of Ecuador (2015). Official Register 449, October 20, 2008, amendment on December 21 .

Cooperativas de las Américas, Region de la Alianza Cooperativa Internacional, https://www.aciamericas.coop/Principios-y-Valores-Cooperativos-4456, https://www.aciamericas.coop/Que-es-la-Alianza-Cooperativa-Internacional

Duarte, T.; Ruiz, M. (2009). Emprendimiento, Una Opción para el Desarrollo (Entrepreneurship, An Option for Development), Scientia et Technica, ISSN: 0122–1701, https://goo.gl/ik1BIX,3(43),326–331

Duarte, T. y Ruiz, M. (2009). Emprendimiento, una opción para el desarrollo, Universidad Tecnológica de Pereira, Scienta et Technica Año XV, No. 43, Diciembre, https://www.redalyc.org/articulo.oa?id=84917310058

Gavilanes, L. (1995). *EI FEPP: Llamada, Pulso y Desafío (Call, Pulse and Challenge)*. Quito: FEPP Press.

INEC. (2010). *National Population and Housing Census*.Press SectionPopulation and Housing Censuses. https://www.ine.es/en/prensa/censos_prensa_en.htm

Bocina, La. (2012). *Voces convocando al desarrollo (The Horn, Voices calling for development) Nr. 160*, FEPP Social Group, Quito, September–October

Organic Law of Popular and Solidary Economy (2018). Official Register 444, May 10, 2011, modified in 2018. https://www.coops4dev.coop/en/4devamericas/ecuador

Ministry of Economy and Finances (2018). 27 Ministerial Agreement 0115, September, 2018. https://www.hacienda.gob.es/en-GB/el%20ministerio/paginas/el%20ministerio.aspx

Miño, W. (2013). *La historia del cooperativismo en el Ecuador, (History of cooperativism in Ecuador)*. Quito: Ministry of Economic Policy Coordination.

Molano, L. (2007). Identidad cultural un concepto que evoluciona. OPERA. 7.7, *Universidad Externado de Colombia*, noviembre, https://revistas.uexternado.edu.co/index.php/opera/article/view/1187

Naranjo, E. (2009). *Análisis de la evolución histórico-cultural del proyecto de desarrollo comunitario en la Parroquia Salines de la Provincia de Bolivar (Analysis of the historical-cultural evolution of the community development project in the Salinas Parish of the Province of Bolivar), Polytechnic Magazine* (30). Quito: National Polytechnic School.

Noorth, L. (1999). El Programa de Salinas. Una Experiencia de Desarrollo Microregional, en Manuel Chiriboga (Ed.) Cambiar se Puede *(The Salinas Program. An Experience of Microregional Development in Manuel Chiriboga (Ed.) You Can Change It,) 1999. FEPP rural development experiences in Ecuador. Quito, Abya-Yala Editorial/ FEPP*. Quito: FEPP Press.

Ortega, R. (2018). Degree thesis, Análisis técnico-conceptual y propositivo sobre las sociedades cooperativistas en el marco de la cohesión territorial para el desarrollo rural. (Technical-conceptual and propositive analysis of cooperative societies in the framework of territorial cohesion for rural development), *Case of the Salinas de Tomabela parish in Ecuador*. Cuenca: University of Cuenca.

PDOT GAD Parroquial Salinas, (2015). http://app.sni.gob.ec./sni-link/sni/PORTAL_SNI/data_sigad_plus/sigadplusdiagnostico/0260012690001_PDyOT%20GAD%20SALINAS%20DIAGNOSTICO_07-09-2015_10-54-20.pdf

Pope Paul VI, (1967). *Populorum Progressio Encyclical, Rome.http://www.vatican.va/content/paul-vi/en/encyclicals/documents/hf_p-vi_enc_26031967_populorum.html*

Polo, A. (2015). *La Puerta Abierta. 30 años de aventura misionera y social en Salinas de Bolivar, Ecuador (The Open Door. 30 years of missionary and social adventure in Salinas, Bolivar, Ecuador)*. Quito: Abya Yala/FEPP Print, fourth edition.

Polo & Borja. (2005). La experiencia de desarrollo de Salinas de Guaranda, Ecuador LEISA, Revista de agroecología, volumen 21, Nr. 2, Lima, http://www.leisa-al.org/web/images/stories/revistapdf/vol21n2.pdf

Pomeroy, Ch. (1986). *La sal en las culturas andinas, (Salt in Andean cultures) Andean World Serie*. Quito: Abya-Yala Editorial.

Resultado del Censo. (2010). de Población y Vivienda en el Ecuador, Fascículo provincial Bolívar, https://www.ecuadorencifras.gob.ec/wp-content/descargas/Manu-lateral/Resultados-provinciales/bolivar.pdf

Richard, H. (2019). *Principios fundamentales de la Economía Solidaria, Red de Educación y Economía, Septiembre*, https://drive.google.com/file/d/0B8AnZOkxJwzGTIdrdjJIYjNLRU9KZGJTVTJiaFZNdnJIMmOw/view

Situación de la niñez y adolescencia en el Ecuador, una mirada a través de los ODS, 2018, Observatorio Social del Ecuador, https://www.unicef.org/ecuador/SITAN_2019_Web.pdf

Up de Graff., F. (1996). Cazadores de cabezas del Amazonas. Siete años de exploraciones y aventuras (1894-1901) *(Headhunters of the Amazon. Seven years of explorations and adventures (1894-1901))*. Quito: Abya-Yala Editorial.

Vargas J. e Ibáñez E. (2003). Análisis y reflexiones sobre la transmisión intergeneracional, Universidad Nacional Autónoma de México, Campus Iztacala, Revista Electrónica de Psicología Iztacala, Enero de, http://www.revistas.unam.mx/index.php/repi/article/view/21690/20428

Vaudagna, M. (2012). *El Evangelio y la Quesera, historia del desarrollo comunitario en Salinas de Bolivar (The Gospel and Cheese makers, a history of community development in Salinas, Bolivar)*. Quito: Abya-Yala Editorial.

6 Socio-technical regimes to understand grassroots innovations and natural capital in Chile

Nancy Sarabia and Jordi Peris

Introduction

Chile is currently living a process of political and social crisis, within a global health and climate emergency and on the brink of an economic crisis. All these processes are not independent but interconnected with each other. The social explosion in Chile began in October 2019 and sought to change the neoliberal development model, established in the country about 40 years ago. The main effects of this model were a marked socio-economic inequality (OECD, 2020) with serious environmental impacts, together with the imposition of a successful social imaginary based on consumerism, individualism and competition (López, 2013). All these factors had together led to a deterioration in the quality of life.

This development model has transcended all spheres and dimensions of Chilean society, including the socio-technical agri-food system, on which this chapter is focused. Chile bases its economic growth on the exploitation of its natural resources (OECD, 2018), mainly mining, forestry, agriculture, fishing and aquaculture. It has a free market policy that encourages the entry of foreign capital and the privatization of agricultural land use and water rights, concentrating capital in national and transnational elites (Campos, 2019). This process generates a large-scale food production system with a high degree of intensification, productive efficiency and industrialization that is oriented towards the agro-export market. However, the economic success generated by this model leaves out small-scale farmers. They make up the majority of the country's productive sector and must compete in the national market with the prices of unregulated imported foodstuffs sold in oligopolistic chains and large shopping centres.

Throughout the country, climate change generates droughts with great impacts on the productive, environmental and social sectors. In addition, monopolization of water use by large agricultural producers, mainly in central Chile, leaves entire communities without water for human consumption (Bolados et al., 2017; Escenarios Hídricos 2030, 2018).

In cities, marked inequality is also observed in the food sector, where 27% of the population does not have access to a healthy diet (MINSAL, 2015). In poor neighbourhoods, commerce is barely diversified and concentrates on lower priced, highly processed and industrialized foods with high caloric value and low nutritional quality. The Pan American Health Organization (PAHO) describes them as obesogenic environments (JUNAEB, 2019; FAO, 2019; PAHO, 2015). In addition, new lifestyles are generating new consumption habits worldwide, increasing nutritional problems such as overweight and obesity, which in Chile reaches figures of 74.2% nationally (MINSAL, 2017a).

Along this chapter, a theoretical review of the Chilean agro-food system will be carried out, using the theoretical framework of studies on transitions to sustainability. It allows a holistic approach to understanding complex problems. The multi-level perspective (MLP) framework will be used to structure the chapter, describing the foodscape, the established regime and the emerging niches addressing different global controversies and challenges.

In the chapter, some disruptive and innovative niche initiatives are analysed. On the one side is the Food Labelling and Advertising Act, in force since 2016. It mandates a warning on the labelling of products according to their saturation of fat, calories, sugar or sodium, along with a ban on advertising unhealthy foods to children. These standards contribute to the democratization of decision-making and food purchasing and production behaviour. On the other side is the important increase of collective disruptive initiatives that are framed under the concept of Social Solidarity Economies (SSE). They are related to contemporary global movements of responsible consumption, agro-ecological production, food sovereignty, circular economy and the common good. SSE are born from social movements responding to the social, economic and environmental needs of the agri-food system.

This study will be contextualized in the moment of socio-political, environmental, health and climate emergency crises, which influence the transition process of the country. The civic re-articulation that is going on is fed by, and at the same time, nourish the existing disruptive spaces in the field of agri-food. In addition, the chapter highlights the key factors for the agri-food transition, through some examples identified in the Chilean agri-food system, based on some studies on the theory of transitions to sustainability (Ingram, 2015; Wolfram, 2016; Frantzeskaki et al., 2018).

Dynamics of transformation in the agri-food system in Chile

MLP is a framework that provides different elements to understand social transitions to sustainability as the result of complex dynamics.

It focuses on the interactions of three levels: landscape (or global trends at the macro level), regime (dominant rules and status quo at the meso level) and niches (or new configurations and disruptive initiatives at the micro level) (Geels, 2002; Geels & Schot, 2007; Frantzeskaki et al., 2018).

A foodscape in dispute

The agri-food landscape is shaped by the dominant development policy macro trends. They are mainly based on economic growth with a disregard of the ecological capacity of the land and the environmental and social impacts. In that sense, capitalism has become a meta-narrative of global scope, transcending all the different spheres and dimensions of life (Letelier et al., 2019; Dardot & Laval, 2009; Boltanski & Chiapello, 1999), including the agri-food system. The MLP has been used in several studies to describe transition processes of the agri-food systems. El Bilai (2019) makes a systematic characterization of the food landscape that includes: 1) globalization and internationalization of agro-food markets, 2) generation of instability and commercial speculation, 3) global interdependence in the health, oil and financial crises, 4) population growth and social inequality, and 4) changes in eating habits and lifestyles. All these elements make up an agri-food landscape with important social impacts, loss of biodiversity, environmental deterioration and climate change. The latest land report of the Intergovernmental Panel on Climate Change (IPCC, 2019) indicates that agro-food system is one of the main affected by climate change and, at the same time, is one of the main responsible for it. It produces between 21% and 37% of greenhouse gas emissions.

As a counterpart to this foodscape, macro policies have been promoted within the framework of the Sustainable Development Goals (SDGs). They provide specific guidelines for action through international treaties and conventions (El Bilai, 2019). Some relevant examples are the Milan Urban Food Policy Pact (MUFPP) and the FAO Framework for the Urban Food Agenda. Both of them promote local food governance and involve cities as the places where food systems can be regulated and food consumption is concentrated. Their aim is to integrate food into urban planning (Cabannes & Marocchino, 2018).

Another macro trend is the recent recognition by FAO (in April 2018) of agroecology as a sustainable agro-food productive alternative. It highlights that, by combining traditional knowledge (indigenous and peasant) and scientific knowledge, agroecology applies ecological and social approaches to agricultural systems and focuses on the beneficial interactions between plants, animals, humans and the environment. In fact, agroecology also includes territorial and participatory eco-social policy approaches, in which it makes a symbiosis with food sovereignty, a concept that was created by Via Campesina in 1996. Additionally, it was also integrated in the Popular Agrarian Reform in the year 2000. All these show that the concept has been gaining global pre-eminence since 2007, especially after the International Forum on Food Sovereignty and the Nyéléni Declaration (Campesina, 2016), when it first became a relevant element of the current macro trends of the agro-food landscape.

Context and tensions in the agri-food regime

Transformation of regimes are the key process for sustainability transitions (Ingram, 2015; Frantzeskaki et al., 2018). According to these authors, the regime is a "dominant conglomerate of structures (physical, institutional, environmental...), cultures (prevailing perspectives) and practices (rules, routines and habits)" (Rotmans & Loorbach, 2010). The regime refers to the dominant status quo and "business as usual" and it is actively oriented to resist change in the quest to preserve itself.

The current agro-food regime is characterized by an agro-industry and agrobusiness model where food becomes a commodity and the priority is to buy and sell it. Elements such as ecological footprint, labour justice, food waste and health are left in a secondary position. All these elements pose key controversial ethical issues. In fact, it has been expressed that agriculture has lost its culture and its vital eco-social value (Esquinas, 2020,;Vivero-Pol, 2017). McMichael (2009) calls it a corporate food regime that embodies the productivist paradigm rooted in the green revolution. Within it, the food systems take an industrial approach, mainly oriented towards the production of large quantities of standardized foods (Gaitán-Cremaschi et al., 2019; Therond et al., 2017; Lang & Heasman, 2015). It has been also called the neo-liberal food regime (Otero, 2013), where the Supermarket Revolution, overproduction and dumping in a highly unequal global market generate accumulation and dispossession (McMichael, 2005). In this line, the Marabá Declaration warns of the alliance between financial capital, agribusiness, the State and the mass media (Campesina, 2016). Chile's agro-food regime has an important neoliberal structure and agro-export focus. Conventional production on different scales (monocultures with agrochemicals) covers almost 100% of the total volume of plant products marketed nationally (Gaitán-Cremaschi et al., 2019). However, these same authors identify other types of production and commercialization of plant foods in Chile. They include agro-ecological production at different scales and a hybrid system of organic production associated with monocultures for the industrial market in the form of "green corporate" (Ríos & Núñez, 2016) and "green capitalism" (Gudynas, 2010). Therefore, the hegemonic model does not cover everything. Saravia et al. (2018) highlight the heterogeneities and emergence of other forms of economy that are born from the resistance and questioning of the regime, as well as from the recovery of history, experiences and particular knowledge of the territory.

A historical glance at the development of the Chilean agri-food regime

Since the process of European colonization and settlement in Latin America, land ownership was associated with wealth and power. Extensive territories were given to different representatives of the conquest. Later on, the political vicissitudes gave rise to new groups of powerful large landowners (Alegrett, 2003). Between 1840 and 1850, the internal food demand expanded as a result of population growth, urbanization and "early industrialization". This coincided with the beginning of the wheat export cycles (Llorca-Jaña et al., 2017) causing the expansion of agricultural areas in the period between 1850 and 1930. Robles (2003) interpreted this period as a transition to agrarian capitalism through a "land route". On the one hand, it displaced the border of indigenous territories, dispossessing them of their lands. On the other hand, it decreased the land ration of tenants (workers of farms and estates) marginalizing them. In 1920, the development of agrarian capitalism not only implied the proletarianization of the rural workers, but also the transformation of their collective action through the formation of unions "workers' councils" and the participation in the Workers' Federation of Chile (FOCh) as well as in political parties (Robles, 2003). This process was also characterized by unequal access to irrigation technology and machinery by the aristocracy, which had a high correlation with the political elite (ibid). In 1929, the international economic and stock market crisis led to the Great Depression, with 20% unemployment in Chile's workforce and high infant mortality figures (Belmin et al., 2018). Food played a key role in the debates on economic recovery, which was considered as essential for the workforce. At the Latin American level, it was important to create the Pan American Sanitary Bureau (PAS) in 1902. Together with ILO (International Labour Organization) and the governments of the region, it coordinated the health policies for tackling the phenomenon of malnutrition and the promotion of popular restaurants (Cueto, 2004; Belmin et al., 2018).

In 1962, Chile joined the agrarian reforms that had previously been initiated in Mexico, Bolivia and Cuba (Alegrett, 2003). The expropriation and redistribution of land was an attempt for the socio-political integration of the peasantry (Thezá et al., 2017). In the 1970s, agrarian reform was stepped up and a policy of price surveillance for basic foodstuffs was developed, along with a State network of collectively run shops and food distribution sites. There was a specific consideration for the popular sectors and the development of a fairer and more equitable consumer market (Frens-String, 2018).

However, the situation changed with the military coup in 1973. Through a dictatorial regime, Chile became a pioneer of the neoliberal economy and the development of the corporate food regime. The system believed in market self-regulation and free competition (Otero, 2013). At normative level, the neoliberal economic model culminated in the 1980 Constitution, permeating all areas and dimensions of Chilean society. In terms of ideology and labour culture, individualism and competition were promoted, repressing and dismantling solidarity relations and membership of trade unions (López, 2013). The extraction of natural resources and the reconcentration of land destined to monoculture and export were promoted. The entry of foreign capital and the privatization of agricultural land and water rights were endorsed, concentrating capital in national and transnational elites (Campos, 2019). Rural peasants and indigenous sectors were abandoned by the State in favour of promoting large-scale models for export purposes (Altieri & Rojas, 1999).

In the 1990s, with the return to democracy, strengthening of rurality and support to small and medium producers was encouraged. However, technical assistance was implemented with a vertical approach based on positivist scientific knowledge (Montalba et al., 2016). It included guidelines towards modernization of conventional agriculture that was dependent on external inputs. Specialization in monoculture was promoted. The idea was to generate clusters of producers to reach a larger scale for their integration into the market. Local and ancestral knowledge was devalued (íbid). Some farmers kept it, and others made hybridization of techniques, but in all cases it was difficult to reach the formal market and the scale to which the advisory programmes were oriented. In addition, there was an increase in the dependence on off-farm wage labour, which became increasingly precarious (Saravia et al., 2018; Valdés, 2015; Fundación Sol, 2011).

The strategy of the neoliberal system was maintained and various free trade agreements (FTAs) were signed. With an industrial organization of medium to high concentration, the most favoured agents were the fruit exporting companies, the forestry industry, the agro-industrial subsectors playing a decisive role in the performance of the chain (sugar, barley, milk, rice), the vertically integrated companies (poultry and pigs), the wine companies and the meat, juice, pasta, dehydrated and frozen industries (Portilla, 2000). According to Fundación Sol (2008), between 1990 and 2006, export returns grew by 332%. The agro-exporting model of fruit increased the labour market, mainly that of "seasonal workers", a niche occupied mainly by rural women and/or vulnerable families. It prompted the government to enact new laws to protect this working class. However, there are still ethical gaps such as the right to organize and participate in the development of regulations concerning decent wages, biosafety conditions and awareness of the exposure of pesticides (Correa, 2018; Valdés, 2015). In 2006, government promoted the slogan "Chile Potencia Alimentaria y Forestal" with the idea of positioning itself globally as an agro-exporting country. Accordingly, it adapted its export products to foreign market trends and opportunities (Becerra, 2019; Campos & Polit, 2011). In 2015, only the productive forestry and agricultural sector generated 9.2% of average employment and 3% of national GDP (Gumucio & Amunátegui, 2017). If the food processing activity is added, these figures increased to 24.9% of employment and 8.6% of GDP, representing 26.2% of total exports. It positions the agro-food sector as the second most important for the country's economy after mining (Transforma Alimentos, 2018).

As of 2016, the agro-export policy is focused on the "Healthy Food Strategic Plan", with the objective of doubling the value of healthy food exports and positioning the country as a reference in healthy eating by 2025. This plan is promoted by CORFO (Corporación de Fomento de la Producción) through its Transforma Program of public, private and academic collaboration. Additionally, the National Food and Nutrition Policy counts on public-academic participation and collects information from civil society. It is aligned with the SDG and it is being constructed as a reference framework since 2018.

However, Chile's international image as an emerging country based on an open economy, political stability and ideal for foreign investment was shattered with the social explosion of October 2019. Citizenry rose up demanding "dignity", "an end to privileges" and a structural change of the neoliberal model of the country that was the cause of a deep environmental and social crisis characterized by inequality. In fact, Chile is the third most unequal country in the OECD (2020),with an excessive concentration of wealth and patrimony in elites that disrupt the entire system with their influences at political, social and cultural levels. It forms an oligarchic power that weakens democracy (von Wolffersdorff, 2019). According to the Global Wealth Report (Credit Suisse Research Institute, 2019), Chile's GDP per adult is a third higher than Argentina's and 70% higher than Brazil's, but its average wealth is five times that of Argentina and more than double that of Brazil. However, the Gini coefficient of Chile's wealth is 0.8, which is a high rate in the international standards. Only 0.01% of the population controls 10% of GDP (Oficina Económica y Comercial de España en Chile, 2019) and 70,000 adults in the top 1% of global wealth holders. With the arrival of the Covid-19 and the period of quarantine and sanitary cordons, more attention was given to vital needs, such as food. In households, the daily process of preparing food at home was recovered. However, the fragility and dependence of the large food supply chains became visible by amplifying inequality and food insecurity. The response was an increase of SSE alternatives.

The conflict on water

There is a multidimensional water crisis in Chile. It encompasses a physical dimension related to drought, climate change and impacts on quantity and quality and also an anthropic dimension with social, political, economic and cultural implications (Oppliger et al., 2019). These dimensions are interrelated and co-dependent. From the physical point of view, in the period between 1985 and 2015, increase of temperature began to be more consistent throughout the territory, especially in the valley and pre-cordillera zones (Vargas et al., 2017). The indicators of the National Environmental Information System, between 1972 and 2018, show that the rainiest periods decreased at national level with the only exception of the highlands. The trend in almost the entire country clearly points towards persistent meteorological droughts (Escenarios Hídricos 2030, 2018). In the anthropic dimension, there is a strong competition in the demand for water, especially in the areas comprehended between the center-north and the center-south of the country. Key sectors in water consumption are mining, drinking and sanitation water, hydropower and forestry. The two latter ones are the most vulnerable in terms of sustaining their current activity due to the limited availability of both at surface and groundwater (ibid).

From the normative aspect of the anthropic dimension, Chile has had a land water code since at least 1908. It experienced a radical change in 1981, when the right to water was separated from land and the commercialization of water rights was allowed as a private good, protected by the State, under the protection of the Constitution of 1980 (Alvez, 2020). Since then, "the rights of individuals over water, recognized or constituted in conformity with law, will grant their owners the property over them" (íbid). The water market was then created, with a low capacity for control, creating water hoarding and overexploitation of the resource, mainly by large mining, forestry and agro-export companies. The poor distribution of water causes serious social impacts, leaving communities without water, migrations and damage to the ecosystems that sustain life and its biodiversity (Fragkou, 2020). This same academic highlights more problems of the anthropic political dimension, such as the fragmentation of the ecosystemic management of water between: 1) fresh and sea water, 2) industrial and human use and 3) gentrification in water access and traditional access ways. In cities, there is no participation in decision-making. People do not know the source of the water they drink, being only customers of the sanitary companies, which in Chile are private. In the northern part of the country, there is distrust in the quality of water. It destroys household appliances and makes people buy bottled water, with an increase in water expenses and in the contamination by plastic bottles (idem).

According to a study carried out between 2008 and 2018, there are 106 decrees of water shortage, 14 decrees of river depletion and 152 areas of water restriction mainly in the central zone (Fundación Newenko, 2019). In addition, 47.2% of the rural population does not have regular access to drinking water through formal networks, which is related to multidimensional poverty as reported in the Caracterizacion Socioeconomica Nacional (CASEN) survey in 2015 (Fundación Amulén, 2019; Frene, 2020). In March 2015, 194 communes in the country (56% of the total) were declared in agricultural emergency due to drought (Escenarios Hídricos 2030, 2018). The agricultural sector requires approximately 70% of freshwater in Chile, being the main consumer sector. Consequently, it is most affected by droughts at the national level (MOP, 2013). Stehr et al. (2010) carried out a modelling of the water response of the central-southern zone of the country and in most of the future scenarios, there is a clear reduction in the average monthly and annual flows. According to the OECD (2012), by 2050 more than 40% of the world's population will be living in areas with severe water stress. Therefore, the water crisis is a growing and structural problem.

Food inequality and obesity

New lifestyles in cities, related overload of work and multiple occupations generate little time to cook and eat at home. Additionally, the easy access to snacks, ready-to-eat dishes, proximity of local restaurants and multinational fast food chains generate new consumption habits worldwide, increasing nutrition problems such as overweight and obesity. The expansion of supermarket chains and hypermarkets and the preponderance of large food processing industries have made ultra-processed products available everywhere and at lower prices than nutritious ones (FAO, 2019; PAHO, 2015). FAO studies show that there is a strong correlation between the increase in sales of ultra-processed food products with urbanization and deregulation of markets which favours large food industries. Chile is one of the main per capita consumers of ultra-processed food and beverages, and it is the second in Latin America (2009–2014) (FAO, 2019). The ultra-processed foods have a low nutritional quality and are usually highly palatable, almost addictive (PAHO, 2015). They increase energy intake and exposure of populations to excessive amounts of sugar, sodium and fats, displacing healthy eating (PAHO, 2019). In Chile, Cediel et al. (2018) showed that ultra-processed foods represent 28.6% of the total energy intake and 58.6% of added sugar intake. According to the Ministry of Health of Chile (2017), obesity and overweight in the country reach 74.2%, while in child population there is an upward trend that reaches 50.7% in pre-schoolers (JUNAEB, 2019).

In cities, marked inequality is also observed in the food sector, where 27% of the population does not have access to a healthy diet (MINSAL, 2015). In poor neighbourhoods, commerce has little diversity and it is concentrated in lower priced, highly processed and industrialized foods with high caloric value and low nutritional quality (JUNAEB, 2019; FAO, 2019; PAHO, 2015). These inequalities can be seen in the 2019 study by JUNAEB (Junta Nacional de Auxilio Escolar y Beca del Ministerio de Educación), carried out at national level, which found that students from more vulnerable sectors are 38 times more likely to be obese. In contrast, the wealthiest sector is 28 per cent more likely to be normal weight. This is related to the absence of a transversal educational programme (students, parents, teachers, etc.) on sustainable nutrition, as well as on the fact that the cost of living in Chile is high. According to OECD and FAO data (2013), it is one of the countries where food prices have increased the most. The Report of the Economic and Commercial Office of Spain states that Chile is relatively expensive for Spanish expectations. It is due to the fact that there is little macro competition in almost all productive sectors because of the concentration of supply and power in the determination of prices. In comparison to other countries, the cost of living is higher and wages are lower. The minimum wage is equivalent to US$ 394 (Dirección del Trabajo, 2020) and the average wage is US$ 718 (INE, 2019), where 53.1% of workers earn less than US$ 500 (Fundación Sol, 2019). According to the Superintendency of Banks and Financial Institutions (today's Financial Market Commission), Walmart Chile alone had issued 1,420,885 credit cards in 2019, a figure that is equivalent to almost 10% of all active credit cards in the country. This means that at least this percentage of Chilean households get into debts to be able to eat (Arboleda, 2020).

With the social outburst in 2019, several supermarkets, smaller markets and restaurants were closed to prevent looting and damage. This led to a series of layoffs, since a large proportion of labour contracts were informal and temporary (OECD, 2018). Layoffs have been amplified by the Covid-19 quarantine, and the national unemployment rate has increased by 1.9 percentage points over the same period of the previous year (INE, 2020). In parallel, food insecurity in Chile's most vulnerable sectors is dramatically increasing.

Niches: building alternatives for the transition to sustainability

Niches are the locus of radical innovations. They provide a place for learning processes and a space for social innovation networks (Geels, 2005). Niches are experimental environments where norms and practices deviate from the prevailing regime ones. Regime changes begin when practices and norms developed in niches become more widely adopted (Frantzeskaki et al., 2018).

Social organizations, social and urban solidarity economies

With the recent social burst in Chile, social needs and fragilities of the system became evident. It generated an important process of empathy, reflection and national collective awareness about different dimensions of the situation of the country. The national scale massive social movement put pressure on the dominant regime to transform it. Citizenry has expressed itself in constant and crowded protests. It has generated a social reorganization around a deep reflection prospect of Chilean future. It has been articulated around citizen-territorial councils and it has promoted a boom in collective initiatives of various kinds, both formal and informal in the cultural, social and economic realm.

Di Girolamo (2020) highlights that urban orchards and supply co-operatives have increased both in number and in participants, as well as the communities and networks for basic multidisciplinary social support (health, food, economy, etc.). Practices such as barter, collective solidarity savings and common pots have also gained presence. Historical expressions such as mutualism, trade unionism, co-operativism, reciprocity and more contemporary ones such as fair trade, common good and responsible consumption had a diversity of economic manifestations that can be labelled under the name of "Social Solidarity Economy" (SSE) (Letelier et al., 2019). The coronavirus quarantine has increased unemployment and the difficulty of accessing food. As a response, communication and organisation of neighbours have been strengthened in the search of practical solutions. These networks have responded with agility to the critical needs of society and some of them have materialized in disruptive initiatives which are inspired by a fairer and/or more agro-ecological food model. It has generated an alternative economy to the dominant model (Saravia et al., 2018; Cid & Latta, 2015). Social organisations and SSE have shown alternative ways of establishing social relations contrary to the dominant competitive and individualistic view. They have advanced initiatives based on trust and active social participation. In 2015, the social economy sector was made up of some 247,559 formal organisations or companies. This non-market sector was made up of community organisations and private non-profit associations, corporations or foundations. These figures are equivalent to 3.8% of the employment and 3.7% of the Chile's GDP (Letelier et al., 2019). However, these same authors conclude that a significant gap can be found between the formal criteria for classifying social economy entities and the substantive reality of their operation.

Rural social organizations, social and rural solidarity economies

At the productive level, there are agro-ecological peasant organizations and cooperatives initiatives, such as the Participatory Guarantee Systems (PGS), which are emerging as disruptive initiatives under a sustainable and alternative paradigm to conventional agriculture. All around the country, several larger scale producers of apple trees, blueberries and vineyards have begun a transition based on agro-ecological principles. There are also NGO experiences that show that basing rural development strategies on family farming and peasant knowledge, combined with elements of modern agroecology, not only ensures the maintenance and continued use of valuable agrobiodiversity, but also allows for the diversification of agricultural areas that ensures a variety of ecological services vital to food security (Altieri, 2016).

However, different types of farmers can be found. There are farmers who produce organic food because it is a better business and the farmers who produce organic food to contribute to a sustainable way of life. Between those two extremes, there is a whole universe of farmers who consider both elements to a greater or lesser extent (ODEPA, 2019). In 2019, there were 19 PGS registered at the national level, according to the data from the Agricultural and Livestock Service (SAG) collected by the Office of Agricultural Studies and Policies (ODEPA). These organizations have a relevant role in self-certification and represent a little more than 15% of the Chilean organic products consumed in the country (íbid). Law 20.089 creates and regulates the National System of Certification of Organic Agricultural Products. It is established that organic, ecological or biological denominations can only be contained in products that have been certified by either a certifying company registered in the SAG Registry or a member of a formalized social organization system (PGS). In Chile, there are three certifying companies for organic products in the domestic market. The certification is a service that is paid annually and has a fixed base cost close to 2500 USD (ODEPA, 2019). This cost operates as an entry barrier for small-scale production units. It becomes a questionable commercial alternative, especially if it is only focused on agro export due to the volatility of the market (Altieri and Rojas, 1999). However, self-certification plays a relevant role in guaranteeing validation, innovation and differentiation in the market. It also promotes self-management and empowerment of producer organizations around the flow of knowledge and maintenance of agro-ecological and sustainable techniques. Something similar occurs with the SIPAM (Important Systems of the World Agricultural Heritage), SIPAN (Sistemas Importantes del Patrimonio Agrícola Nacional) and Manos Campesinas seals. Geographical indications (GIs) or territorial marks are also ways to support endogenous innovation. They are not intended to change the food regime, but to protect certain qualities of the territory, culture and particular techniques in the long term (Belmin et al., 2018). Most of these organizations are supported by INDAP (Instituto de Desarrollo Agropecuario), a government institution that traditionally promoted conventional productive development, but it has gradually included agro-ecological advice in pilot projects.

The SSE around the management of water resources comprises the rural drinking water committees and cooperatives (RWCs). They have been collectively managing the water supply for their members for over 50 years in an autonomous and non-profit manner. FENAPRU, the National Federation of Rural Drinking Water, represents approximately 1730 committees and rural drinking water cooperatives (FENAPRU, 2016). It participated actively in a multisectoral effort with various state agencies for the development of Law 20,998 on Rural Sanitary Services, a regulatory framework that defines the regulatory action and subsidiary role of the State. This law has among its objectives: 1) strengthening the management capacity of community organizations, 2) protecting the operational territories currently served by RPAs, 3) incorporating the dispersed rural sector, with priority given to areas declared as water scarce, 4) the participation of leaders in a National Advisory Council and in Regional Advisory Councils and 5) incorporating the collection and treatment of wastewater, both in investment and in advisory and assistance. Law 20998 was enacted in 2017 with the participation of RPAs, which gave it relevance and legitimacy (Schuster & Tapia, 2017) for moving towards freshwater governance in the rural sectors. Currently, legal teams are in the last stages of revising the regulations of the Law that "Regulates Rural Sanitary Services" (MOP, 2020).

There are other important and contingent political and regulatory processes that also constitute key opportunities for change. The first is the approval of the National Rural Development Policy in May 2020, which will be in charge of 14 ministries and will have a National Council composed of representatives from the public, private and civil society sectors. The second is the Climate Change Bill, which is under study. However, it has been questioned that in the processing of the project, there is a precarization of the right to citizen participation (Madariaga, 2020).

Niche-regime interaction as spaces for social innovation

There are other interesting disruptive initiatives that are essential for understanding transitions. They are related to the articulation between policy, food regulation and SSE, as well as to the creation of spaces of interaction between niches and regime. One clear example is what happened between the RPAs and the generation of the Rural Health Services Law. Ingram (2015) highlights that these spaces of niche-regime linkage are diverse and complex. They proceed with a continuous adaptation among different types of actors that open opportunities both for the absorption of disturbances by regime actors to maintain their functions and for developing different kinds of adaptation pathways by the regime. In that sense, policy instruments aims to reformulate regime tensions and generate a pressure for change. They also aim to promote reconfigurations to advance developments on a new desired trajectory (Geels, 2002; Smith et al., 2005; Smith, 2012).

Democratization and politicization of food

A disruptive initiative at the national level of public policy is the pioneering Law 20,606 on "Nutritional Composition of Foods and their Advertising" or "Labelling Law" (MINSAL, 2012). After 10 years of process, it was approved in 2016 as a public policy of structural character to reduce obesity and increase the consumption of healthy foods (FAO & PAHO, 2017). The law enforces a front labelling of food packages with black hexagons like the "stop" sign. That way, it warns about processed food products that are high in calories, saturated fats, sugars and sodium. It also includes a ban on the sale of food around schools and restricts the advertising of unhealthy foods to children. Law No. 20,869 on "Food Advertising" (MINSAL, 2015b) complements the "Law on Labelling" and adds regulations on the advertising of breast milk substitutes.

On the Law of Labelling, Bustos (2019) says: "This was a first step in the democratization of food, where the consumer has clear information to make decisions at the time of purchase, a change that is not easy for the food industry, where they were also invited to make a reformulation of their food towards healthier foods". According to the CADEM Survey (2018), 64% of Chileans said they looked at food stamps before choosing a product and had changed the products they usually consumed for others with fewer stamps. A total of 58% changed their usual brands, 57% stopped buying a product and 38% modified their children's homemade school lunches.

It is also important to acknowledge the efforts made by the Law 20,780, which in its Article 42 enacts the increase of the tax on sugar and alcoholic beverages (MINSAL, 2017b; FAO, 2017; Lira, 2019). In the 18 months following the implementation of the tax increase, the purchase of beverages with a high sugar content fell by 23.7% (Taillie et al., 2020). According to Olea (2019), 4.32% is due exclusively to the change in the tax.

However, some experts propose changing it to a specific tax and to increase its rate... "it is very low and still does not compensate for the externalities of consumption, which generates significant costs to the health system that we all finance with our taxes" says the public health academic Cuadrado (2020,).Another experts in Nutrition and Dietetics says, "although the tax increase was low and there is no campaign or incentive to avoid the consumption of sugary drinks, there was a decrease, which is not the result of the tax, but of campaigns that the same companies are carrying out and that have led them to reduce the amount of sugar by themselves and thus avoid the black stamps" (Durán, 2018). Coca Cola admitted that only in Chile, it has reduced 38,000 tons of sugar through a reworking of different recipes. It has also proposed that 50% of its sales become sugar free (or reduced sugar) products (Vercelli, 2019). In June 2019, the third stage of the "Labeling Law" was initiated, integrating small and medium enterprises, which had been given more time to adapt and tighten the limits on calories, saturated fats, sugars and sodium to reach what was recommended by experts. On 26 June 2019, FAO recognized the promoters of this Chilean initiative with the Jacques Diouf Award, noting that "the law represents an example of policy change supported by the mobilization of a wide range of actors such as consumers, science, academia and a vast coalition of members of different political parties" (FAO, 2019).

Public procurement policy for local foods

Public purchase of food from local and ecological producers is recommended at the international level (FAO, 2013, 2015, 2017, 2020). It strengthens territories and family farm economy and promotes healthier food. In Chile, there are experiences scattered throughout the country, such as the sale of organic quinoa from a PGS in Tarapacá to a government concession for the School Food Program (ODEPA, 2019). Along the same lines, in 2017 the School Feeding Programme included an obligation for companies to purchase a minimum quantity (15%) of raw materials at the territorial level (region) from small producers, or a minimum of 10% of inputs from deprived areas of the country. This obligation extends, as of 2020, to all regions of the country, and companies that deliver the service in the Metropolitan Region must compulsorily purchase 50% of their inputs in deprived areas (JUNAEB, 2016). In the context of Covid, this initiatives could also be applied to the State purchases of food to cover food insecurity in vulnerable sectors through the delivery of boxes with food to families (Painel, 2020,).Although this regulation is incipient and focuses more on the local elements than on the agro-ecological or organic ones, it is an interesting niche-regime articulation to be developed, for example, by progressively extending these requirements to all purchases by public institutions of the State (universities, hospitals, municipalities, armed forces, etc.). It could also encompass a percentage of demand for agro-ecological or organic products, which would encourage transition to more sustainable and healthy production models.

Conclusions

Chile's current panorama of ongoing multidimensional crisis (political, social, economic, environmental, health, climate, ethics) unquestionably generates a historical turning point, a process of transition and radical change that will transform the country. The social outburst in 2019 has generated spaces of reunion and social rearticulation that confront a long historical process of individualism and competition promoted by the neoliberal model. This process of questioning the rules of the game, of collective reflection and citizen participation, has also generated an effervescence of new disruptive and collective food initiatives to respond to social needs, especially those not attended by the government. Existing cooperatives, associations and disruptive practices have also been strengthened through an increasement of their participants and the incorporation of niche actors with contemporary narratives linked to ideas such as solidarity economy, sustainable food, fair and responsible trade and the common good. Likewise, existing niches and their networks have been a key element in the articulation and coordination of collective reflection processes such as citizen councils. They have functioned as intermediaries by bringing people together into a more massive social movement. Therefore, a favourable scenario has been created for the rapid development of an empowered social movement, vital in the transition processes to sustainability.

Following the MLP framework, Chile is currently experiencing a great pressure on the neoliberal regime that transcends the agro-food field (meso level). These pressures come both from the landscape (macro level) and from the niches (micro level). In fact, niches are multiplying exponentially, challenging the regime by questioning their rules of the game and the established belief system. At landscape level, macro political trends related to SDG, climate change and water rights generate pressure and advance narratives with a chance of opening windows of opportunity for change. These global political macrotrends could be the basis for a future Constituent Convention process for a New Constitution. This reformulation of the constitutional charter could be a key window of opportunity for transition processes, together with a change of government that is more in line with the new narratives of eco-social justice and sustainability, so that the capacities for transition to sustainability can flow.

According to transition theories, effective governance is a central factor in a socio-technical system's transition to sustainability. This involves not only niches, but also niche-regime interfaces. In Chile, there are important and incipient experiences of niche-regime articulation. On one side, the Rural Health Services Law has been able to generate a governance space for law making processes. It has constituted a National Advisory Council and several Regional Advisory Councils. That way, social innovation and transdisciplinary (including local knowledge) is addressed. On the other, a public food policy has been recognized at the international level for their ability to stress the food regime and create major changes in consumption and corporate production behaviours towards a healthier supply. It is the law on labelling and advertising of packaged foods. Additionally, another interesting niche-regime interface with the potential of enabling transition processes is the public procurement policy for local products.

These three cases highlight the importance of the regulatory aspect in strengthening, integrating and coupling innovation. Both niche-regime relations and effective food governance have yet to make significant progresses in the country. An opportunity for their development at the municipal level would be the signing of the Milan Urban Food Policy Pact (MUFPP), which gives specific guidelines for the establishment of territorial food governance. Municipalities are the ones that subscribe this international protocol and there are interesting experiences in other territories where the Milan Pact has triggered transition capacities. However, up to now, no city in Chile has signed it up.

Acknowledgements

This work was funded by the National Commission for Research in Science and Technology (CONICYT) of Chile. Special thanks to Martín Arboleda and Cristina Galvez for their initial guidance and to Paulina Terrazas and Verónica Ocaña for their help and support.

References

Alegrett, R. (2003). *Evolución y tendencias de las reformas agrarias en América Latina*. Roma: FAO. http://www.fao.org/3/j0415t/j0415t0b.htm#TopOfPage (Accessed on 19May2020).

Altieri, M., & Rojas, A. (1999). Ecological impacts of Chile's neoliberal policies, with special emphasis on agroecosystems. *Environment, Development and Sustainability*, *1*, 55–72. https://doi.org/10.1023/A:1010063724280.

Altieri, M. (2016). Una estrategia agroecológica en Chile como base para la soberanía alimentaria. *Ambiente y Desarrollo de CIPMA*, 24–29. Retrieved from: http://agroeco.org/wp-content/uploads/2016/01/CIPMA-Altieri.pdf (Accessed on 3 June 2020).

Alvez, A. (2020). El agua: la crisis que viene. En: 4° Sesión del Ciclo Ecoderecho. Foros Virtuales para una Constitución del Siglo XXI. Organiza Centro de Derecho Ambiental, *Universidad de Chile*. https://www.facebook.com/1353506178038527/videos/267054941139448 (Accessed on 3June2020).

Arboleda, M. (2020). Towards an agrarian question of circulation: Walmart's expansion in Chile and the agrarian political economy of supply chain capitalism. *Journal of Agrarian Change*, *20*, 345–363. https://doi.org/10.1111/joac.12356.

Becerra, M. J. (2019). *Interview by* Let's Foods Cities [video]. En: "El Sistema Alimentario de Valparaíso, Chile". https://letsfoodcities.com/home/les-villes/valparaiso (Accessed on 6 June 2019).

Belmin, R., Casabianca, F., & Meynard, J. M. (2018). Contribution of transition theory to the study of geographical indications. *Environmental Innovation and Societal Transitions*, 27, 32–47. http://dx.doi.org/10.1016/j.eist.2017.10.002.

Bolados, P., Henriquez, F., Ceruti, C., & Sánchez, A. (2017). La eco-geo-política del agua: una propuesta desde los territorios en las luchas por la recuperación del agua en la provincia de Petorca (Zona central de Chile). *Revista Rupturas*, *8*(1), 159–191. https://doi.org/10.22458/rr.v8i1.1977.

Boltanski, L., & Chiapello, E. (1999). *Le nouvel esprit du capitalisme*. Paris: Gallimard. 980 p.

Bustos, S. (2019). *Interview by* Let's Foods Cities [video]. En: "El Sistema Alimentario de Valparaíso, Chile". https://letsfoodcities.com/home/les-villes/valparaiso (Accessed on 6 June 2019).

Cabannes, Y. & Marocchino, C. (Eds). (2018). *Integrating Food into Urban Planning*. Rome: UCL Press; FAO. http://www.fao.org/3/CA2260EN/ca2260en.pdf (Accessed on 22 August 2019).

CADEM Survey. (2018, December). El Chile que se viene. https://www.cadem.cl/encuestas/el-chile-que-viene-diciembre-2018/ (Accessed on 3June2020).

Campos, V. (2019). *Interview by* Let's Foods Cities [video]. En: "El Sistema Alimentario de Valparaíso, Chile". https://letsfoodcities.com/home/les-villes/valparaiso (Accessed on 6 June 2019).

Campos, J., & Polit, E. (2011). Nuevos enfoques para Chile Potencia Alimentaria y Forestal. Oficina de Estudios y Políticas Agrarias – ODEPA. Santiago de Chile. https://www.odepa.gob.cl/publicaciones/articulos/nuevos-enfoques-para-chile-potencia-alimentaria-y-forestal (Accessed on 3 June 2020).

Cediel, G., Reyes, M., da Costa, M. L., Martinez, E., Monteiro, C. A., Corvalán, C., & Uauy, R. (2018). Ultra-processed foods and added sugars in the Chilean diet (2010). *Public Health Nutrition*, *21*(1), 125–133. https://doi.org/10.1017/S1368980017001161.

Cid, B., & Latta, A. (2015). Agro-ecology and food sovereignty movements in Chile: Sociospatial practices for alternative peasant futures. *Annals of the Association of American Geographers*, *105*(2), 397–406. https://doi.org/10.1080/00045608.2014.985626.

Constitución Política de la República de Chile (1980).

Correa, G. (2018, 25 de Agosto). Mujeres temporeras marchan hasta el Congreso en Valparaíso para exigir sus derechos. *El Desconcierto*. https://www.eldesconcierto.cl/2018/08/25/mujeres-temporeras-marchan-hasta-el-congreso-en-valparaiso-para-exigir-sus-derechos/ (Accessed on 11May2020).

Cuadrado, C. (2020, Febrero 13). *Interview by* Marcela Gómez [digital media]. Pese a una caída del impuesto, los refrescos sin azúcar suben de precio. *Pauta*. https://www.pauta.cl/economia/impuestos-al-azucar-encarecieron-refrescos-cuyo-gravamen-disminuyo (Accessed on 3June2020).

Cueto, M. (2004). *El valor de la salud: historia de la Organización Panamericana de la Salud*. Washington: OPS.

Credit Suisse Research Institute. (2019). *Global Wealth Report 2019*. file:///C:/Users/Administrador/Downloads/global-wealth-report-2019-en%20(2).pdf (Accessed on 3June2020).

Dardot, P., & Laval, C. (2009). *La nouvelle raison du monde: Essai sur la société néolibérale*. Paris: Editions La Découverte. 498 p.

Di Girolamo, G. (2020 27 de Abril). Vida comunitaria: un antídoto contra la crisis. *Rev. Paula, La Tercera*. https://www.latercera.com/paula/vida-comunitaria-crisis-economica-coronavirus-redes-solidarias-abastecimiento-trueque/ (Accessed on 3June2020).

Dirección del Trabajo. (2020). Ingreso mínimo. https://www.dt.gob.cl/portal/1628/w3-propertyvalue-22104.html (Accessed on 3June2020).

Durán, S. (2018, Julio 4). *Interview by* Cecilia Yáñez [media]. Consumo de bebidas azucaradas disminuyó 21% tras impuesto. *La Tercera*. https://www.latercera.com/nacional/noticia/consumo-bebidas-azucaradas-disminuyo-21-tras-impuesto/229718/ (Accessed on 3June2020).

El, Bilali H. (2019). The multi-level perspective in research on sustainability transitions in agriculture and food systems: A systematic review. *Agriculture (London)*, *9*, 74. https://doi.org/10.3390/agriculture9040074.

Escenarios Hídricos 2030. (2018). Radiografía del Agua: Brecha y Riesgo Hídrico en Chile, Chile. Fundación Chile, Santiago. https://fch.cl/wp-content/uploads/2019/12/resumen-radiografia-del-agua-1.pdf (Accessed on 17June2020).

Esquinas, J. (2020, Mayo de). Sostenibilidad y ética en el sistema agroalimentario Quo vadis Terra?. En: *Ars nesciendi* "el arte de conocer la propia ignorancia". *II Sesión ciclo de conferencias online*. Fundación Instituto de Agricultura Ecológica y Sostenible -FIAES.

FAO. (2013). Alimentación escolar y las posibilidades de compra directa de la agricultura familiar: Estudio de caso en ocho países. *Brasil*. http://www.fao.org/3/a-i3413s.pdf (Accessed 17June2020).

FAO. (2015). Las compras públicas a la agricultura familiar y la seguridad alimentaria y nutricional en América Latina y el Caribe Lecciones aprendidas y experiencias. *Brasil*. http://www.fao.org/3/a-i4902s.pdf (Accessed on 17June2020).

FAO. (2017). Guía para implementar estrategias locales de compras públicas a la agricultura familiar campesina. *Bogotá, Colombia*. http://www.fao.org/3/a-i7504s.pdf (Accessed on 17June2020).

FAO; OPS. (2017). Aprobación de nueva ley de alimentos en Chile: resumen del proceso. *Santiago, Chile*. http://www.fao.org/3/a-i7692s.pdf (Accessed on 17June2020).

FAO, OPS, WFP y UNICEF. (2019). *Panorama de la seguridad alimentaria y nutricional en América Latina y el Caribe 2019*. Santiago. 135. Licencia: CC BY-NC-SA 3.0 IGO. http://www.fao.org/3/ca6979es/ca6979es.pdf (Accessed on 17June2020).

FAO. (2019). FAO reconoce internacionalmente Ley de etiquetado. *Noticias, Oficina Regional de la FAO para América Latina y el Caribe*. http://www.fao.org/americas/noticias/ver/es/c/1199927/ (Accessed on 17June2020).

FAO. (2020). Marco de la FAO para la alimentación y la nutrición escolar. Roma, *Italia*. http://www.fao.org/3/ca4091es/CA4091ES.pdf (Accessed on 17June2020).

FENAPRU (2016 18 de Noviembre). Declaración Pública emitida por FENAPRU. *Fund. Newenko*. http://newenko.org/2016/11/18/declaracion-publica-emitida-por-fenapru/ (Accessed on 3June2020).

Fragkou, M. (2020). El agua: la crisis que viene. En: 4° Sesión del Ciclo Ecoderecho. *Foros Virtuales para una Constitución del Siglo XXI, Organiza Centro de Derecho Ambiental*. Universidad de Chile.

Frantzeskaki N., Bach M., Hölscher K., & Avelino F. (2018). Introducing sustainability transitions' thinking in urban contexts. In N. Frantzeskaki, K. Hölscher, M. Bach, F. Avelino (eds), *Co-creating Sustainable Urban Futures. Future City*, 11. https://doi.org/10.1007/978-3-319-69273-9_3

Frene, C. (2020). *El agua: la crisis que viene. En: 4° Sesión del Ciclo Ecoderecho. Foros Virtuales para una Constitución del Siglo XXI. Organiza Centro de Derecho Ambiental*, Universidad de Chile.

Frens-String, J. (2018). Communists, commissars, and consumers: The politics of food on the Chilean road to socialism. *Hispanic American Historical Review*, *98*(3), 471–501. https://doi.org/10.1215/00182168-6933567.

Pobres de agua Radiografía del agua rural de Chile. (2019), *Visualización de un problema oculto. Santiago*, Chile: Centro de Derecho y Gestión de Agua UC Fundación Amulén.

Fundación Newenko. (2019). Escasez hídrica en Chile: Desafíos en el consumo humano y perspectivas en modelos comparados. *Santiago, Chile*. http://newenko.org/estudio-2019/ (Accessed on 3June2019).

Fundación Sol. (2019). Los verdaderos sueldos de Chile: Panorama actual del valor de la fuerza de trabajo usando la ESI 2018. Documentos de trabajo del área de salarios y desigualdad. Retrieved from: http://www.fundacionsol.cl/wp-content/uploads/2019/08/Los-Verdaderos-Salarios-ESI-2018.pdf (Accessed on 3June2020).

Fundación Sol. (2008). Caracterización del Sector Agro-Exportador Chileno: Una mirada general. *Cuadernos de Investigación* (8). http://www.fundacionsol.cl/wp-content/uploads/2010/09/Cuaderno-8-Sector-Agro-Exportador.pdf (Accessed on 23April2020).

Fundación Sol. (2011). Precariedad laboral y sistema productivo en Chile. *Serie "Ideas para el Buen Vivir", N°1, Área Tendencias del Trabajo*. http://www.fundacionsol.cl/wp-content/uploads/2011/12/Ideas-1-Tendencias-del-Trabajo2.pdf (Accessed on 4May2020).

Gaitán-Cremaschi, D., Klerkx, L., Duncan, J., Trienekens, J., Huenchuleo, C., Dogliotti, S., Contesse, M., & Rossing, W. (2019). Characterizing diversity of food systems in view of sustainability transitions. A review. *Agronomy for Sustainable Development*, *39*, 1. https://doi.org/10.1007/s13593-018-0550-2.

Geels, F. W. (2002). Technological transitions as evolutionary reconfiguration processes: a multilevel perspectiva and a case-study, *Research Policy*, *31*(8–9), 1257–1274. https://doi.org/10.1016/S0048-7333(02)00062-8.

Geels, F. W. (2005). *Technological transitions and system innovations: a co-evolutionary and socio-technical analysis*. Cheltenham: Edward Elgar.

Geels, F.W., & Schot, J. (2007). Typology of sociotechnical transition pathways. *Research Policy*, *36*(3), 399–417. https://doi.org/10.1016/j.respol.2007.01.003.

Gudynas. (2010). The political ecology of the global crisis and the limits of benevolent capitalism. Íconos. *Revista de Ciencias Sociales*, *36*, 53–67. https://doi.org/10.17141/iconos.36.2010.391.

Gumucio, A., & Amunátegui, R. (2017). *Aporte del sector a la economía de Chile al 2030. En: Agricultura Chilena, Reflexiones y Desafíos al 2030*. ODEPA. Santiago, Chile. https://www.odepa.gob.cl/publicaciones/documentos-e-informes/agricultura-chilena-reflexiones-y-desafios-al-2030 (Accessed on 3June2020).

Instituto Nacional de Estadísticas, Chile – INE. (2019). *Resultados de la Encuesta Suplementaria de Ingresos en la Región Metropolitana de Santiago, período 2014-2018*. Secretaría Regional Ministerial de Desarrollo Social y Familia, Santiago, Chile. http://www.desarrollosocialyfamilia.gob.cl/storage/docs/DOCUMENTO_ESI_2014-2018_RMS.pdf (Accessed on 17June2020).

Instituto Nacional de Esadísticas, Chile – INE. (2020). *Boletín Estadístico: Empleo Trimestral N°, 259*.

Ingram, J. (2015). Framing niche-regime linkage as adaptation: An analysis of learning and innovation networks for sustainable agriculture across Europe. *Journal of Rural Studies*, *40*, 59–75. https://doi.org/10.1016/j.jrurstud.2015.06.003.

IPCC. (2019). Special Report on Climate Change, Desertification, Land Degradation, Sustainable Land Management, Food Security, and Greenhouse gas fluxes in Terrestrial Ecosystems. *Summary for Policymakers*. https://www.ipcc.ch/srccl/ (Accessed on 3June2020).

JUNAEB, (2016). *Junaeb deberá adquirir insumos de productores locales y zonas rezagadas para el Programa de Alimentación Escolar*. https://www.junaeb.cl/archivos/24859 (Accessed on 17June2020).

JUNAEB, (2019). Presentación de resultados: Mapa Nutricional 2019, *Chile*. https://www.junaeb.cl/wp-content/uploads/2013/03/Mapa-Nutricional-2019-1.pdf (Accessed on 17June2020).

Campesina, La Vía. (2016). Conferencia Internacional de la Reforma Agraria Declaración de Marabá. En: Land Research Action Network (LRAN). *Nuevos desafíos y estrategias en la defensa de la tierra y el territorio. N°4 Informativos LRAN*. https://www.social.org.br/files/pdf/1_NUEVOSDESAFIOSCompletoESPANHOL.pdf (Accessed on 23April2020).

Lang, T., & Heasman, M. (2015). *Food wars: the global battle for mouths, minds and markets*. London: Routledge.

Letelier, E., Vanhulst, J., Cid, B., & González, R. (2019). Panorama de la economía social en Chile: la brecha entre definiciones y sustantivas. *Revesco*, *132*, 144–168. http://dx.doi.org/10.5209/REVE.65484.

Lira, M. (2019). *Normativas y políticas contra la obesidad en Chile. U de Estudios, JUNAEB. Santiago*. https://www.junaeb.cl/wp-content/uploads/2013/03/Normativas-y-pol%C3%ADticas-contra-la-Obesidad.pdf (Accessed on 17June2020).

López, A. (2013). *Desarticulación y resistencia. Movimiento obrero y sindicalismo en dictadura. Chile y Argentina, 1973-1983. Tesis para optar al grado de Magíster en Estudios Latinoamericanos*. Santiago, Chile. Universidad de Chile.

Llorca-Jaña, M., Robles, C., Navarrete-Montalvo, J., & Araya, R. (2017). La agricultura y la élite agraria chilena a través de los catastros agrícolas, *c.*1830-1855. *Revista Historia*, 2(50), 597–639.

Madariaga, M. (2020). Participación Ciudadana en el Proyecto de Ley Marco de Cambio Climático. Policy brief N° 20, Observatorio Ley de Cambio Climático. http://leycambioclimatico.cl/policy-brief-participacion-ciudadana-en-el-proyecto-de-ley-marco-de-cambio-climatico/ (Accessed on 16June2020).

McMichael, P. (2005). Global development and the corporate food regime. *Research in Rural Sociology and Development*, *11*, 265–299.

McMichael, P. (2009). A food regime genealogy. *The Journal of Peasant Studies*, *36*(1), 139–169. https://doi.org/10.1080/03066150902820354.

Ministerio de Obras Públicas-MOP. (2013). Estrategia nacional de recursos hídricos 2012- 2025. https://www.mop.cl/Documents/ENRH_2013_OK.pdf (Accessed on 3June2020).

Ministerio de Obras Públicas-MOP. (2020). Proyecto del Reglamento Ley 20.998. *Programa de Agua Potable Rural. Dirección de Obras Hidráulicas.* http://www.doh.gov.cl/APR/Paginas/proyectoreglamento.aspx (Accessed on 3June2020).

Ministerio de Salud de Chile-MINSAL. (2012). Ley 20.606 Sobre Composición Nutricional de los Alimentos y su Publicidad. https://www.leychile.cl/Navegar?idNorma=1041570 (Accessed on 17June2020).

Ministerio de Salud de Chile-MINSAL. (2015). Infografía: El impacto económico de las Enfermedades No Transmisibles (ENT) en Chile en tres dimensiones, *En: Boletín semestral, Economía y Salud 2016* 1(10). Chile: Ministerio de Salud.

Ministerio de Salud de Chile-MINSAL. (2015b). Ley No 20.869 Sobre Publicidad de los Alimentos. Chile. https://www.leychile.cl/Navegar?idNorma=1083792 (Accessed on 17June2020).

Ministerio de Salud de Chile-MINSAL. (2017a). Primeros resultados de Encuesta Nacional de Salud 2016–2017. Retrieved from: https://www.minsal.cl/wp-content/uploads/2017/11/ENS-2016-17_PRIMEROS-RESULTADOS.pdf (Accessed on 3 June, 2020)

Ministerio de Salud de Chile-MINSAL. (2017b). Política Nacional de Alimentación y Nutrición. http://www.bibliotecaminsal.cl/wp/wp-content/uploads/2018/01/BVS_POL%C3%8DTICA-DE-ALIMENTACI%C3%93N-Y-NUTRICI%C3%93N.pdf (Accessed on 3June2020).

Montalba, R., Infante, A., Contreras, A., & Vieli, L. (2016). Agroecología en Chile: precursores, pioneros y su legado. *Agroecología*, *11*(2), 69–76. https://revistas.um.es/agroecologia/article/view/330111 (Accessed on23 April, 2018).

Nyéléni (2007). Declaration of Nyeleni. *Forum for Food Sovereignty*. https://nyeleni.org/spip.php?article290 (Accessed on 17July2019).

ODEPA. (2019). *Caracterización de la cadena nacional de productos orgánicos*. Santiago, Chile: Ministerio de Agricultura. https://www.odepa.gob.cl/wp-content/uploads/2020/01/InfCadenaOrganicaNacional2019.pdf (Accessed on 3June2020).

OECD. (2012). *Environmental outlook to 2050: The consequences of inaction*. Paris: OECD Publishing. https://doi.org/10.1787/1999155x.

OECD; FAO. (2013). *Perspectivas Agrícolas 2013*. Texcoco: UAC. https://doi.org/10.1787/agr_outlook-2013-es.

OECD. (2016). *Chile: Prioridades de políticas para un crecimiento más fuerte y equitativo*. Paris: OECD Publishing. https://doi.org/10.1787/9789264251199-es.

OECD. (2018). *Estudios Económicos de la OCDE: Chile 2018*. Paris: OECD Publishing. http://www.oecd.org/economy/surveys/Chile-2018-OECD-economic-sruvey-Spanish.pdf (Accessed on 20June2020).

OECD. (2020). *Income inequality (indicator)*. 10.1787/459aa7f1-en (Accessed on 20June2020).

Oficina Económica y Comercial de España en Chile. (2019). Informe Económico y Comercial: Chile 2019. 46 p. https://www.icex.es/icex/es/navegacion-principal/todos-nuestros-servicios/informacion-de-mercados/paises/navegacion-principal/el-mercado/estudios-informes/DOC2019821888.html?idPais=CL (Accessed on 20June2020).

Olea, I. (2019). Efecto del aumento del impuesto a las bebidas gaseosas azucaradas en Chile: precios y comportamiento del consumidor, *Tesis para optar al grado de Magister en Economía Aplicada.Memoria para optar al Título de Ingeniero Civil Industrial*. Santiago, Chile: Universidad de Chile.

Oppliger, A., Höhl, J., & Fragkou, M. (2019). *Water scarcity: disclosing its hybrid origins in the Bueno river basin* (pp. 9–27). Chile: Revista de Geografía Norte Grande 73. http://revistanortegrande.uc.cl/ojs/index.php/nortegrande/article/view/1098 (Accessed on 3June2020).

Otero, G. (2013). El régimen alimentario neoliberal y su crisis: Estado, agroempresas multinacionales y biotecnología. *Antípoda. Revista de Antropología y Arqueología*, *17*, 49–78. http://dx.doi.org/10.7440/antipoda17.2013.04.

PAHO. (2015). *Alimentos y bebidas ultraprocesados en América Latina: tendencias, efecto sobre la obesidad e implicaciones para las políticas públicas*. Washington, DC: Departamento de Enfermedades no Transmisibles y Salud Mental. https://iris.paho.org/bitstream/handle/10665.2/7698/9789275318645_esp.pdf?seque (Accessed on 3June2020).

PAHO. (2019). Alimentos y bebidas ultraprocesados en América Latina: ventas, fuentes, perfiles de nutrientes e implicaciones. *Washington, DC*. Retrieved from: https://iris.paho.org/handle/10665.2/51523 (Accessed on 3June2020).

Painel, V. (2020 Abril 13) *Interview by* Radio Minga [audio]. Cooperativa Mapuche llaman a que se operativicen fondos fiscales ante emergencia sanitaria. https://radiokurruf.org/2020/04/13/audio-cooperativa-mapuche-llama-a-que-se-operativicen-fondos-fiscales-para-adquisicion-de-produccion-local-ante-emergencia-sanitaria/

Portilla, B. (2000). La política agrícola en Chile: lecciones de tres décadas. *Serie Desarrollo Productivo*, *68* 79p. CEPAL. https://repositorio.cepal.org/handle/11362/4674 (Accessed on 23April2020).

Ríos, S., & Núñez, N. (2016). Organic agrifood chain in southern Chile: tensions conditioning its potential value. *Estudios Sociales*, *25*(47), 39–62. https://doi.org/10.24836/es.v25i47.308.

Robles, C. (2003). Expansión y transformación de la agricultura en una economía exportadora. La transición al capitalismo agrario en Chile (1850-1930). *Historia Agraria*, *29*, 45–80.

Rosset, P. (2018). Reforma agraria popular: El nuevo llamado a la reforma agraria en el siglo XXI. En: Land Research Action Network (LRAN). *Nuevos desafíos y estrategias en la defensa de la tierra y el territorio. N°4 Informativos LRAN.*

https://www.social.org.br/files/pdf/1_NUEVOSDESAFIOSCompletoESPANHOL.pdf (Accessed on 23April2020).

Rotmans, J., & Loorbach, D. (2010). Towards a better understanding of transitions and their governance, a systemic and reflexive approach, as Part II. In J. Grin, J. Rotmans, & J. Schot (eds), *Transitions to sustainable development: new directions in the study of long term transformative change* (pp. 105–120). London: Routledge.

Saravia, P., Carroza, N., & Cid, B. (2018). Economic heterogeneity in territories of the Valparaíso Region - Chile: Approaches and emergence of other economic forms. *Población & Sociedad [online]*, *25*(1), 103–131. http://dx.doi.org/10.19137/pys-2018-250104.

Schuster, J. P., Tapia, F. (2017). El Modelo de Gestión Comunitaria del Agua Potable Rural en Chile: Contexto Institucional, Normativo e Intenciones de Reforma. *Foro Jurídico*, 16, 110–120. http://revistas.pucp.edu.pe/index.php/forojuridico/article/view/19865 (Accessed on 17June2020).

Smith, A., Stirling, A., & Berkhout, F. (2005). The governance of sustainable sociotechnical transitions. *Research Policy*, *34*(10), 1491–1510. https://doi.org/10.1016/j.respol.2005.07.005.

Smith, A. (2012). Capítulo VI Traduciendo sustentabilidades entre nichos ecológicos y regímenes socio-técnicos. En:. In H. Thomas, M. Fressoli, & G. Santos (eds), *Tecnología, desarrollo y democracia: nuevos estudios sobre dinámicas socio-técnicas de exclusión/inclusión social.* Buenos Aires: Ministerio de Ciencia, Tecnología e Innovación Productiva de la Nación.

Stehr, A., Debels, P., Arumi, J. L., Alcayaga, H., & Romero, F. (2010). Modelación de la respuesta hidrológica al cambio climático: experiencias de dos cuencas de la zona centro-sur de Chile. *Tecnología y ciencias del agua*, *1*(4), 37–58.

Taillie, L. S., Reyes, M., Colchero, M. A., Popkin, B., & Corvalán, C. (2020). An evaluation of Chile's law of food labeling and advertising on sugar-sweetened beverage purchases from 2015 to 2017: A before-and-after study. *PLoS Medicine*, *17*(2), e1003015. https://doi.org/10.1371/journal.pmed.1003015.

Transforma Alimentos. (2018). Programa Estratégico Nacional. *Santiago*. http://transformaalimentos.cl/assets/docs/documentos/2018-Transforma_Alimentos-Brochure.pdf (Accessed on 3June2020).

Therond, O., Duru, M., Roger-Estrade, J., & Richard, G. (2017). A new analytical framework of farming system and agriculture model diversities. A review. *Agronomy for Sustainable Development*, *37*, 21. https://doi.org/10.1007/s13593-017-0429-7.

Thezá, M., Flores, D., & Gac, D. (2017). Reforma Agraria en Chile, ¿Palimpsesto de otra ruralidad? Reflexiones y propuestas. *Polis, Revista Latinoamericana*, *47*, 137–164. https://journals.openedition.org/polis/12499 (Accessed on 28April2020).

Valdés, S. (2015). Feminización del empleo y trabajo precario en las agriculturas latinoamericanas globalizadas. *Cuadernos De antropología Social*, *41*, 39–54. https://doi.org/10.34096/cas.i41.1595.

Vargas, X., Mcphee, J., Vicuna, S., Suarez, F., Meza, F., Daniele, L., Rondanelli, R., Lagos-Zúñiga, M., Mendoza, P., Bambach, N., Boisier, J.P., Cepeda, J., Vasquez, N., Morales, D., Sandoval, J., Negri, A., & Caro, A. (2017). Actualización balance hídrico en Chile. Metodología y desafíos de modelación, *En: XXIII Congreso chileno de ingeniería hidráulica, Sociedad Chilena de Ingeniería Hidráulica*. Chile: Valparaíso.

Vercelli, D. (2019, Septiembre 11). *Interview by* Rosario Zanetta [digital media]. La fórmula de coca cola para lograr vender más productos sin azúcar. *PULSO Boomerg*. https://www.pauta.cl/negocios/bloomberg/el-camino-de-coca-cola-para-reducir-el-azucar

Vivero-Pol, J. L. (2017). Food as commons or commodity? Exploring the links between normative valuations and agency in food transition. *Sustainability*, 9(3), 442. 10.3390/su9030442

von Wolffersdorff, J. (2019, Noviembre 7). *Interview by* Joannon, F [video]. Jeannette von Wolffersdorff y la desigualdad social: "Repensemos la posición de la elite con la idea de repartir patrimonio". *El Mostrador*. https://www.youtube.com/user/mostradortelevision/videos (Accessed on 3June2020).

Wolfram, M. (2016). Conceptualizing urban transformative capacity: A framework for research and policy. *Cities*, *51*, 121–130. https://doi.org/10.1016/j.cities.2015.11.011.

Yáñez, J.C. (1930-1950). Los pobres están invitados a la mesa. Debates y proyectos transnacionales de alimentación popular en América del Sur. *Historia Critica*, *71*, 69–91. https://doi.org/10.7440/histcrit71.2019.04.

Part III

Social Innovation and Human Capital

7 Entrepreneurship, associativity and social technologies in rural communities

A reading from the Papal Encyclical Laudato Si in Colombia

Marietta Buchelli and Juan Fernando Álvarez

Introduction

One of the greatest challenges facing the Colombian economy is to provide its citizens with conditions for their mobilization as actors in the social, economic, environmental, political and cultural development of their territories. The above in a context where rural territories have not received the same level of public endowments as urban areas. The efforts that the State has made to face this challenge go hand in hand with the support of social organizations and aim to promote a shared commitment in the management of the local and strengthen actions that contribute to the efficient functioning of the markets.

The Catholic Church also supports communities and a tool for this are the Papal Encyclicals that serve as guiding exhortations for the Church's task to face the great problems of humanity and build a new society. The Papal Laudato Si Encyclical of 2015 advocates collective responsibility based on a change in culture and knowledge, emphasizes the local actor and goes towards an alternative economy to protect the common home. Said encyclical revives the discussion of promoting peasant associativism that had enlivened the encyclical Populorum Progressio of March 26, 196, which had repercussions in some rural and small municipality cooperatives in Colombia.

The objective of the chapter is to demonstrate how some transformative organizational ecosystems in Colombia define response strategies to the challenges of the society-nature relationship that are framed within the Papal Laudato Si Encyclical, which offers action alternatives to this relationship to confront the ecological situation of the world. This chapter also aims to observe the response strategies to these issues through the practices followed by six solidarity organizations in Colombia based in rural areas. To achieve its aims, this article is divided into seven sections. After this introduction, a brief approach is made to the existing relationships between the management of organizations from a society-nature perspective, organizational ecosystems. Also, an analysis is made of the Encyclical Laudato Si as a critical approach to global agendas that do not advocate limitation in economic growth. In the third section, the case study and its observation units are justified as the methodology used.

In the fourth, the information gathering tools carried out and the relationship made between organizational management, cooperative principles and Laudato Si are studied in depth. The fifth presents the main findings of the study in the selected organizations. In the sixth, the findings are discussed in light of the socioeconomic context, poverty, inequality, the persistence or otherwise of different magnitudes of violence and the related possibility of constituting civil groups and the environmental context. In the last section, the conclusions are presented and discussed.

Relations between the management of solidarity organizations from a society-nature approach

Management sciences have taken science concepts such as biology to explain the trajectory, emergence and evolution of organizations. For authors such as Mars and Bronstein (2018), the notion of an organizational ecosystem implies that human systems and organizational systems work as ecosystems and also exhibit desirable properties that are similar to what one would see in nature. Anthropology makes its contribution to the observation of organizations. González and Acevedo (2012: 21–23) point out the importance of the society-nature interaction from culture and human activity channeled in the forms of human organization. Organizations contain human activities that allow it to transform as a system.

The concept of Ecosystem, in biological terms, contains five features which can be combined with an organization's system to understand its evolution. The characteristics of the Ecosystem are, according to Mars and Bronstein (2018: 384): "a) they consist of a set of nodes, within which multiple players function and interact; b) nodes are linked to each other by flows of information and resources; c) not every node is linked, and those that exist vary in strength and direction (positive, neutral or negative); d) nodes grow, shrink, are added, and are lost over time; e) nodes emerge from bottom-up processes and persist or fail based on how they are networked; they are not designed for particular functions".

Mars and Bronstein (2018) make an analogy between the biological ecosystem and the organizational ecosystem, arguing that nodes correspond to various organized human groups; nodes have flows of information and resources such as people and money; organizations face changing and fast environments like any ecosystem. In summary, the authors argue that the biological perspective allows us to have a better understanding of human organizations, the networks and the systems that compose them, as well as the patterns and processes associated with the changes in these systems over time. Regarding the global agendas, Francisco criticizes them, arguing that the agendas prepared to respond to the environmental crisis have not had satisfactory results due to the lack of a political will that allows their practical execution. This statement supports the position of authors, such as Sachs (2017: 2582), for whom the 2030 Agenda does not recognize the limits of growth and that instead this proposal is to maintain the model that responds to this characteristic. The encyclical makes exhortations that translate into methodological proposals, orientations and actions for both development practice and religion (Deneulin and Zampini-Davies, 2017). Francisco's Carta Magna proposes an individualized action in each condensed state in what encompasses the concept of Common Good and supported in a cultural revolution. Sachs reinforces the above arguing that the encyclical attacks the economic and financial systems that take away from the common good (Sachs, 2017: 2581). Culture turns to environmental ethics in relation to those responsible for the environmental problems mentioned in the current debates on the moral responsibility of the individual and of the institutions in the face of these problems.

According to Sachs (2017), the encyclical presupposes that the looting of the planet has already exceeded the ecological limits without solving the problem of poverty while this great dilemma of our day is far from being addressed by the 2030 agenda. The author maintains that the agenda is protecting the growth model, a model that has always been prioritized over the protection of nature. The same author notes that goal 12 of the 2030 agenda emphasizes the proper use of resources. Instead, Laudato does suggest a strategy embedded in the change of culture based on the fact that it is the rich who have to change, not the poor; it is wealth that needs to be relieved, not poverty; the common good is the great unknown of the neoclassical economy (Sachs: 2017: 2580, 2581).

Barkin begins his essay on a new social paradigm with a vision that regroups what Laudato Si proposes and what the debate on social and solidarity economy emphasizes. For the author, "The crises we suffer today are the result of the centralized form of capital accumulation... the result of the dominant paradigm based on market rationality. To face this situation, new social contracts are needed, taking into account the contributions of the social, solidarity and ecological economy disciplines... that offer other ways of raising the fundamental problem of the society-nature relationship" (Barkin, 2012: 42). Research such as that by Alió y Fransualdo de Azevedo (2015) answers these questions. In their article, the authors analyze the population's ability to become an active social actor in the process of change towards a more just society with better relations of balance with nature. They start from the hypothesis that social and solidarity economy enterprises form new forms of organization that have a very positive impact on socio-ecological transformation.

Continuing with Barkin, the author emphasizes the accumulation of capital in few hands, product of the productive organization of the current system. His argument dialogues with what Francisco maintains in part 104 of the encyclical "... GM crops imply concentration of productive land in the hands of a few" (Laudato, Si). The same author expresses that "in this production system, human misery has been unprecedented in the history of 'civilizations,' accompanied by the degradation of many ecosystems around the world" (Barkin, 2012: 42). To his concern, the encyclical states "Poor countries need to have as a priority the eradication of poverty... and pay attention to the high consumption of privileged sectors" (Laudato Si, 172).

Barkin argues that studies of social economy and solidarity economies lack the seals of acceptance or legitimacy that the fields arising from the recognition of the environmental crisis enjoy. In this regard, the Pope also calls for the solidarity organization: "In some places, cooperatives are being developed for the exploitation of renewable energies... while the existing world order is impotent to assume responsibilities, the local organization can make a difference" (Laudato Si, YEAR: 179).

Therefore, this chapter identifies transforming ecosystems as organizations that influence the territory based on self-managed practices. Emphasis is placed on the organization as a repository of management practices that produce integral transformations, both within the organization and the environment in which they operate. Using an interdisciplinary perspective with an emphasis on the society-nature relationship, it is argued that this relationship is supported by civil society organized in various forms. Then, civil society creates different expressions of collective forms of grouping to address any common cause. In this document, the collective forms are related to the companies of the social and solidarity economy. This is why it is imperative to understand transformative organizational ecosystems in terms of their role in the society-nature relationship.

Methodology

The methodological approach is a case study which has different perspectives. For some teachers, it is a complete research methodology (Eisenhardt 1989; Robson, 1993; Yin, 1994); for other researchers, the approach is a description and analysis, in depth of a limited or circumscribed system (Merriam, 2002: 40). According to Yin (1994), a case study is an empirical investigation that examines a contemporary phenomenon in a real context when the boundaries between the phenomenon and the real context are not clearly evident; this is why multiple sources of evidence are required (Yin, 1994: 17). In this proposal, the types of case study proposed by Yin (1994) are followed, defining that the best option, for the research proposal, is the multiple case study with three observation units. The option is justified because the purpose of the research is to highlight a phenomenon, which, without being rare, has not yet been available to the scientific community (Yin, 1994). The selection of cases rests on heterogeneous and homogeneous criteria. Heterogeneous in relation to the sector of the economy to which they belong. This criterion allows to extend the robustness of the conclusions and make them transferable to other cases. Homogeneous in that they favor an innovative perspective of intellectual debate in relation to the Solidarity Economy and its contribution as a management strategy to the challenges of Laudato Si. The observation units are sub-analysis units that allow the depth of the case study to be expanded (Yin, 1994).

The definition of the multiple case study is:

Solidarity management in response to the challenges of the society-nature relationship expressed in the Laudato Si:

a. The case of Solidarity Microfranchises which are "a business model aimed at the vulnerable population, which seeks to transfer to the associates of a solidarity company the tools necessary to operate a business that has been successful and profitable - or projected to be. It can be replicated on a smaller scale with a relatively low investment (UAEOS, 2015). The micro franchise comes about from the promotion of the Colombian State through two public bodies that, after a public call, choose a private operator. The operator, Morrosquillo Institute Corporation, has the function of promoting cooperative associativity in communities in the Gulf of Morrosquillo. The organizations that emerge from the process of associative development are called Solidarity Microfranchises.
b. the case of the Association of fish farmers of the Villeros dam, Department of Córdoba, Colombia, as a case of local public development,
c. the case of two groups of solidarity organizations from the tertiary sector located in the department of Antioquia:

i. credit cooperative and family recreation- Creafam-; Credit union San Pío X -Coogranada- and Cooperativa Infantil Granadina - Cooingra- in the Municipality of Granada and
ii. the Pío XII Savings and Credit Cooperative of the Municipality of Cocorná.

Observation unities were defined as:

a. The orientations of Laudato Si and its relation to the principles of the doctrine of the Solidarity Economy.
b. The practices of solidarity organizations and their impact on the understanding of the territory.

Data gathering tools

Twenty interviews were conducted between 2017 and 2018 of people linked to the cases and to promoters and officials of the City Halls in the case areas. Three workshops were held to identify the relationship between Laudato Si and the management of organizations. The workshops were attended by management associates of each case study (Table 7.1).

The Laudato Si relationship, management practices and society-nature relationship were approached taking the principles of solidarity economy with the numbers of the Laudato Si convergent with the principles. This exercise was carried out taking into account that social and solidarity economy organizations orient their practices based on their organizational identity. In the workshops, it was found, in situ, whether such theoretical convergence of orientations, exhortations and speeches have or not a handle on the management practices of the organizations under study. Table 7.2 shows the selected numerals of the encyclical that were discussed both in the workshops and in the interviews.

Findings

After conducting the workshops in each of the areas with the selected organizations, a collective approach to the society-nature approach was found and an understanding of the territory nuanced by the contexts of development of the experiences that prevent generalizing common trajectories from the point of view of organizational results.

Case a. Solidarity micro franchises

Most of the links in the economic circuit were organized except for workers linked to the kitchen trades, who in turn received equipment to make a semi-industrial process for preserving fish and other seafood. This linked to the little support after the creation of companies, by the public financing agencies, generated a high dependence on the private promoter who, finding no possibility of participation in the conduct of business, by determination of the entities public funding, ended up gradually separating from the microfranchise program. Without accompaniment, farmers, merchants of basic products such as groceries, fishermen and cooks tried to maintain their associative ties but the impossibility of generating commercial outlets to maintain the companies to which they were linked as owners and managers, paying the high fees

Table 7.1 Relation of interviews carried out between 2017 and 2018

No.	*Interview*	*Organization*	
1	Director of the operative institution that supports microfranchises	Institute of Morrosquillo	Municipality of Montería, Córdoba Departament
2	Associate	Cooperative La Gloria	Vereda La Gloria, Municipality of San Antero, Córdoba Departament
3	Owner of the shop – Microfranquicia-	Country Shop (Terra&Mar –Social Food)	
4	President of the Association	Association of Fish Farmers Represa de Villeros	Municipality of Coveñas, Sucre Departament
5	Interview of two civil servants	Mayorship of Coveñas	
6	Group interview with three associates	COOGRANADA	Municipality of Granada, Antioquia departament
7	Associate	COOGRANADA	
8	Associate	TEJIPAZ	
9	Directive associate	COOINGRA	Municipality of Granada, Antioquia departament
10	Group meeting with five associates	CREAFAM	Municipio de Granada, Antioquia
11	Historian from Granada	Granada	Municipality of Granada, Antioquia
12	Manager	Cooperative Pío XII from Cocorná	Cocorná, Antioquia
13	Associate	Cane sugar association –Asociación de productores de panela (Asopaco)	Municipality of Cocorná, Antioquia
14	Associate	Propez Association off ish farmers of the municipality Cocorná	Municipality of Cocorná, Antioquia
15	Entepreneurs	Visit to ventures -COPLÁTANO. Cocornense association of banana producers (Acoplátano) in the municipality of Cocorná -Aromatic project	Municipality of Cocorná, Antioquia
16	Solidarity network markets	Manager	Municipality of Granada, Antioquia

Source: Compiled by the authors.

Table 7.2 Numerals of the Laudato Si that converge with the principles of the social and solidarity economy

Numerals of Laudato Si´	*Convergence of solidarity economy-environment*
5, 23, 25, 44, 47, 48, 50, 51, 53, 54, 56, 57, 127, 128, 224	**Economy-environment relationship.** Diagnosis that evidences relations between the ecological crisis (climate warming) with its consequent need for ecological conversion and the importance of a change in the hegemonic production and consumption models (consumerist, short term, technocratic, with intensive use of fuels, extractivist model, with relationships of domination between countries, inequitable, exclusive, speculative, with divinized marketing)
63, 66, 160	**Ethical-economical horizons to solve the environmental crisis of the "Common Home"**
30, 37, 58, 109, 111, 152, 153, 157, 197, 211	Need for theoretical-practical perspective of State intervention for the defense of the public (democratization of water, housing, transport, among others)
49, 93, 112, 125, 129, 143, 144, 145, 147, 148, 179, 206, 213, 219, 232	Importance of community actions (cooperatives, associations, among others) and cultural diversity as alternatives for economic and environmental development

Source: self-made.

to lease spaces for agricultural production and maintaining equipment for fishing, caused a dent and a hard organizational setback. In turn, the canning equipment ended up abandoned very close to the establishment of restaurants that only wanted to link to the project to improve their commercial infrastructure.

Case b. Association of fish farmers of the Villeros Dam

The association of fish farmers of the Represa de Villeros had a productive vocation to raise fish in the Villeros Dam of the Municipality of Coveñas, also in the Gulf of Morrosquillo but in the Department of Sucre. After a conflict over the use of water from the Dam for its productive activity and whose main antagonist was a military detachment that protects one of the most important oil-pipeline interconnections in Colombia, Caño Limón - Coveñas, fishermen were displaced from the place of their economic activity. Fishing and raising fish in a dam is relatively simple but generates water pollution for human consumption. To resume their business, the fishermen met with officials of the

Municipality of Coveñas and technicians of the same entity operating the solidarity microfranchises. However, the result was different. The Morrosquillo Institute Corporation managed to adapt an innovative system of production and breeding of weights under a system of swimming pools or ponds that had the characteristic of making use of bacterial biotechnology to make the least possible use of water in the process.

The initiative promoted through resources of the Mayor's Office was just the beginning of an accompaniment process between the municipal public body and the technical operator that resulted in a technical, financial and associative viability expressed in the generation of a breeding and cultivation model of clean fish that in turn serves as an economic complement to the work of the partners involved and that has improved their employability and heritage, as well as serving to expand the capacities of the members of the association of fish farmers.

Case c. Solidarity organizations in the municipality of Granada and Cocorná

In the east of the Department of Antioquia, the Municipalities of Granada and Cocorná are configured as exemplary territories for the development of cooperative actions for the common good. This territory is of agricultural vocation and in its history it has been able to recover after a process of cruelty against civil society by the main armed groups related to guerrillas and paramilitaries, some of the worst that Colombia suffered.

Years before the destruction, these Antioquia towns were exemplary scenarios of the cooperative movement of all of their population by three cooperatives which divided the more than 15,000 families available to be associated. But the destruction and resurgence of war brought about the displacement of the great majority of its inhabitants. For example, in the last census of the Municipality of Granada, 10,000 inhabitants were registered and after the worst moments of the war, after the explosion of a bomb in the community, it was recorded that there were only nine people left in the municipal area.

At the end of the 20th century, after the destruction, massacres and kidnapping of the inhabitants of these Municipalities, the savings and credit cooperatives of these towns provided the economic and social organization means to rebuild them. The economic means were sought by activating the accumulated social contributions of the partners willing to rebuild the town and their aggregation served as a counterpart for the request for resources to the State for reconstruction. In addition, they established incentives for entrepreneurship projects in the town, such as zero interest loans, co-financing of projects and technical support to projects. This was very significant in the municipality of Cocorná where the Pío XII cooperative has been the financing and management entity of the majority of economic initiatives such as transport, tourism, associated work, producer association, among others.

The means of social organization consisted in appealing to the cooperation between cooperatives to make use of the facilities of other cooperatives in cities where the inhabitants of these municipalities who fled the violence went and thus identify, congregate and generate collective actions such as fairs of recollection of resources for reconstruction. This happened in the Municipalities of Cocorná and Granada. These strategies were joined by the creation of a cooperative for children and young people to motivate the civic reconstruction of the citizens of the Municipality. The children's cooperative in Granada, COOGRANADA, was created as a hybrid institution supported by the two main cooperatives of the Municipality, COOGRANADA and CREAFAM, which economically disputed the resources of the residents of the Municipality. However, in the social aspect, they cooperated for what they considered the common good. The following video shows part of the experience of the children's cooperative (CREAFAM TV, 2017). By 2019, these cooperatives are the fundamental bastion of the development of their territory. Their initiatives transcend the economic sphere and end up bringing together initiatives for the environment, the strengthening of culture, education for cooperation and the development of participation. Obviously, this has had an impact on the state authorities coming from the cooperative structure or must be endorsed by them to have social validity. Thus, in the towns of Granada and Cocorná, the vestiges of a common message are printed on each corner: Cooperation as an alternative for citizen construction, reconstruction and co-construction.

Discussion

In this chapter, the cases analyzed are limited to territorial particularities related to the socioeconomic context such as poverty, inequality, persistence or not of different magnitudes of violence and the related possibility of constitution of civil groups and the environmental context. For example, in the case of the Gulf of Morrosquillo, the evidence documented by other research shows how there is a cause-effect relationship (and vice versa) between poverty and environmental destruction and also shows how public discourse continues to feed such a negative circle since it considers that the three sources of economy are: intensive fishing, harmful livestock and beach, sea and party tourism. In the case of the east of Antioquia, the cooperatives set up self-management practices given the absence of the State and thereby rebuilt their villages and their economy and energized their local development by appealing to the economic networks and circuits. Therefore, in Morrosquillo there was an attempt to exogenously promote development and in Antioquia the promotion was endogenous. The organizational practices found go against the discourse of local development promoted by the Public Administration. The solidarity organizations visited develop initiatives for sustainable agriculture, community tourism, artisanal fishing and fish farming, appealing in all cases to social, indigenous and vernacular technologies that exemplify the society-nature relationship. Just as the practices developed in the cases analyzed are close to the Laudato Si, also from an applied reading of the Laudato Si, there are clues and paths to meet the challenges of the organizations and contribute to managing their sustainability.

Conclusion

The study reinforces the contribution of the association, of social and solidarity economy organizations to the territories. Each case represents what development support agencies as well as what is expressed in the scientific literature show about territory, community and economy. The text constitutes a basis for projecting the study towards the comparison of Laudato Si and the 2030 Agenda in terms of the importance of local organizations as executors of the society-nature relationship; social and solidarity economy organizations that, because of their roots in the local, have an understanding of the territory with sufficient strength to be the protagonists of the global agendas.

In the case of the cooperatives studied, it is evident that management practices have emphasized the protection and reinforcement of their territory, such as the initiative to maintain the memory of the events with the construction of the "Hall of Nevermore", a local museum that reflects what happened in the municipality of Granada. The case cooperatives have been protagonists of the protection of their community and of understanding the territory as a space that goes beyond the politically defined, for example, the reconstruction actions of the municipality of Granada carried out by displaced partners. In these cases, there is a reorientation of the political control of the territory; this aspect can be further investigated with the same cases or with others, which contributes to strengthening the guidelines of the Laudato Si and other agendas. In addition, the recreational aspect is absent or invisible taking into account its importance for the reconstruction of a territory. The cooperatives studied have as one of their pillars the recreational as a tool of peace and progress.

Regarding the economic space understood as the place of production and exchange, the case of microfranchises and the case of fishermen reflect different orientations. In microfranchising, it is not possible to identify a defense of the territory, but endogenous isolated initiatives that protect, stimulate and redirect the market, as in the case of fish farmers.

These cases reflect an endogenous local development that needs to be visible to address some deficiencies such as certain forms of public financing that harm the local development or the small concurrence of small organizations to the project financing market due to the educational level and technological access of their Associates. Publicizing these cases increases the potential that these organizations have because they have innovative production processes and carry out an economy that allows them to have links with various instances of the territory, such as city halls and other forms of organization. Subsequent research can also emphasize the limitations of the social and solidarity economy and its contribution to the global agendas, the successes of this economy and the requirements to strengthen its contributions to the global agendas in concurrence with all other ways of creating economies.

References

Alió y Fransualdo de Azevedo. 2015. *La Economía Social y Solidaria en la transición ambiental, Mercator, Fortaleza, 14*(3), 89–108. set/dez. 2015 10. 4215/RM2015.1403.0006.

Álvarez, J. 2019. La economía solidaria en Colombia y las estructuras de apoyo estatal: disonancias y expresiones de una economía en construcción. In J. Álvarez, C. Marcuello, L. Morais, M. Radrigán, & J. De Sá (coordinadores), *En Anuario iberoamericano de la economía social No.3-2018*. Valencia: OIBESCOOP - CIRIEC.

Álvarez, J., Zabala, H., García, A., & Orrego, C. 2015. *Marco para el fomento de la economía solidaria en territorios rurales de Colombia*. Bogotá: UAEOS.

Barkin, D. 2012. Hacia un nuevo paradigma social. *En: Polis, Revista de la Universidad Bolivariana, 11*(33), 41–57.

Centro de Memoria Histórica. 2016. *Granada: Memorias de guerra, resistencia y reconstrucción*. Bogotá: Imprenta Nacional de Colombia.

COOGRANADA. 2015. *Informes de gestión COOGRANADA*. Recuperado de: https://www.coogranada.coop/coogranada/informes

Deneulin, Zampini-Davies. 2017. Engaging development and religion: Methodological groundings. *World Development*, 99(201), 110–121.

Eisenhardt, K. 1989. Building theories from case study research. *The Academy of Management Review, 14*(4), 532–555.

González, F., & Acevedo, D. 2012. *La Institucionalización del tema ambiental en la universidad. JavegrafN6. Pontificia Universidad Javeriana Bogotá, impresiones Estudio de caso: historia y gestión del Instituto de Estudios Ambientales para el Desarrollo – IDEADE- Ensayo Ambiente y Desarrollo*, Pontificia Universidad Javeriana. https://revistas.javeriana.edu.co/index.php/teoxaveriana/article/view/20967

Mars, M., & Bronstein, J. 2018. The promise of the organizational ecosystem metaphor: An argument for biological rigor. *Journal of Management Inquiry*, 27(4), 382–391. 10.1177/1056492617706546

Merriam, S. B. A. 2002. *Qualitative Research in Practice: Examples for Discussion and Analysis* (1st ed.). San Francisco, CA: Jossey-Bass.

Robson, C. 1993. Real World Research: *A Resource for Social Scientists and Practitioner-Researchers*. Oxford: Blackwell Publishers Inc.

Sachs, W. 2017. The Sustainable Development Goals and Laudato si': varieties of Post-Development? *Third World Quarterly*, *38*(12), 2573–2587. https://doi.org/10.1080/01436597.2017.1350822.

Yin, R. K. 1994. *Case Study Research Design and Methods: Applied Social Research and Methods Series* (2nd edn.). Thousand Oaks, CA: Sage Publications Inc.

CREAFAM TV 2017 (Productor). (30 de agosto de). Video Institucional COOINGRA. Reecuperado de: https://www.youtube.com/watch?v=WK1Mta1XFCc

UAEOS 2015 (Productor). (22 de junio de). Video Experiencia Cap 2_2015 Microfranquicias Solidarias - Magangué, Bolívar {DVD}. Recuperado de: https://www.youtube.com/watch?v=EE1M4QgEuf0

8 Cooperativism in Acapulco, México

Roberto Cañedo Villareal, María del Carmen Barragán Mendoza, and Daniel Francisco Nagao Menezes

Introduction

This work arises as a result of the participation of the authors as registered university researchers in the call for the performance of the Sixth Academy of Social and Solidarity Economy (SSE) in the city of Puebla, Mexico, sponsored by the International Labor Organization (ILO) and the National Institute of Social Economy (INAES) of Mexico. The event was held on November 23–27, 2015 in the city of Puebla, Mexico, this being its sixth edition at the international level (previously held in Turin, Italy, in 2010; in Montreal, Canada, in 2011; in Agadir, Morocco, in 2013; in Campinas, Brazil, in 2014; and in Johannesburg, South Africa, in July 2015).

Within the framework of the South-South Cooperation Program of the Puebla event, researchers from universities in Brazil, Colombia and Mexico showed interest in doing joint work, given the context of unemployment and violence in these countries and the proposed alternative development of the SSE at the international level.[1] To the extent that the SSE appears as a central axis of the lines of work shared by the researchers, the interest for the conditions and actual issues in the construction of the Social Economy Sector Organizations (SESO) in different territories of Latin America led to the need to identify and characterize the strategic stakeholders involved in these processes *in situ*.

Considering that these SESO take different shapes, depending on their own historical process of construction, we consider our interest in projects located in specific territories of our countries as a form of accumulation of experiences that allows us to understand the particular processes of these constructions and their problems, while noting that the results of this research are not generalizable, but that they aim to identify remarkable findings and factors, matter of possible scientific hypotheses of future works.

In this sense, the research shows the distance between the theory and practice of solidarity in some Latin American territories. We start from the philosophical sources of being, of the human being in particular (in the perspective of Heidegger[2] and of the epistemologies of the south), which implies, in practice, being democratic, supportive and environmental defenders, which should mark the alternative proposal in the socio-economic and political field of the practices of cooperation and solidarity of that movement.

We consider, from the results obtained, that the approach to the other economy involves the construction of new identities, both for the recognition of economy as a social construction and not conceived as hitherto, as a fact of natural and a historical evolution, and the recognition of the participants as conscious subjects of this construction. That is, to put at the center of the new economy, the well-being of humankind and the conservation of nature, a binomial that we consider indissociable for the new way of interpreting social welfare.

With this conceptual framework, we designed a research tool from which we applied a series of focus groups with semi-structured interviews with cooperatives and university experts in the City of Campinas, State of Sao Paulo and rural cooperatives, housing and savings, in the city of Manaus, in the Brazilian Amazon (2017); we also conducted non-structured interviews in the City of Pereira, Department of Risaralda, in the center-west of Colombia, with experts from different countries, in particular, Colombians, on social innovation, environment and territory, and the approach to projects of a different nature, but which had at its core the social innovation for the attention and preservation of the environment. Finally, semi-structured focus groups and interviews were carried out in the municipality of Acapulco in the State of Guerrero, Mexico, with cooperative projects in the process of building the Acapulco rural area and strategic agents of the Social and Solidarity Economy Network of Guerrero (REDESSGRO).

After the processing of the collected information, a text analysis was carried out in the phenomenological perspective,[3] from which conclusions have been obtained: 1) there is a considerable distance between the philosophical foundations of solidarity, and in particular of cooperativism, and the daily practice of this alternative of economic and social development; and 2) the practical problems of the productive processes of cooperatives, although they require professional technical and financial assistance for the generation of new projects and/or for the accompaniment in their consolidation process as such, are profound definitional problems, such as those of decent employment and of organizational origin, that have to be treated in the field of Social Research, referring to the being and its solidarity and sustainable consciousness, without which, we believe, there will be no possibility of existence for the new economy.

Background: the socio-economic and political conditions of Brazil, Colombia and Mexico

Brazil

With a territorial area of slightly more than 8.5 million km^2, which currently accounts for about 47% of South American territory, and about 205 million inhabitants, it was a colony of the kingdom of Portugal until 1822, when it gained its independence. Brazilian society is considered to be multi-ethnic, consisting primarily of descendants of Europeans, Indigenous People, Africans and Asians.

During the period of conquest and colonization, which officially began in 1534, the main economic activity was focused on the extraction of Brazil's Palo, a product that was used as a kind of dye in the textile industry, although sugar production quickly became its main export product, and it was accompanied by a very significant increase in the import of African slaves. The sugar production was maintained during the XVI century and until the end of the XVII century, when they discovered gold mines in what is now known as Minas Gerais, Mato Grosso and Goiás, which solidified the Portuguese occupation in the region. The coffee production boom would have an important impact on the Brazilian economy and, at the same time, the development of a process of diversification of primary production in the following centuries, thus generating important infrastructure throughout the communications network, which would allow for quick development, to such a degree that it is currently considered the largest Latin American economy. Its economic activities are primarily located in agricultural, livestock, industrial, high-tech production, and financial services, among others.

Today, in the north of the country, primary activities (sugar cane and livestock) predominate, and the central-south relies on livestock activity to develop commercial activities with the products of the other regions of the country, which also explains their rapid and important population growth and, to a great extent, the political power of these regions (Sao Paulo, Minas Gerais and Rio Grande do Sul), which would relate to the period of the dictatorship (1964–1985). It is important to point out this last aspect, because this will be the context in which various political, workers and civil society organizations begin a process of anti-dictatorial struggle, based on food and employment needs, which the dictatorship had deepened. The emergence of the Workers' Party (PT) takes place in this same context and will be an obligatory reference point in order to understand the cooperative movement and, in general, the SSE in Brazil.

It is in the South (Porto Alegre, municipality of Rio Grande do Sul) that the first solid expressions of the advance of a community alternative to the economic policy of the dictatorship are given, since in 1986 one of the first mayors (prefeitos) of the left was elected,[4] "Alceu Collares of the

Partido Democratico Trabalhista (PDT) as mayor and later, in 1989, Olívio Dutra of the Partido dos Trabalhadores (PT)" (Hernández and Eduardo, 2016, p. 63). Perhaps the "participatory budget" not only has been one of the leftist political flags to access power in Brazil, but also one of the most important expressions of popular participation, as stated by Hernández and Eduardo (2016, p. 64).

This enabled the creation of local institutions during the 1990s to support and develop businesses, especially in the south and northeast of Brazil. This process of institutionalization was the basis for the creation in 2003 of the National Secretariat for Solidarity Economy (SENAES), which created a national policy to support the Solidarity Economy throughout Brazil. With the withdrawal of the Partido de los Trabajadores of the central government, the SENAES underwent a process of weakening and in 2019 it was extinguished.

Mexico

In view of the serious marginalization suffered by important sectors and regions of Mexico, the SSE has presented itself as a viable opportunity to confront it. But, although this perspective could be adapted to the structural functioning of the capitalist system, without a doubt, the impact of neoliberalism in the employment and income of families in the last decades in the region has forced the population to confront the social inequality from a qualitative transformation of the fight against poverty, marginalization and violence by large sectors of society in such a way that the Social and Solidarity Economy focuses more and more in the territory than in the market, without it ceasing to be an important topic on their current agenda, in the short and long term. In this sense, the SSE opens its alternatives to a more holistic vision of development and not just the economic aspect. Statistics, in this sense, are an important reference for a perspective on the situation of regional development; however, they are insufficient and have to be interpreted more qualitatively than quantitatively.

Take, for example, the age group of young people between 18 and 23 years of age; only 33.2% are accessing any type of education, while, for the particular case of the State of Guerrero, the place where we carried out the interviews, only 18% access education; on the other hand, 50.6% of the population in Mexico, in 2016, was in poverty, and in Guerrero it was 64.4% (CONEVAL, 2016). These few data can show us the difficult economic and social conditions in which the population of our region finds itself. This has created a push to look for alternative paths to get out of this situation.

In Mexico, the SSE, in all its expressions, already has a considerable presence in the national territory, even if it is not identified with this name, nor it has the visibility it requires. The most salvageable thing for the subsistence, social coexistence and defense of the territory is that they have built, and continue to build, in the heat of daily struggle, sometimes in contexts of criminal violence and government repression, others in the heat of religious and originary spiritualities, some more in the radical revolutionary perspective, or in some combination of all these, but all converge in the search and construction of a new economy.

There is a pre-Columbian tradition of Solidarity Economy in Mexico; among the Mayans and Aztecs, this was an institutional form of production and distribution, as was the *tequio* in the southern states of the country and the *gozona* (Gwzon) among the Zapotecs of Oaxaca, and there are many regional experiences in Mexico of the humanist relationship of the economy of the native people with work and nature. The point is that we do not have to go far, to other continents or cultures outside our America, to find a platform for building modern SSE in the region, since many of these traditions of solidarity cooperation remain active or ready to be recovered by actions directed by government programs or direct actions of civil society.

We consider it necessary; however, to make a few clarifications on this matter. In the first place, while the multifaceted expressions of the SSE in this region have ancestral sustenance, they have been beaten and minimized since the establishment of the Spanish colony and in the advent of neoliberalism they have tried to make them disappear (the sale of the ejido in Mexico, for example) or, at least, to prevent them from being visible; or, they have been allowed to die of starvation, which has led to their potential physical extinction, but not the indigenous worldview that remains in the Mexican people.

These kinds of SSE expressions are mainly located in the rural areas of our country, which are vast territories of our region and which, when forgotten by neoliberalism's policymakers, are located in unconnected links of the value chains of many and varied agricultural products, with little possibility of obtaining financing to generate added value, or broken or non-existent marketing channels for their products. But, more importantly, these forms of production are also expressions of forms of solidarity in social-communal coexistence, which have to do with the environment and the peaceful coexistence among its members, today more than ever, required for the reconstruction of the social fabric that has been devastated by criminal activities and governmental corruption in our territories. The native people of Mexico are currently a potential source of SSE construction. The problem of the market is thus very important in this case, but no more than the recovery of the territory, with all that this implies.

The above has to be valued in terms of Mexican reality. Today, Mexico is a large region that is troubled by poverty, violence, injustice and dispossession of all kinds; although in the urban areas of this region there is an atmosphere of insecurity, in the rural areas, with some fortunate exceptions, it is often dangerously inaccessible and the inhabitants of these regions live in daily turmoil. For this reason, considering any alternative development in this type of region necessarily involves discussing the problems of governance, democracy and the real powers, national and international, which are the actors involved in these spaces. The market is one more variable in this complex model of development with multiple variables, among which some are deeply explanatory of the social phenomenon we live today.

In the second place, despite the policy of undermining the pre-Columbian expressions of collective work, emerged in the region, from the beginning of the XIX century, other forms of organization of the SSE. We refer to the cooperative movement which, by its structuring, systematization and substantiation, has become the most representative expression of the SSE in Mexico. Its emergence can be placed in 1839, as in that year he laid the foundation of the *Savings Account of Orizaba*, and in 1873 the *First Cooperative Workshop*, the precursor of the first *Cooperative Society of Mexico*, integrated by 26 tailors of the City. Although it is not possible, nor appropriate, to historically or spatially frame the evolution of the cooperative movement in Mexico, we can only say that from the XX century this process has been promoted and influenced, with different depth and ideological biases, by the action of the catholic church, special international programs of the United States of America in the region (in particular the United States Agency for International Development, USAID), by international organizations such as the International Labor Organization, Trade Union Organizations with some consolidation (such as the International Cooperative Alliance, ICA), the different national States and, in recent decades, by a sort of organizations which we could identify as revolutionary. This implies that "cooperativism" becomes a polysemic term in Mexico, if it is classified, either according to its ultimate objectives or as a theoretical construct.

Anyway, the point is that cooperativism has become almost a synonym of SSE in Mexico, as it was said, and its maturation, in every sense, makes it a fundamental and strategic agent for this development alternative in the region. Currently, there are enough legal and legislative bases for institutional recognition of cooperativism in Mexico. This does not mean that it is in every sense, nor that there is sufficient precision in this regard for useful legislation on cooperativism, a task that is already being worked on by some national, regional and international organizations and academic institutions, but that a legal framework for the functioning and recognition of its economic and social importance has been built.

There are other problems of Mexican cooperativism that need to be addressed in a coordinated way by the strategic actors of this movement, such as the necessary generational change of the cooperativists, the creation of adequate financial structures for their healthy expansion, or the design of public policies and programs that have to become permanent and indispensable for the promotion and consolidation of co-operatives. According to some organizations, however, there is a need to arrive at conceptual and organizational convergences of the cooperative movement in order to advance properly.

Colombia

It has a population of over 48 million people, making it the third most significant population in Latin America after Brazil and Mexico. Approximately 70% of its population live in urban areas, above the global average. Its immigration is mainly Spanish, American and currently Venezuelan.

It is the fourth economy in Latin America (ANDI, 2013), only after Brazil, Mexico and Argentina. Although it is true that its main and emblematic traditional production is coffee (the fourth world producer and first in Arabic coffee, National Federation of Coffeemakers of Colombia, 2011), it is also very competitive in livestock (having the most important cattle herd in Latin America), but, in general, the agricultural sector appears with a contribution of about 7% of the national GDP. Its industrial development is also important, particularly in the medium- and high-tech goods industry, achieving growth rates of more than 30% per annum and, to a lesser extent, but also remarkable, in the construction sector.

Although the Colombian economy as a whole has been experiencing significant growth since 2000, the fact is that when it reached its most remarkable moment in 2011 (7.4%), a marked deterioration began, leading it to rates below 3%, between 2016 and 2019, reaching to submerge about 30% of the population below the poverty line (expansion, 2019), thus expressing a constant increase in social inequality.

In addition, Colombia is experiencing a strong social crisis. Its levels of corruption ranked 98th out of 175 countries evaluated by Transparency International in 2016. Its judicial system is also in crisis, as only 13% of reported cases are resolved (Urueña and Manuel, 2017). But perhaps the biggest problem, in social terms, that lives in its contemporary history is its internal armed conflict. After Syria, Colombia is considered as one of the countries with the largest forced internal population displacement product of the presence of the *guerrillas* of the extreme left, of the extreme-right paramilitary, of drug cartels and organized crime, a conflict that dragged on since the decade of the sixties of the last century, despite significant advances in its fight against the drug trade and the attempts ranging from treaties of peace with the *guerrillas* (ACNUR, 2017). In this scenario, today the SSE has an evident presence in Colombia that allows us to glimpse good omens of democratic and sustainable transformation for the future of the country, as we will see later.

Cooperative movement and the Social and Solidarity Economy

Values of the SSE in the territory

SSE as an alternative to neoliberalism is relatively recent, not more than a couple of decades, although its backgrounds can be traced from the very birth of industrial capitalism, as was the founding of the Equitable Society of the Rochdale Pioneers in Britain. This cooperative was born as a response to the employment crisis generated by the production transformation process during that period because the unemployment situation generated for the inhabitants of this city led them to become the first consumer cooperative for the purchase of their basic necessities. While it is true that before this cooperative there were others, the remarkable thing about its foundation is that this cooperative society issued what we know today as the Rochdale Principles, which are assumed by the modern world cooperative movement, and which are nothing more than a series of democratic participation principles of its members, of community interest, of solidarity and not individualism.

Although cooperativism, by its own characteristics, is, or should be, an expression of SSE, this does not necessarily happen, according to some of the results of our own research. Because of their mission, as we mentioned, the cooperatives attached to the SSE are only those that function democratically (with a horizontal organization and administration), sustainably (responsible for the environment) and solidary (that respond to the needs of the community and its partners). The above is, of course, a controversial definition and classification; however, it allows to make a clear first distinction between those cooperatives with a conscience of social equity, acting sustainably and in solidarity with those that lack at least one of these properties. Thus, we can find cooperatives that are born with the sole purpose of improving, in different proportions, the income of their organizations through the sale of their products or services and that may, therefore, have a hostile or irresponsible attitude towards the people of the cooperative itself, as well as towards the community and/or be predatory of the environment. The interpretation of some of our research findings allows us to identify some of the apparent causes that give rise to these externalities of ideal cooperativism, and that required a minimal contextualization of the territory as has been done.

Conceptual theoretical framework: the SSE from epistemologies of the South

It was felt that the research on SSE in the territory required a theoretical perspective different from the canons established by normal science (in the Kuhn perspective), both in the social sciences in general and economic science in particular, as well as to dare to use both an alternative vision, as are *Epistemologies of the South*, and a methodology that conforms to that perspective, as the research is phenomenological. Based on this, a theoretical perspective of a development model is presented of specific communities in Brazil, Colombia and Mexico, according to an intercultural program that glimpses the recovery of the contributions of the original cultures, and of alternatives of social innovation based on what is observed in the field. This is intended to provide information for the creation of a conceptual and methodological theoretical base for community work in the perspective of epistemologies of the south, using as a reference the cooperative experiences identified in these countries. The objectives proposed relate both to the expressions of *monoculture* and to the *ecologies* proposed by Boaventura de Souza applied to the studied projects and to describe and reinterpret their situation.

In addition, the theoretical-methodological basis requires evidence of some variables and indicators that can serve as parameters of information applicable in future research interventions, which implies describing the process in which the strategic actors of the solidarity cooperatives are found regarding the ideological alienation to the capitalist market (conceived as an axis of social welfare construction, in the sense of the classical economists and the Paretian Optimum) and the new holistic vision of the SSE.

The aim is to recover knowledge in the field of microdialy strategies and practices in the intersubjectivities of cooperatives and collective projects that allow understanding of the processes of generation and reproduction of social imaginaries, in order to try to visualize the contributions of the original cultures based on the design of perception instruments of the SSE, and to enable the generation of inputs for the presentation of public policy proposals and programs aimed at reducing social inequalities, asymmetries in the construction of power and the sustainable relationship between the human being and the nature.

The aim was to follow Santos (2006) in the need to arrive at more complex rationalities that exceed the imposed Western perception of *totality*, transforming our reality beyond understanding; the above implies, as the author argues, to combat the metonymic reason from a sociology of absences and thus avoid the reproduction of the nonexistent for the hegemonic powers. Boaventura, in this way, identifies these absences from its monoculture generating sources. Let's go through them:

> *Of knowledge and rigour:* where "scientific" knowledge disqualifies another knowledge. The shape it takes is ignorance.

> *Of linear time*: it considers the advance of history as a linear passage; the countries of the future are the developed, civilized; the others are

the backward, primitive. Its shape is residual.

Of the naturalization of differences: the differences between poor and rich, white and non-white, men and women and so on are "natural". Its shape is "inferiorize".

Of the dominant scale: there is always a dominant scale in things; it is structured under the aegis of the developed world, universalism or globalization; the local does not count. It takes the shape of local or private.

Of capitalist productivism: the development of a society is conceived only under the economic growth of the market; nature and the human being are usable and disposable parts; its shape "unproductivity".
In such a way, this capitalist *rationality* leads us to conceive that the one who does not share it is: ignorant, residual, inferior, local or particular and unproductive. To this end, it proposes to confront the monoculture with five *ecologies*:

Of knowledge: incorporate non-western knowledge into universal knowledge and use it as counter-hegemonic spaces.
Of temporalities: respect and give meaning to times that are outside the hegemonic linearity of history.

Of recognition: eliminate differences that denigrate, humiliate or undermine people and stay with those that are our own and do not hurt.

Of "trans-scale": move to *glocalization.*

Of productivities: rescue the non-capitalist forms of production that humanize the human being.

On the other hand, Boaventura De Sousa's criticism of prolific reason attempts to "contract the future, for a concrete future, of realistic utopias", which suggests giving rise to the *Sociology of emergencies,* promoting, caring for, and developing decolonizing social expressions through a *translation procedure* of knowledge that seeks cooperation without homogenization. The *epistemologies of the south*, in this sense, consider that "there is no global social justice without global cognitive justice" (Santos, 2006; pp. 22–33).

As we can see, the aim was to locate the way in which monocultures and ecologies described by the strategic agents of the cooperatives of Campinas, Pereira and Acapulco are expressed.

At this point, it is necessary to emphasize that the SSE has been objectified in the construction of a new type of cooperatives, whose center of conformation is reciprocity, understood as a central value of Human Relations, "a reciprocity that re-emerges and re-expands as:

a. Organization of production, exchange or distribution, and reproduction;
b. Associated with the community as a collective authority structure;
c. Social equality of individuals within diversity and the heterogeneity of individual and collective identities;
d. Horizontality of the relations between the individuals of all identities, starting with the differences between the sexes and sexualities;
e. Relations of use and reproduction with other living beings and
f. A culture of co-responsibility in the existence of the universe", which Aníbal Quijano calls "Bio-economy" (in Díaz-Muñoz, 2012, p. 8).

Methodology: construction of the basis for the observation of the SSE in the territorial experience

For the fieldwork, a platform for the database was built identifying the spaces, variables and indicators of the daily experiences in the SSE undertakings. The way to recover this information was carried out centrally through focal groups; this technique was applied with undertakings of the cities selected under the following scheme:

General purpose

Identify monoculture expressions in light of Boaventura Dos Santos' ecological counter-hegemonic proposal.

Specific purposes

Describe and reinterpret the following duos (monoculture-ecology):

a. Of knowledge and rigour – Of knowledge (axis 1)
b. Of linear time – Of temporalities (axis 2)
c. Of naturalization of differences – Of recognition (axis 3)
d. Of the dominant scale – Of the "trans-scale" (axis 4)
e. Of capitalist productivism – Of productivity (axis 5)

The investigated universe

Nine projects were visited, five Brazilians, two Mexicans and two Colombians, and they are listed below:

a. Cooperative "Nossa Senhora Aparecida" (plastic recycler), of the Catholic Church "Batel", in Campinas, Brazil

b. RECICAMP (Plastic Recycling Cooperative), in Campinas, Brazil
c. Cooperative No. 1 (indigenous fishing and agricultural project), a community of Liberation, on an island on the Amazon River, in Manaus, Brazil
d. Cooperative 2 (indigenous project, seven etnias: Mura, Pa Ari, Chi Una, among others, of artisan products), Community of Libramiento, island over the Amazon River, in Manaus, Brasil
e. Community Bank Cooperative ARUAK, on the outskirts of the city of Manaus, Brazil
f. Cooperativa "Julia Ramírez Blanco" (artisan producers of candy), in the town of Tres Palos, in Acapulco, Guerrero, Mexico
g. Escuela Campesina, Ecotourist Cooperative Society of Fishing and Artisan in Barrio las Playas, Acapulco, Guerrero, México
h. Fundación Crisol (displaced project), in the town of Cerritos, Pereira, Colombia
i. Parque Otún Quimbaya, of the Yarumo Blanco Foundation, in the town of Corregimiento de La Florida, in Pereira, Colombia

Results and discussion

After carrying out a text analysis of the transcript of the focus groups and the semi-structured interviews, the following observations were collected from each of the axes, spaces of research.

Of knowledge

A constant in most of the projects observed is the low level of education of its members; however, the use of one's own knowledge has real impact on rural projects, not in urban ones.

In the first case, we believe that it is due to the nature of the products (handcrafts and foods of different kinds, among others) because these have characteristics that are the result of historical community knowledge. Thus, we were able to find a rich variety (in every sense) of proposals of typical handcrafts, food and sweets of the region that were not only a clear expression of their deep knowledge, but also showed evidence of the conservation and cultural enrichment of their territory (this was particularly observed in the Brazilian Amazon and the rural and coastal areas of Acapulco, in Mexico and Pereira, in Colombia). In almost all cases, it should be emphasized that the presence of the spirit, and knowledge of the projects regarding the preservation and care of nature, was evident, as well as a perfectly clear conception and promotion of SSE in the cases studied in Colombia and Mexico, not in those in Brazil. However, one aspect that the interviewees pointed out was the constant appropriation of their own knowledge by private sector business corporations, without receiving any kind of recognition from them. However, there are cases such as those in

Acapulco, Mexico, where the cooperativists themselves have created spaces for the reproduction of their knowledge with a clear impact on the territory, as is their "Escuela Campesina".

While the products of the urban projects are rather part of the nearest modernity, it requires rather new knowledge, absent in the cultural history of the projects of the territory in question. This has led to entrepreneurship becoming more dependent on external market knowledge, moving away from their own knowledge. This does not mean that innovation in the entrepreneurship is absent; on the contrary, there is a clear willingness to build own knowledge that impacts the technical process of production, or the services offered by the project (which in some cases were plausible proposals), to a greater or lesser degree, and which are transmitted from the older cooperativists (with greater knowledge and roots to the project) to the younger ones in most of the observations made.

In any case, what predominates in each type of project is the clear need to sell, which is completely understandable. The problem is that the market seems to end up orienting its day-to-day work and subsuming its own knowledge, which becomes distant from the values of the SSE.

On the other hand, what was also observed is that, on a regular basis, the managers of the cooperatives are usually the ones with the greatest schooling, in one type of enterprise or another; this, it seems, has to do with the geographical (in the case of rural) and labor (in the case of urban) spaces, since in the first case, it is common to note the absence of educational opportunities, given the limited educational supply in the territory and, in the second, that urban cooperatives tend to absorb the victims of unemployment, in general those with the least resources for their training and education.

In both cases, the state appears to be absent from its obligation to train and educate citizens, both because of its negligence and because of its inability to do so. It is worth noting, on the other hand, that a constant observation in the projects was the presence of the Catholic Church, not only in the process of creating cooperatives, but in their development and consolidation, which is perceived as a project dependence (at least of its administrators) towards this institution, although this was not entirely exclusive of other religious proposals in the observed projects.

Of temporalities

Although the cooperativists, in general, retain hope for the success of their project, in the observed environment there is a perception of inability to arrive at change. Even clearer, the hope of the base cooperative seems to shelter in the assistance and external support more than on their own capabilities, particularly in the cases of Mexico and Brazil and, to a much lesser extent, in Colombia. The hope that is based on their own resources is expressed primarily in the leaders of the projects and in those who accompany them (advisers), that is, in the strategic agents of the SSE (such as university researchers and the church). This has given rise to the fact that while there are structured and active proposals of SSE networks, these seem to be supported, fundamentally, by the "external" agents that "drag" the projects behind them.

The technical advice of the university students and the logistical support of representatives or allies of the church appear to be the scaffolding in the construction of the SSE in the studied territories. In this way, for example, the laws in force to support and promote the SSE, in their different expressions, are usually translated into the territory by the university students, as well as the links with the different government bodies related to them. Thus, divorcing the theory of the practice promoters of the entrepreneurs subject's practice of the SSE in the territory. Despite these disagreements, the SSE is covering different spaces in a slow but steady walk in the technical-productive, legislative and marketing aspects, as well as the ideological heart of the SSE. While showing a lack of deeper impact of SSE values among the cooperativists and their surroundings, it is clearer in the Mexican and Brazilian cases than in the Colombian case.

Of recognition

One of the aspects that we consider to be transcendental and indispensable in the consolidation of a counter-hegemonic alternative to the neoliberal vision of the economy is the values inculcated in the construction process of the SSE. In this space, we consider that there are project expressions that seem to denote favorable conditions to advance the alternative proposal, since the real leadership of the women in the studied projects is evident (although not formal, as we will see); besides, there is a clear absence of counter values such as *machismo*, racism, homophobia or religious intolerance, mainly in Colombia and Mexico, not so in Brazil. There are still some signs to overcome, such as the high presence of men in the boards of directors or executive commissions of the productive units (more evident in Mexico and Colombia than in Brazil) as well as the declared existence of selfishness in interpersonal relations or the distrust among the cooperativists.

Of the trans-scale

In the field of the impacts that hierarchies of different kinds usually cause within the projects, we can point out that in some cases more deeply than in others, the members of the management bodies appear distant and clearly differentiated from the base of the cooperativists, although we consider that in most cases there is no perverse intention to generate this situation, but we found a type of disposition from the cooperative base to generate it. We must make it clear that we are aware that the distribution of functions is one thing and the administrative and power hierarchies is another, both in rural and urban areas. In short, it is not clear, however, whether democratic participation is an everyday act or at least practiced in the special moments of transcendental decision-making.

One aspect to note is that alongside the typical productive activities of the unit we almost always find leisure, cultural and sports activities, among others, that accompanied the economic work, both in Colombia and in Mexico and Brazil. This is more evident in the rural area than in the urban places, which demonstrates the cultural identity of the projects in relation to their territory and a deep feeling of roots in the cases studied in the three countries.

Of the productivities

One constant that is identified in the self-diagnosis of the projects observed is their perception of financial requirements to increase their productivity, which is based on the permanent need for government support; this is more noticeable in the cases studied in Brazil and Mexico and to a lesser extent in those in Colombia, without meaning that there is no longer any type of support from the State. However, the prospects of going forward with the support network of other projects of the SSE are present, in diverse manners, in all cases, without disregarding the conditions of economic crisis in each country.

The relationship between the development of the collective projects studied and the personal development of their members seems to not be fully aligned; this is more evident in the Brazilian cases since in the questions in the focus groups about their personal expectations, many of them explicitly expressed their character as transient members of the projects while finding something better, a permanent job that guaranteed their future, with social security and retirement; that is, they thought about the material security that they did not see in the cooperative. In this sense, it seems that the values of the SSE were not as deeply rooted as one would wish them to be in the base subjects, and although this situation appeared more clearly in the Brazilian cases, they were also present in the Colombian and Mexican cases, although to a much lesser extent. While it is remarkable that the strategic agents of change have promoted and supported the conscious and democratic participation in the projects, it is also true that the dependence, sometimes obvious and sometimes subtle, of the base on the leaders of the projects is evident, which leads not to endorse the ideal of transformation or to conceive themselves as real agents of change from the base.

Thus, it was perceived that there is greater interest in preserving entrepreneurship technically and financially as a platform for the personal security of employment and monetary income, which leads us to consider the need to continue to deepen the investigation of the problems of the cooperative, of the collectivist and solidarity being, as a central element of the decolonization or de-alienation of the strategic subjects of the other economy. One element to highlight is that the projects in Colombia and Mexico are very clear about the need for care and preservation of the environment as an integral part of their performance; in Brazilian cases there is also this provision consciously, although to a lesser extent. However, in this respect, a constant perception in the previous spaces of participation of the projects is present again, and that is that the clarity of the values of respect for nature is very firm in the forefront of all the projects, but not so evident in the base participants. For example, in the case of rural cooperatives in Brazil, based on an Amazon Island, the legislation that makes their territory a protected region appears to them as a limitation of their development as cooperatives because it limits or even prohibits commercial exploitation activities of the territory, including commercial fishing.

Conclusions

The international movement of the SSE is becoming more visible every day; its expressions in different territories, however, are quite dissimilar. In many of the so-called "developed" countries, the influence of the SSE has been consistent, and, in some way, it has been consolidating development strategies within and outside the hegemonic market model today. On the other hand, in many of the countries that are not in that area of development, the situation is more varied, and their backgrounds have a greater conjugation with the territory; that is, their practices and problems are more intricate with problems of land, water, governance and, of course, with the market. This chapter showed the distance between the theory and the practice of solidarity in specific projects in Latin American territories. The above implied starting from the philosophical sources of being, and of the human being in particular (in Heidegger's perspective and the epistemologies of the south), which involved observing the supposed solidarity and socioeconomic perspectives of this movement, in order to enter into solidarity practices *in situ* and obtain an approach to its problems and expectations.

In this way, we have made an observation that shows, in the first place, the evident distance between what we consider should be expressed as being supportive and being supportive in practice, the real being, the being in the territory and, in the second place, intrinsically related to the above, the ranking of the problems perceived as critical by the members of the bases of the projects studied and that are closer to the common problems of any other citizen who is out of the SSE movement. Thus, the people and enterprises of the Latin American territories, apparently, prefer the necessary solution to their problems to increase their income and to achieve stability and permanence in decent employment.

The conclusions of this work are related to the ideological perspective of a solidary, democratic and sustainable movement, as is the SSE, which, essentially, has not permeated beyond the circle of promoters of this alternative of economic and social development, many times, that conceptual and ideological baggage "above" of the administrative leaders of the cooperative enterprise of the territories studied has remained. This does not imply, however, that very important objective steps are not already being taken in the construction of an alternative for humanist and sustainable development for the Latin American region. Understanding what the being is, and the human being in particular, could lay the foundations for appropriate protocols for the construction of any alternative democratic and sustainable society.

Notes

1 The dynamics of academic linking of researchers of the Autonomous University of Guerrero, Mexico (UAGro), Mackenzie Presbyterian University, Brazil (UPM) and the Pontificia Universidad Javeriana, Colombia (PUJ) allowed the Doctoral position of Mexican researchers at the UPM in Brazil in 2016, a position in Manaus, in the Brazilian Amazon, as well as another position in the Department of Risaralda, Colombia, sponsored by the Middlesex University in Great Britain and the University of UNIMINUTO in Colombia, which consolidated the ties of academic exchange between researchers in these three countries and sponsors of the SSE in Latin America.

2 From this perspective, human experience ceases to be a simple presentation of objects and it becomes a dynamic process in which people's consciousness participates in an intentional relationship between the supposed objects and the subjects; therefore, objects are not studied, but phenomena (which is intended). Heidegger identifies the human being just like the Dasein; its essence resides in its existence; its point is to exist in the world. The Dasein occupies the world affectively; its understanding of the world is not cognitive but existential, projects possibilities.

3 "… a category of research designs that extract descriptions from observations that take the form of interviews, narrations, field notes, audio and video recording, all kinds of written records, photographs or movies and artifacts".

4 "Between these political forces, it is important to highlight the Workers' Party (PT) […] At the end of the decade of the eighties, the PT, in coalition with other political forces of the left, won the local elections in several major localities in Brazil -São Paulo, Porto Alegre, Santos, Belo Horizonte, Campinas, Vitória, Goiâna - and introduced in all of them, institutional innovations that encouraged popular participation in municipal government" (Santos, 2004: 16).

References

ACNUR (2017). *Global trends. Forced displacement in 2017*, https://www.acnur.org/stats/globaltrends/5b2956a04/tendencias-globales-desplazamiento-forzado-en-2017.html

Aguilar Hernández, & Eduardo, E. (2016). *The social production of the territory under the solidarity economic logic, the case of the Guajuviras neighborhood in Canoas, Rio Grande do Sul, Brazil, Benemerit Autonomous University of Puebla, Faculty of Economics, Center of Economic and Social Development Studies*, http://www.economiasolidaria.org/documentos/la_produccion_social_del_territorio_bajo_la_logica_economia_solidaria

ANDI (2013). *National Association of Businessmen of Colombia*, Colombia: Balance 2011 and Perspectives 2012. Financial Sector. https://web.archive.org/web/20130605193822/http://www.andi.com.co/Archivos/file/CEE/ANDI_Balance2011_perspectivas2012.pdf

CEPAL and CIA (2019) World Factbook, https://www.indexmundi.com/map/?v=69&r=ca&l=es, accessed on May

CONEVAL (2016). https://www.coneval.org.mx/coordinacion/entidades/Guerrero/Paginas/Pobreza-2016.aspx, accessed on May 2019

Charry Urueña, & Juan Manuel (2017). *The Profound Crisis of Justice*, https://www.semana.com/opinion/articulo/la-crisis-de-la-justicia-colombiana/519271

Díaz-Muñoz, Guillermo (2012). *Between the local and the global in the south of Jalisco: the citizen alternative regionalization before the dominant regionalization, Technological Institute of Higher Education of the West, Institutional Repository of ITESO*, https://rei.iteso.mx/bitstream/handle/11117/1295/ENTRE%20LO%20LOCAL%20Y%20LO%20GLOBAL%20EN%20EL%20SUR%20DE%20JALISCO.pdf?sequence=2

Expansion (2019). *GDP Colombia second quarter of 2019*, https://datosmacro.expansion.com/pib/colombia, accessed on May 2019

National Federation of Coffeemakers of Colombia (2011). *Protected Geographical Indication for Colombian coffee*, https://www.federaciondecafeteros.org/buencafe-fnc-es/index.php/comments/indicacion_geografica_protegida_para_el_cafe_colombiano/

Hamui-Sutton A, et al. (2013). *Technique in focal groups, Journal of research in medical education, Faculty of Medicine, National Autonomous University of Mexico*, MexicoHerrera, Juan Published by Elsevier (2008). The cualitative research, Vurtua Collection UdeG, http://biblioteca.udgvirtual.udg.mx/jspui/handle/123456789/1167

Santos, Boaventura De Sousa (2004). *Democratize democracy. The Paths of Participatory Democracy*, México, FCE

Santos, Boaventura De Sousa (2006). *Renew critical theory and reinvent social emancipation, meetings in Buenos Aires*. Buenos Aires: CLACSO, http://biblioteca.clacso.edu.ar/clacso/coediciones/20100825032342/critica.pdf, November 2016

International Transparency (2016). *Know the new ranking of corruption in Latin America*, https://rpp.pe/mundo/latinoamerica/conoce-el-nuevo-ranking-de-corrupcion-en-america-latina-noticia-1026247, accessed on May, 2019

9 The relationship with knowledge, skills of entrepreneurs and companies' internal factors

Findings from collective enterprises in Colombia

Ana Milena Silva Valencia

Introduction

This research refers to the identification and analysis of the factors that explain the success in the creation of solidarity organizations in a context of crisis in Colombia. As a research topic, the evolution that entrepreneurship has had as a scientific field and in the generation of knowledge should be highlighted. However, this theme is in the gestation stage or beginning in countries like Colombia, where its emergence is basically confined to the last ten years. Organizations have been limited by their inventory of resources and capabilities. Therefore, entrepreneurship has proven to be a strategy in which despite the adversities in the environment, whether due to economic, political or social crisis, entrepreneurship requires personal qualities that make it possible to gain access to valuable, differential and complementary resources and/or capabilities. This research analyzes entrepreneurship from the theory of Resources and Capabilities defining resources as "the assets, organizational processes, attributes, information and knowledge controlled by a company that allow it to achieve and implement strategies that improve its effectiveness and efficiency" (Barney, 1991).

Taking as reference one of the seminars of the venture, Schumpeter (1934), who disseminated the concept of creative destruction suggested that organizations must, on the one hand, have sufficient stability to allow them to manage their learning leading to continuous growth and, on the other hand, need to have sufficient flexibility to face their environment, which is constantly changing and highly competitive.

This research identifies the success factors in the formation of solidarity or non-profit economy organizations in Colombia since 2009. It analyses their influence on social, environmental and economic effectiveness, factors that are latent in organizations and factors that are included in the international agenda on social responsibility that organizations must legitimize regardless of their legal nature. In this sense, Elkington's[1] model known as triple income statement links these three dimensions: social, environmental and economic and the interaction that results from them.

In the Colombian context, there has been an increase in unemployment rates since 2009, these being in percentages close to 10% in recent years. In 2015, the unemployment rate was 8.2%.[2] It is here that entrepreneurship takes shape and presents alternative solutions in difficult situations, and so entrepreneurship is an adequate way to generate sources of work and income through conformation of organizations where the human being prevails as the subject and purpose of the economy. This research aims to explain how entrepreneurial skills and knowledge (KSE) and internal company factors (CIF) have an influence or are related to economic, social and environmental factors. Several authors from the approach of the theory of resources and capabilities state that "a company is a collection of resources, a knowledge tank to the extent that resources have individual competencies and are capable of providing diverse services. The way to use and dispose of this collection of resources, between different uses and in the course of time, is determined by administrative decisions" (Penrose's, 1959, cited in Ibarra, 2004).

The theory of resources and capabilities takes into account the strengths of the organization represented in resources and capabilities that allow it to have a competitive advantage and products and services that are difficult to imitate. The resources and capacities of companies can be translated as that endowment or inventory of resources that is the result of its own history and that this composition can be maintained over time (Peteraf, 1993).

The empirical verification was carried out in a sample of cooperatives in Colombia, using a research methodology with a quantitative approach, in which the Multiple Regression Analysis was used and as a previous analysis to select the variables the MCA (Main Components Analysis). This work's purpose is to answer the following research question: How do entrepreneurial skills and abilities (ESA) and internal company factors (ICF) influence or relate to economic, social and environmental factors? In order to answer this research question, the objective was to identify the social, economic and environmental factors of solidarity economy organizations that were constituted in crisis situations in Colombia through the influence of internal factors and entrepreneurial capacities.

Methodology

For the year 2015, 1450 cooperatives were registered in Colombia before the Superintendence of the Solidarity Economy, 147 in Valle del Cauca and to date 70 such organizations have been registered in the Chamber of Commerce of Cali. To conduct a deeper and more detailed study, it was focused only on the cooperatives established in the city of Cali, which were analyzed throughout the research process. According to the Chamber of Commerce, of the 70 registered cooperatives, 40 are multi-active, 26 of associated work, 2 are integral, 1 specialized in savings and credit and 1 classified as a pre-associated work cooperative.

Taking into account the population under study, for research purposes a sample of 65 active cooperatives formally established between 2009 and 2015 and registered in the Chamber of Commerce of the city of Cali were chosen. During this period, information was obtained from each organization, which was extracted through the application of a survey of the entrepreneurs or managers of the organizations studied in the months of March and April 2016 and the database provided by the Chamber of Commerce of Cali. A group of interviewers and the researchers visited the cooperatives by appointment and other visits were made without appointments.

In this investigation, the Multiple Linear Regression Analysis was used to establish the relationship that is generated between a dependent variable, in this case the Economic, Social and Environmental factors, and a set of independent variables, such as the knowledge and Skills of the Entrepreneur (KSE), each with its items or indicators and the Internal Factors of the Company (CIF). This is how the model equation would be represented: $Y = a + b1x1 + b2x2 + \ldots + bnxn + e$, where Y is the dependent variable to predict how the skills, knowledge and internal factors of the companies have a direct reaction or not with the economic, social and environmental factors and *an* and b are the parameters that are unknown and are going to be estimated.

Literature development and review

There are various modalities of entrepreneurship and one of them precisely impacts a change in society which in turn benefits not only an owner or a single entrepreneur but also several people. This is what is known as social entrepreneurship, which was introduced by Bill Drayton, who founded the Association of Innovative Social Entrepreneurs in the United States (ASHOKA, 2009). The social entrepreneur innovates and generates social change[3] for the benefit of a community, region or country.

Another nuance of entrepreneurship is known as cooperative entrepreneurship, which has its beginnings at the time of the industrial revolution (1844). Its history stands out as a group of workers of a textile company in England who made the decision to form their own company, thus leaving the exploitation processes where they were submitted by an employer (Serrano, 2007). The cooperative entrepreneur starts his business through a company collectively form, non-profit or for profit, depending on the legislation in the countries, that benefits only the people who make up the collective organization, whether as partners or associates. And finally, there is a traditional venture that is characteristic of capitalist companies where individual capacities and profitability prevail in the hands of a few people or an individual entrepreneur.

To be able to create a company, you must start by recognizing an entrepreneurial opportunity, a definition of this could be: "Entrepreneurship opportunities are those situations in which new goods, services, raw materials and organizational methods can be sold and introduced at a price higher than its production costs". In order to define entrepreneurship, it is necessary to mention the first person to introduce a contribution to this topic in the economic literature, Cantillón, who defined the entrepreneur as the "agent that buys the means of production at certain prices and combines them in an orderly way to get a new product from there". In addition, he says that the entrepreneur does not have a safe return on his economic activity and is the one who assumes the risks that may arise in the market. Subsequently, Burnett the French economist, affirmed that the entrepreneur is "a new leader, forecaster, risk taker and project evaluator, and that mobilizes resources from a low performance area to a high productivity one". In addition to this, he highlighted the importance of entrepreneurship for society in general, rather than for a single individual (Formichella, 2004).

Subsequently, the Austrian school emphasizes this issue, which says that the entrepreneur is the one who identifies opportunities in the market using his knowledge and being creative when entering it. In the same way, they say that importance should not be given to the outcome but to the market process, and the importance of competition, since this is what leads to discovery and creativity (Perdomo Charry, 2010). Social entrepreneurs have taken great strength in the business world. These types of entrepreneurs have considered social needs as an opportunity and not as a problem, seeking in this way to contribute and improve the well-being of the individuals who together represent a community. According to the European EMES research network created in 1996, the social enterprise "is defined as an organization created in order to achieve a goal related to benefiting a community".

This company is made up of a number of people who seek to achieve their objectives through cooperation, and where the dynamics of profits vary from a conventional capitalist company. In this case, dividends are generally reinvested in the company in order to improve the product or service they offer and finally contribute more effectively to the social problem that is being worked on. In this order of ideas, "entrepreneurship implies turning a new idea into a successful innovation using skills such as vision, creativity, persistence and risk exposure" (Grau, 2012). As Pomerantz states, social enterprises must be based on traditional and innovative business methods, with the purpose of incorporating strategies that lead them to success in a faster and safer way.

The theory of solidarity entrepreneurship arises from the analysis carried out by Gide (1968), who states:

> the associations in which workers will perceive the integral product of their work, because they will possess their production instruments; associations that will suppress the intermediaries, because they will change their products directly, associations that will not mutilate the individual because the individual initiative will be preserved as the hidden spring that will move each one of them and that on the contrary will protect against the hazards of the life through the practice of solidarity; associations, in short, that without suppressing the emulation that is indispensable to progress, will attenuate the concurrence and struggle, suppressing most of the causes that put men in conflict in our time.

From an economic perspective, there are other authors who write on the subject. Luis Razeto, with his experience in Chile, analyzed how certain communities undertook economic organizations with their own initiatives and resources in order to help themselves collectively. Razeto also proposes comprehensive economic theory with the aim of understanding social and solidarity relations and that make up a rationality different from state or market organizations. It also proposes factor C as that social energy that energizes the processes that are undertaken. The ultimate goal of a solidarity venture is not the maximization of the capital factor or the obtaining of profits, but to achieve better benefits for the greatest number of people and their communities.

Solidarity ventures have their particular characteristics that differentiate them in other ways: they are self-managed, since entrepreneurs are managers, workers and users of services. Solidarity economic ventures cover various forms of economic organizations that originate in the free association of workers based on principles of self-management, cooperation, efficiency and viability.

Figure 9.1 presents in a general way the basic model with each of the variables, both independent and dependent. The selection of the model is

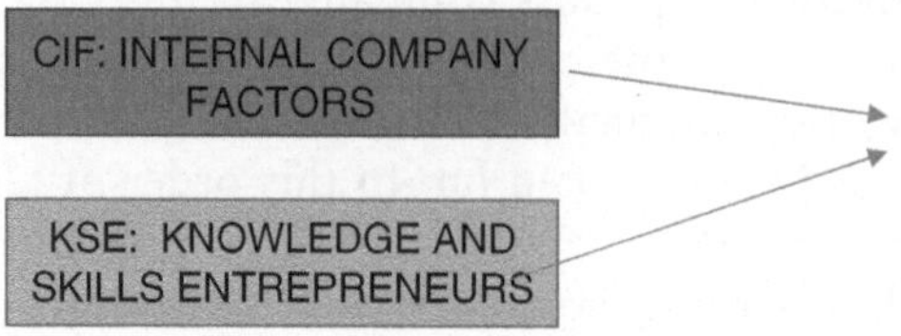

Figure 9.1 Factors determining the success of the creation of SMEs.
Source: elaborated by the authors.

based on or taken up from the proposal presented by the researchers Campos Climent et al. (2014) in their study on the determining factors in the success of the creation of small and medium enterprises: case of cooperatives in Spain.

It is worth noting that this same model was validated for the new cooperatives formed in Colombia in times of crisis or more specifically at the time of the peace dialogues between the years 2009 and 2015. The same latent variables proposed by the already mentioned researchers were maintained.

In this regard and in relation to the model, the research took into account the internal factors of the company, which were grouped into different functional areas: Marketing, Provisioning, Production, innovation, Human Resources, Finance and Management (Campos Climent et al., 2014) and how these influence social, economic and environmental factors. With reference to the individual level, the entrepreneur's perceptions of the importance of internal factors in the creation and success of companies were taken into account. The idea with the empirical research process is to analyze the effects that these independent variables (internal company factors and the knowledge and skills of the entrepreneur) have on the degree of social, economic and environmental success (dependent variable) in a population of cooperative organizations little studied by researchers. The background of the investigations has shown results of these factors and the influence on success for capitalist or lucrative companies.

The theory states that the success of the entrepreneurial activity will depend on the knowledge and skills that the entrepreneur has. As examples of key factors in this process they are the ability to learn from the experience and training received.

On the other hand, the theory states that entrepreneurs who believe they have the appropriate knowledge and skills to create and develop a company tend to generate favorable expectations regarding results, although in other jobs it is expressed that entrepreneurs have more knowledge and skills to identify businesses or start businesses other than social ones (Alonso and Galve, 2006). The perspectives of entrepreneurs in the process of creating a company with respect to their internal factors can be a determining element in success (Baron, 2004).

Returning to Herron and Robinson, (1993), Barba and Atienza and García, Martínez and Fernández, in the words of Campos Climent et al. (2014). "The creation and success of a company depends largely on the motivation and skills of those who begin the process of creating a company; as indicated in other studies: entrepreneurs who consider they have appropriate skills and knowledge to create and develop a company, usually generate results and therefore business performance" (pp. 5-7).

According to what Veciana stated in relation to the business perspective and when analyzing the internal factors that determine success in creation, these factors are considered as strengths and can positively influence the success of the creation of companies, as stated or corroborated in other research projects (Alonso and Galve, 2006). The internal factors correspond to the main functional areas of the company, and these influence the success of the performance, as described and verified in research already carried out (Herron and Robinson, 1993; Alonso and Galve, 2006).

When some resources are scarce, it can also influence the difficulty of achieving success when the company is formed, as Gartner puts it. If the organization optimizes the use of resources, efficiency translates into economic advantages for it and for its stakeholders; that is, if the organization manages environmental processes, it will generate not only competitive advantage but the creation of new products or services that would be reflected in income. Given the previous reference, this study aims to verify the following hypotheses:

H1. The economic factor of the newly created cooperatives is positively related to the knowledge and skills of the entrepreneurial group and the initial endowment of internal factors of the company.

H2. The social factor of newly created cooperatives is positively related to the knowledge and skills of the entrepreneurial group and the initial endowment of internal factors of the company.

H3. The environmental factor of the newly created cooperatives is positively related to the knowledge and skills of the entrepreneurial group and the initial endowment of internal factors of the company.

Discussion

When carrying out the analysis of the chosen sample, it was obtained that, in 2012, 21 cooperatives were formed (see Figure 9.1). It should be noted that 2012 was when the peace dialogue process began and it was also when the largest number of cooperatives in the sample was created, followed by 2015 in which 15 cooperatives were created. An increase is observed during 2012, of 250% compared to the previous year; however, during the years 2013 and 2014, there was a decrease of 62% and 75%, respectively, compared to the previous year. For the year 2015, a 650% growth of the number of cooperatives created can be observed compared to 2014.

Figures 9.2 and 9.3 show the percentage of cooperatives created from 2012 to 2015 compared to the percentage of cooperatives created from 2009 to 2011. In this graph, it can be clearly seen that the percentage from 2012 to 2015 is higher; therefore, it can be affirmed that

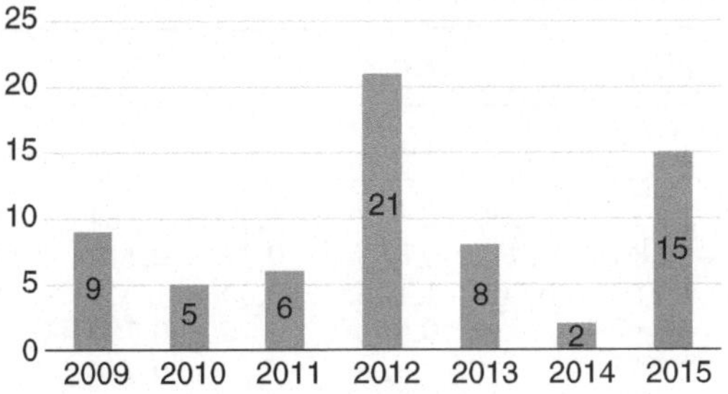

Figure 9.2 Conformed cooperatives.

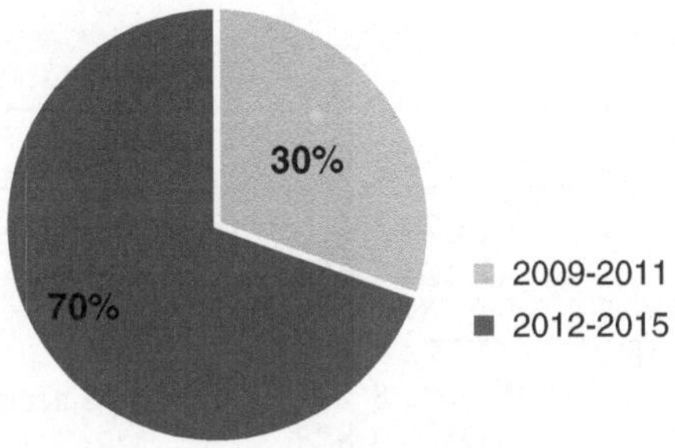

Figure 9.3 Percentage of cooperatives.

during the period of the peace dialogues in Colombia (2012–2015), there had been an increase in the number of cooperatives formed in the city of Cali.

Table 9.1 presents the summary of results of the linear regression and Table 9.2 presents the summary of the hypothesis contrast.

Taking into account the results and observing charts 1 and 2, the adjusted R2 of equation 1 or H1 takes a value of 0.74, which means that the KSE (knowledge and skills of the entrepreneur) and the CIF (internal factors of the company) jointly explain 74% of the EF (economic factor) of the cooperatives that were formed in the context of crisis. In addition, the ANOVA test of the same equation was statistically significant (0.01), which indicates that the equation is statistically significant and therefore it is possible to reliably explain the EF of cooperatives based on the application of KSE and the use of the CIF. Regarding the interpretation of the estimated B in the equation, it can be said in the case of the first hypothesis that as the entrepreneur's KSE increases, the EF worsens. The opposite occurs with the CIF that has a positive influence; that is, as these internal factors increase, the economic factor improves, among the most significant factors of the (KSE) and that presents an important level

Table 9.1 Summary of linear regression results

	FE		*FS*		*FM*	
	Valor	*Sig*	*Valor*	*sig*	*Valor*	*Sig*
Constant	1,372	1,000	2,308	1,000	1,761	1,000
KSE	−0,286	0,042	0,055	0,24	0,113	0,400
ICF	1,110	0,000	1,126	0,000	1,022	0,000
RR2	0,750		0,836		0,785	
r2 Corregida	0,742		0,828		0,774	
Durbin-Whayson	1,654		1,888		1,725	
Anova (F)	92,851		103,436		74,190	

**p < 0.05; p < 0.1.

Table 9.2 Hypothesis contrast

Hypothesis	*Equation*	*Parameters*	*Results*
H1	FE = α1 + β1.1 CHE + β1.2 FIE- FE = 1,372 + 0,286 ∗ CHE + 1,110 ∗ FIE	R2 = 74.2%; DW = 1,654; Anova = p < 0.01; VIF = 4,710	It is accepted
H2	FS = α2 + β2.1 CHE + β2.2 FIE + β2.3 FIE- FS = 2,308 + 0,055 ∗ CHE + 1,126 ∗ FIE-0,324 ∗ FE	R2 = 82.8%; DW = 1,888; Anova = p < 0.01; VIF = 5,037-9,630	It is accepted
H3	FM = α3 + β3.1 CHE + β3.2 FIE + β3.3 FE- FM = 1,761 + 0,113 ∗ CHE + 1,022 ∗ FIE + 0,43 ∗ FE	R2 = 77.4%; DW = 1,725; Anova = p < 0.01; VIF = 5,037-9,630-3,995	It is accepted

of correlation for this construction. We have the capacity to predict and anticipate change, modernization in management and the ability to adapt to changes. These factors do not have as positive an impact on the economic factor as if it the do: management.

On the other hand, the adjusted R2 of equation 2 or H2 has a value of 0.828, which means that 82.8% of the Social Factor of cooperatives formed in crisis contexts can be explained with the use of KSE and application of the CIF. In addition, the ANOVA test of equation 2 turned out to be statistically significant at 0.01.

With reference to the interpretation of the estimated B of equation 2, it can be seen that both present (KSE and CIF) positive signs, and so it would indicate that both the knowledge and skills of the entrepreneur and the internal factors of the company have a positive impact on the Social Factor.

Analyzing equation 3, the adjusted R2 takes a value of 0.774, so that 77.4% of the Environmental Factor (MF) of cooperatives formed in the context of crisis can be explained by the application of KSE and CIF. In addition, the ANOVA test of equation 3 was statistically significant, and so the level of reliability of the aforementioned equation can explain the MF based on the application of the KSE and CIF. Regarding the interpretation of the estimated B of equation 3, both the KSE and the CIF have a positive and statistically significant impact on the Environmental Factor.

The H1 of this research proposed that the knowledge and skills of the entrepreneur and the internal factors of the company are variables that are positively related to the Economic Factor of cooperatives formed in the context of crisis. From the estimated B of equation 1 or H1, it follows that the existence of a positive and statistically significant relationship at 0.05 between the CIF and the EE can be verified. In the case of KSE and its impact with the Economic Factor, this relationship has not been statistically 0.05, and so it is possible to accept hypothesis 1 partially.

The H2 of this study proposed that the KSE and CIF have a positive impact on the Social Factor of the newly created cooperatives, the results show R2 adjusted at a high level. In addition, the estimated B for this equation presents positive values, for what would be partially accepted. In relation to H3, it is partially accepted, since CHEs have a non-significant relationship with FM ($0.40 > 0.05$) and FIEs have an impact and are statistically significant.

Conclusions

This study makes its contribution in the social and environmental variables, because according to the hypothesis contrast, both the social factors and the environmental factors are positively related to the knowledge and skills of the entrepreneurial group and to the factors Company interns. In this sense, the Elkington model, known as Triple Bottom Line (TBL) or the triple income statement, links the three dimensions (social, economic and environmental) and its constant and permanent interaction with organizations and their environment, was as well at the end of the 90s, emphasis is placed on the environmental dimension as a result of the crisis in the world on environmental aspects, caused by human behavior, especially the actions carried out by companies. In this context, the environmental discourse began to gain strength in administrative theories and strategies.

The H2 and H3 contrast the validity of the theoretical approaches, confirming the positive influence of the KSE and CIF in relation to social and environmental factors. Other internal factors or indicators were found that, despite being strategic, are not in harmony with the proposed structural model or have a low correlation such as: financial costs, the level of indebtedness and the level of technology. Given that during the periods of crisis in Colombia (2012–2015) there was an increase in the number of cooperatives formed in the city of Cali, it would be good to analyze them once the peace treaty is signed. In other words, to analyze whether this increase in cooperatives is due to the increased demand for labor by ex-guerrillas in society and whether this would bring any social test, if these organizations do not conform according to law.

The study offers input for future research to articulate the relationship of social, economic and environmental factors. In relation to the United Nations' 2030 agenda, specifically, the Sustainable Development Goals, forming new associative forms contributes to poverty reduction and the improvement of living conditions for intended beneficiaries through decent and dignifying work.

Notes

1 Tomado de. 1997. *The triple bottom line of 21st century business.* Oxford
2 According to data obtained from DANE – National Administrative Department of Statistics of Colombia.
3 Regarding Social Change, Saco states that "It is a collective process of lasting alteration over time of the forms of operation and structuring of interactions between individuals or groups that changes the historical course of a collective".

References

Alonso, M. J., & Galve, C. (2006). The entrepreneur and the company: a theoretical review of the determinants of its constitution. *Actions and Social Investigations, 26*, 5–44.

Álvarez, O. L. A., & Salazar, H. Z. (2011). Key conditions for the success and sustainability of solidarity ventures in Medellín. *Economic Semester, 14*, 77–94.

ASHOKA (2009). *Social entrepreneurs in Spain.* http://www.ashoka.es (accessed on 04April2015).

Baron, R. A. (2004). The cognitive perspective: a valuable tool for answering entrepreneurship's basic "why" questions. *Journal of Business Venturing, 19*, 221–239.

Barney, J. (1991). Firm resources and sustained competitive advantage. *Journal of Management, 17*, 99–120.

Bergamini, T. P., Navarro, C. L. C., & López, Á. R. (2014). Análisis del marco económico-jurídico específico para los emprendedores sociales. Un estudio comparado entre diversos países. *CIRIEC-España, 80*, 5–78.

Bergamini, T. P., Navarro, C. L. C., & López, Á. R. (2014). Analysis of the specific economic-legal framework for social entrepreneurs. A study compared between different countries. *CIRIEC-Spain, 80*, 5–78.

Campos Climent, V., Mohedano Suanes, A., & Sanchis Palacio, J. (2014). Determining factors in the success of the creation of small and medium enterprises. *The case of cooperatives in Spain. Valencia. Reversco 119*, 183–207.

Fernández, J., & Arranz, N. (1999). Business cooperation networks: an organization for the next millennium? *Management and Organization, 21*, 12–19.

Formichella, M. (2004). *The concept of entrepreneurship and its relationship with education, employment and local development* (pp. 1–42). Argentina: Buenos Aires.

Gide, Charles (1968). *Cooperativism* (pp. 206–300). Bogotá: Publi-coop.

Glaser, B. G. A. L. Strauss (1967). *The Discovery of Grounded Theory: Strategies for Qualitative Research* (p. 81). London: Wiedenfeld and Nicholson.

Grant, R. M. (1991). The resource-based theory of competitive advantage: implications for strategy formulation. *California Management Review, 33*, 114–135.

Grau, M. (2012). Social entrepreneurs: innovation at the service of social change. "La Caixa" Chair of corporate social responsibility and corporate governance. *Organizational structure, challenges and future perspectives. IESE, 14*, 1–67.

Herrera-Guerra, C. E., & Montoya-Restrepo, L. A. (2012). Approach to the characterization of entrepreneurs endorsed by the Emprender Sincelejo Fund. *Economic Panorama Magazine, 20*, 33–66.

Herron, L., & Robinson, R. B. (1993). A structural model of the effects of entrepreneurial characteristics on venture performance. *Journal of Business Venturing, 8*(3), 281–294.

Ibarra, E. L. T. (2004). *What is behind the decision to cooperate technologically?: Integrative theoretical proposal to explain inter-firm technological cooperation*, 30–56. Doctoral Dissertation, Mexico.

Kirzner, I. M. (1997). Entrepreneurial discovery and the competitive market process: an Austrian approach. *Journal of Economic Literature, 35*, 60–85.

Mair, J. (2010). *Social entrepreneurship taking stock and looking ahead*. Iese Business School - University of Navarra, Pamplona, Spain

Matiz, F. J. (2009). *Research in entrepreneurship, a challenge for the construction of knowledge* (pp. 66–182). Rean: Magazine-School of Business Administration.

Monzón, J. L., & Chaves, R. (2008). The European social economy: concept and dimensions of the third sector. *Annals of Public and Cooperative Economics, 79*, 549–577.

Penrose's, E. (1959). Contributions to the resource-based view of strategic management. *Journal of Management Studies, 41*, 183–191.

Peteraf, M. A. (1993). The cornerstones of competitive advantage: a resource-based view. *Strategic Management Journal, 14*, 179–191.

Raceto, L. M. (1993). From the popular economy to the solidarity economy: an alternative development project. *Labor Economics Program, 3*, 1–45.

Sanchis, J. R., & Melián, A. (s.f.). *Social entrepreneurship and new social economy as a mechanism for socio-labor insertion.* 1–9. http://www.ensie.org/socialeconomyandsocialenterprises

Sanchis, Campos, & Mohedano (2014). Key factors in the creation and development of cooperatives. Empirical study applied to the Valencian community. *Reversco, 199*, 183–207.

Serrano, R. (2007). Critical notes on cooperative democracy. *Cooperativism and Development*, *27*, 64–79.

Silva, A. (2012). Cooperativism and internationalization. *Some management guidelines for cooperativeness. Legis SA, Bogotá, II*, pp. 161–176.

Schumpeter, J. (1934). *The Theory of Economic Development.* Cambridge: Harvard University Press.(New York: Oxford University Press, 1961.) First Publisher in German, 1912

10 Fair trade focus of social joint and engine for the sustainable local development

Experiences in Quito-Ecuador with the American City of Fair Trade

Cesar Augusto Marcillo Vaca, Laura Angélica De La Cruz Guerrero, and Jaime Ramiro Figueroa Fraga

Introduction

Ecuador, like many other countries in Latin America, had to build its own local development mechanisms, based on its experiences, geographical conditions and historical context. During a period of its history, its development model was based on an almost exclusively extractive and export model of raw materials for the benefit of the international market. Progressively, this model has had to take steps to evolvet in the construction of another model which allows local actors to enter themselves in the international market with other types of criteria that can better benefit these producers. Moreover, the creation of effective collective networks of producers have had a different impact on the economical running of their country.

Unlike the classic development models that seek to promote a development based primarily on foreign aid, the model that allowed the construction of fair trade dynamics essentially implied the recognition of the existence of local knowledge, productive traditions and societal organization. It was organized under an economic dynamic that was combined with a solid international movement around a new conception of international cooperation for development based on the principles of "Trade, Not Aid".

This process involved the development of a dynamic of deep transformation paradigms, which did not depend entirely on the outside, but from a logic of own production that is combined with an international movement of greater awareness with a global reduction of inequalities and with a greater awareness of the importance of consumer power in global dynamics. Parallel to this, this situation also implied taking into account the general differences in global economic mutations, where the economic importance of the developed countries is more relevant. A fundamental element of the change in this paradigm was the oil crises caused by the actions arranged by OPEC in the 1970s, of which Ecuador is part of. The awareness of the fundamental role than old countries considered as "peripheral" by the old colonial powers has also been decisive in allowing the consolidation of a new global trading system, based on different premises than the simple law of supply and demand in an increasingly interconnected world.

This convergence of factors is the origin of one of the most interesting and successful experiences on fair trade in the world, which is the case of Ecuador. Obviously, this process has not been without complexities, challenges, errors or even contradictions. However, it is noteworthy that this dynamic of more than 40 years produces results that are increasingly encouraging. Although at the beginning the proposal was fundamentally oriented towards an export dynamic, today Ecuador is in a position to develop and reinforce its own internal market dynamics and to evolve the local networks. It was especially promoted originally by the Catholic Church and non-governmental organizations towards a broader movement, not only on raw materials, but also on new types of products and services, such as tourism and products with greater added value.

These successful experiences are also of great interest for the dynamics of the solidarity economy, which is the economic model in the Ecuadorian legislation. The popular and solidarity economy is the form of economic organization, where its members, individually or collectively, organize and develop processes of production, exchange, marketing, financing and consumption of goods and services to satisfy needs and generate incomes. It is not only because of the relevance of the use of their own mechanisms with new paradigms and economic practices based on different principles than the classical profit of the private economy, or the economic schemes redistributive of the public economy. Moreover, they analyze the relevance of new paradigms in the economic activity: the recognition of the dynamics of local production that guarantee crops and products of a different quality to the mass production provoking innumerable effects on the nature and the social dynamics of the communities, among many other negative factors.

The level reached and officially registered by the Ecuadorian Fairtrade activities oriented abroad motivates its evaluation as to whether associativity constitutes a determining cause for these achievements measured in monetary form (Figure 10.1).

According to these records, the jump is considerable because fair trade exports passed from US $ 23 million in 2010 to US $ 112 million in 2016. Within the 10 Principles of Fair Trade, the number 6 raises the freedom to associate. More people involved in this movement are also forced to comply with the remaining nine principles (WFTO, 2019).

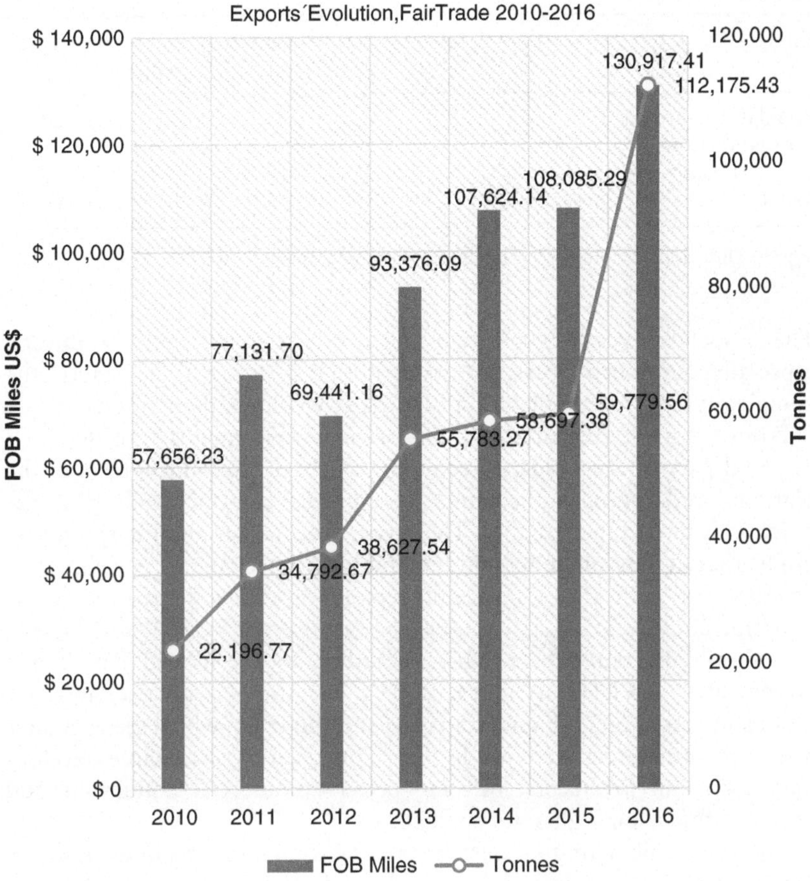

Figure 10.1 National Service of Customs of the Ecuador, SENAE 2016.

Table 10.1 Fair Trade exports in Ecuador 2017 *(value FOB thousands USD)*

Fair trade exports from Ecuador 2017 Thousands USD	
Association exports	59.296
Exports of floricultural plantations	46.779
Private companies expressions	42.964
Total estimated exports	**149.039**

Source: Direction of Commercial Intelligence and investments, PROECUADOR

Table 10.2 Exporters with fair trade certification 2017

Kind	Exports	Does not exports	Total
Popular and solidarity economy (EPS) organizations	20	7	27
Private businesses	34	1	35
Total	54	8	62

Source: Direction of Commercial Intelligence and investments, PROECUADOR

The associativity of Ecuadorian fair trade actors, small producers, especially rural producers, has constituted a strength that faced the complexity and monopolization of current world trade relations.

From the most auscultating point of view, fair trade is considered an essential part of the solidarity economy. Several pronouncements of the National Federation of the Exporters consider that fair trade is an activity with its own personality. Therefore, the analysis and interpretation imply that it has an inherent dynamic and its example enriches and collaborates with the component sectors of the solidarity economy (Guerra, 2009).

It should be remembered that according to the World Fair Trade Organization (WFTO) (Guerra, 2009), fair trade is an exchange relationship based on dialogue, transparency and trust, which seeks greater justice in commercial activity. It contributes to the sustainable development of small producers, offering better commercial conditions and ensuring that their rights are fulfilled.

The economic activities start from the production of goods and services and they are commercialized and conclude with their consumption. Within this framework, fair trade is considered to link solidarity productions, such as food sovereignty products, handicrafts, agribusiness, community tourism and so on, with responsible consumers inside domestic economies and in other countries, especially in the Global North. Likewise, it draws on an ethical and solidarity financing that is different from the objectives pursued by capitalist finances. For the operation of fair trade, associations of small producers, cooperatives, organizations, intermediation and solidarity networks have been generated. On the other hand, there is a responsible consumer who chooses ethical, ecological and small producer groupings.

Ecuador leads fair trade in Latin America because of the figures, but even more by the way that it has been built, which are mostly from rural and depressed areas with a high intervention of the Catholic Church. Also, it is emphasized that historically there has been a very little intervention by the State in the beginning and during the development of fair trade. In recent years, government presence is noted, although still incipient through a policy and small public management actions in this area.

According to the Ecuadorian Fair Trade Strategy, it is not only an international buying and selling activity, but it also has a deep essence expressed in these characteristics.

- It is much more than stamps and certifications.
- It is a mainstay of the solidarity economy.
- It is a strategy towards "Buen Vivir". It means that the National Plan for "Buen Vivir" 2017–2021 is intended as the instrument of social and political dialogue, where the development planning is seen as the space to achieve major national agreements.
- It is a structural tool to eliminate poverty and inequality.
- It is a strategy for territorial equity.
- It is a transversal axis of the process of change of the productive matrix.
- It is a tool to change the rules of national and international trade.
- It contributes to sustainability and sustainability.
- It promotes agroecology and food sovereignty.
- It promotes responsible consumption.
- It has a value chain vision.
- It is associativity and organization.
- It raises awareness and educates society.
- It uses appropriate systems of promotion, recognition, monitoring and control.
- It promotes economic and gender equity.
- It recognizes diverse actors and values the culture and identity of the people.

An apparently favorable environment for solidarity partnerships in Ecuador

The country in 2008 approved the Constitution of the Republic that governs until these days. In article 28, it established that the economic system is social and supportive. Therefore, the economy based on associativity and solidarity was recognized, which had always been in the shadow of public and private economies (Asamblea Nacional. Constitución de la República del Ecuador, 2008). With true hope, in the population and especially in the strata of greater economic deprivation, it was configured that a new era of creation and strengthening of enterprises based on the union of people with principles and values began.

The Organic Law of Food Sovereignty (LORSA) (2009), the Organic Law of Popular and Solidarity Economy and of the Asamblea Nacional. Ley Orgánica de Economía Popular y Solidaria (2011) were quickly approved and subsequently the articles and codes favorable to the so-called Popular and Solidarity Economy (Asamblea Nacional. Ley Orgánica de Economía Popular y Solidaria, 2011). Since 2012, the Fair Trade Agenda began to be built, which would later become the current name of the Ecuadorian Fair Trade Strategy, an instrument aimed at promoting fair and supportive production and marketing.

Several institutions in the administrative framework of the central government appeared to favor the Popular and Solidarity Economy. Therefore, the promotion of the Institute of Popular and Solidarity Economy (IEPS) was created for financing the National Corporation of Popular and Solidarity Finance (CONAFIPS) and for the control of the Superintendence of Popular and Solidarity Economy (SEPS). In addition to several existing public institutions, units linked to this task were organized.

It should be noted that the official recognition, through the Law, was that cooperatives, associations of small producers and community organizations are actors of the Social and Solidarity Economy. These three actors together with the popular economic units basically made up of individual, family, artisanal, commercial microenterprises, care economy (home) and even informal ones are part of the so-called popular economy. The sum of these four actors officially generates the Popular and Solidarity Economy (EPS). However, the first three are associated and supportive, while the popular economic units are individuals and not required to comply with values and principles. In total, the EPS represents between 60% and 64% of the economically active population, around 5 million people (INEC, 2019).

Several sectional public bodies known as Decentralized Autonomous Governments (GADs) have sought to be included in the promotion and support of the EPS, although in the majority very tangentially. In fact, of the 221 municipalities that Ecuador has, only about 10 issued ordinances on the EPS, none have a structured plan of short or medium term and no technical units, except for honorable exceptions.

Regarding fair trade, the Ministry of Production, Foreign Trade, Investments and Fisheries has the Inclusive Trade unit, supported by a fully technical body, which is the Institute for the Promotion of Exports and Investments, PROECUADOR, in charge of both issues mentioned, but this public organization has been absorbed by said Secretary of State.

On the other hand, they have deserved the recognition of Latin American Fair Trade Universities: the UTE EC University with headquarters in Quito, UTE, and the Chimborazo Polytechnic School based in Riobamba, ESPOCH, which have committed to send news, information, photos and videos of the activities they carry out for fair trade. It also has two Latin American fair trade cities: the capital of the country Quito and Riobamba, a historic city in the Ecuadorian Andean center (CLAC, 2016).

Associativity and the construction of local, national and international networks

A horizon that traced fair trade from the South was to combine associativity from small local groups with a global focus, especially in Ecuador. Due to this basic condition, local, national and international networks have been developing rapidly and decades ago.

The associativity of small producers has a very solid base in the Andean communities, which is why in recent years the projection that a solidarity economy must be linked to Good Living was revived, living harmoniously between people, localities and these with nature.

In the interior of the country, there is the network with the greatest geographical coverage, the so-called Social and Solidarity Economy Movement of Ecuador (MESSE). Although it operates without a legal status, it has turned 11 years and it has a horizontal sectorization of: North, Central and South Zone, among its basic axes is fair trade (Aguilar, 2017). Another recognized network is the Union of Peasant Organizations of Cotacahi (UNORCAC, 2019). It was born in 1977, and as the name suggests it consolidates more than 190 organizations between communes, water boards and so on. Thus, we find in each province these networks that carry out their activities in an associative way.

The basic fair trade count in Ecuador: David versus Goliath

A recurring invisibility has marked the trajectory of export fair trade in the country. Policies and actions have always supported the productions of capital companies. This concealment was only revealed in 2010, which is evidenced by the enactment of statistics on external sales of fair trade (Mason & Tapia, 2005).

Making its way into the status quo showed that the expertise to enter the world of global marketing is not only reserved for large national and transnational corporations. In fact, the business intelligence and skills can assimilate people without the levels of education currently required, attending training and continuing popular education (Cunningham, 2005). Almost without exception, the initiators and leaders of Ecuadorian fair trade and even some still today have presented as a common denominator the non-obtaining of titles of third, fourth or fifth level of education. It means college, university, master or PhD degrees.

Fair trade exports have no privilege or special preferences such as those offered to capitalist corporate exporters. Periodically, the State has provided its logistical and financial support for capitalist entrepreneurs to attend fairs and events of any kind, as well as free sample shipments and finally the organization of commercial offices in certain cities of countries of commercial interest. They created tax exemption instruments, credit lines, university education at their service, infrastructure and so on. However, for fair trade, there have been no such perks.

Faced with this unequal structure, fair trade organizations were making their way with the support already indicated by the Catholic Church, external non-governmental organizations and the strong will of these groups of small producers empowered by this way of life and imbued to say enough to the exploitation that was made in the pricing and weighing of products. The list of pioneer names is long; however, we will mention Padre Graziano Mazón, Rubén Tapia, Padre Polo, José Tonello, Vargas family, Rosa Guamán. Also, the emblematic organizations such as Grupo Salinas, Fondo Ecuatoriano Popularum Progressio (Camari), Maquita Cushunchic (MCCH), Sinchi Sacha, Jambi Kiwa, FAPECAFES, Asoguabo and so on. Each one has a history full of vicissitudes with falls, but with triumphs they managed to position this alternative marketing as a Latin American example.

Its recognition was considered for Quito to be designated as the headquarters of the Latin American Community Marketing Network, RELACC, which joins 12 national networks of the region corresponding to Central America, Mercosur and the Andean area. This network began its construction in 1991 and was completed after several meetings in 2001 under the approval of Ecuadorian laws as a private law corporation for social and non-profit purposes and in addition without political or religious affiliations.

The learnings of two Ecuadorian fair trade organizations with certifications: Fair Trade Consortium and Ecuadorian Fair Trade Coordinator

Two international organizations push the consolidation of fair trade in Ecuador. FAIRTRADE (FAIRTRADE, 2017) is linked to the Fair Trade Consortium, while the Latin American and Caribbean Coordinator of Small Fair Trade Producers (CLAC) cooperates with the CECJ. Since the 1970, this activity has been pushed.

The Fair Trade Consortium is a member of the WFTO formed by seven important organizations, namely, Fondo Ecuatoriano Populorum Progressio (Camari), Fundación Chankuap, Gruppo Salinas, Maquita Cushunchic (MCCH), Fundación Sinchi Sacha, Red de Turismo Comunitario Pakariñan y Corporación de Ferias de Loja. The CECJ brings together FAPECAFES, Jambi Kiwa, KOPROBICH, UROCAL, FECAFEM, ASOGUABO, UNOCACE, FOMSOEAN, Cerro Azul Association and Fortalezas del Valle. These consolidated networks have become the force to boost the intensification of the concept and its characteristics of the national and global Fair Trade movement.

Of the US $ 112 million reported from fair trade exports to 2016, according to PROECUADOR, a representative portion belongs to the organizations of these two networks. The first organization that worked since the 1970s with an idea of justice for producers was the Salinas Group in Guaranda, developing and commercializing a great diversity of products and services in a community way. Following the motivation of the Ecuadorian Populorum Progressio Fund (FEPP), in 1981 Camari was born as a solidarity marketer with the mission of promoting the development of communities.

In 1985, Maquita Cushunchic Marketing as Brothers (MCCH) was born, as a direct bridge between rural producers and producers with urban consumers, linked to the Ecclesial Base Communities, first in the south of Quito and then in other cities of the country. Since 1990, other marketing experiences have emerged, such as Sinchi Sacha closely linked to trade and cultural identity issues and Chankuap with a commendable social impact in the Amazon.

All the aforementioned organizations are certified as Fair Trade organizations by the WFTO collective feature that since 2011 prompted them to promote the Ecuadorian Consortium of Solidarity Economy and Fair Trade of Ecuador as a public advocacy space, promotion of fair trade and responsible consumption.

In 2003, the Ecuadorian Fair Trade Coordinator (CECJ) was founded and legalized in 2010 as a National Union of Small Farmers Associations Certified in Fair Trade from Ecuador that groups 11 organizations certified with FLO Seal with a total of 11,138 members and partners who work in the areas of cocoa, coffee, bananas, cereals, aromatic and jams in the provinces of Esmeraldas, Manabí, Los Ríos, El Oro, Chimborazo, Loja, Sucumbíos and Zamora Chinchipe. It is aligned with the objectives and principles of the CLAC to ensure that its organization, production and marketing practices comply with Fair Trade standards. They have developed the SPP Guarantee Seal (Seal of the Small Producer) widespread in the Continent.

Currently, this national movement has been joined by entrepreneurs and various organizations of producers with a variety of products and services aimed at local and international markets with a social and economic impact. It has meant that Fair Trade and Economy Popular and Solidarity in Ecuador contribute positively to the economic development of the country.

Analyzing the current Ecuadorian fair trade system from the work deployed by the Fair Trade Consortium of Ecuador and the CECJ, we can see models of solidarity companies with significant advances, but also with gaps to establish radically creative and timely corrective measures. Thus, in the area of production and services, producers must develop new lines with innovative products without losing the essence of fair trade, since consumer preferences are changing by age and status and especially to meet the needs of the consumers. The quality, presentation and promotion of the product is a challenge of continuous improvement.

Associations of small producers: cultivation of principles, values and harmonious relationship with nature

A deficiency found points to the shortage of information sources in the country with in-depth analysis concerning the numerous cases of small associations that are icons of this movement in the country. Many are known for their products, but not for their history, their origins and their conformation, especially to the obstacles of discrimination in several ways, such as race, gender, income, religion, access to education, political representation, food and housing.

In the Andean communities, the fulfillment of ancestral values, such as ama quilla, ama llulla, ama shua, which means not to be idle, not to lie, not to steal, has united them even by building their own justice, recognized in Article 1 of the Constitution of 2008.

The other major aspect is the veneration of the Pacha Mama as a source of life for the communities. Therefore, the communities celebrate several times a year as a symbol of gratitude for the crops (El Comercio, 2017). This environment derives in the appearance of associations of small producers.

Two Andean values stand out: minga and pamba mesa, whose spiritual essence in the group deepens associativity. "La minga" (WordPress, 2008) translated into a mutual community support for the required activities is the focus on a physical constructive nature, such as irrigation channels, neighborhood roads, communal houses, construction works and repair of each member's property and so on, and also to support in planting and harvesting of the fruits of the land. In addition, the pamba mesa (Marquez, 2015) or sharing food in a communal meal is where everyone contributes with food and they enjoy it in group known as mingas or festivities.

Briefly, the Andean vision of Sumak Kawsay or Buen Vivir derives a conception of the ancestral life of the Andean people that has remained in force in many indigenous communities until today. In Quichua, "Sumak" means the ideal, the beautiful, the good, the realization, and "kawsay" means life, in reference to a dignified life, in harmony, with a balance between the universe and the human being, the community and family. These practices have led to the use of agroecology for planting (Altieri, 2010), development and harvest of agricultural products. Also, they use the so-called social technologies, whose identification has also been enhanced in Latin America.

Field-city, exchange relations

There are full of divergences. The countryside subsidizes the cities based on delivering products at low prices. Even it does not matter in sacrificing the countryside in order to increase the well-being of the city. In addition, they demand clean and nutritious products and so on. It is not exclusive to Ecuador, but to almost all countries; the presence of unequal relations between farmers in the countryside with consumers in cities is always latent. Peasant products have a propensity to be acquired at the lowest prices, reducing to levels below production costs. In the imaginary city, the farmer is free of commitments and it demands less incomes; therefore, they have to pay the minimum for the products.

In the country, the greatest poverty is evidenced in the countryside, precisely because of this structure of prices and lack of economic resources, inputs, land, information, product development, quality, productive capacity, specialized training, organization and so on. They live daily with unfair competition, the exclusionary market, irresponsible consumption habits and insufficient comprehensive public policies that reactivate the production and fair marketing of surpluses. In this difficult reality, producers access and remain in the market under unequal conditions. However, through fair trade rural producers receive a higher price for their products and also sales to the Global North are generated. In fact, they are rewarded with an extra contribution: In the food field, healthy, organic, safe and nutritious products are being offered.

Products and services of a fair trade: quality, volumes and local markets

Achieving appropriate volumes constitute an issue in this area, and many times it has not been possible to meet the requirements for the domestic market and even more for the overseas market. Therefore, the requirement to work in networks is vital. Various efforts made to obtain an entity of its own, which is responsible for the certification and promotion of fair trade in Ecuador. It has not been possible for various reasons; among them, the lack of political decision from government control agencies, the lack of organization and management of producer organizations and the little interest of the private company that minimizes the expectation of development within this marketing system. The questions also go through whether the products are certified nationally or at the local territory level or being the organizations as a whole. These argumentations work among fair trade actors, the public sector and the academy, striving to find the viable and adequate solution for producers and consumers.

A fair trade not certified

It is known that in numerous country organizations of different geographical nature produce and market products and services for the domestic market with large approximations to the 10 global criteria of fair trade (Marcillo, 2016).

As mentioned above, the absence of a national certifying entity for fair trade products and the limited financial resources to access to the registration of a membership cause a lack of interest in small producers to work for a guarantee seal within this system. On the other hand, the low promotion and ignorance of consumers regarding this alternative marketing system, based on compliance with the principles of fair trade does not allow real awareness by the people, who demand quality products to satisfy their needs, thinking about their health and common well-being, based on social and environmental responsibility. Despite the great importance, especially of food production, they do not have specific infrastructure for sale in the localities and go to fairs granted by municipalities in public spaces with minimal adequate hygiene, sun protection, rain or wind protection.

Food sovereignty constitutes an emblem for food production defending the multivariety of supply, rescuing products in danger of extinction, sowing and cultivating together with the realities of mother earth, ancestral knowledge and the influence of the moon and the elimination of the use of chemicals (Kiwa, 2012). Their fight is against junk products and fast food; they appeal for traditional food or slow food. In this context, the offer focuses on grains such as quinoa, amaranth and chocho; exotic fruits such as arazá, chihualcán, babaco, badea, cocoa and its derivatives; and meat from smaller animals such as guinea pig, rabbit, alpaca and vicuña. The medicine goes to the medicinal plants.

Compliance criteria of fair trade cities and universities

The two cities Quito and Riobamba declared as Latin American fair trade cities have met the six criteria established by the Latin American Fair Trade Coordinator (CLAC). Therefore, actions at the municipal level were articulated and sensitized, and then the declaration of the respective mayors was obtained. The local committees were formed and public purchases of the local organisms of this sector are being fulfilled, although not with the desired effectiveness. Moreover, fair trade campaigns are organized to encourage consumers to purchase these products. Educational entities are slowly incorporated into this movement, especially universities focused on research, education and promotion. A very effective link that is being created constitutes the annual celebrations of World Fair Trade Day.

By 2020, Quito will host the International Meeting of Cities for Fair Trade. The designation is a recognition of the trajectory displayed by the city in favor of a different marketing model. More than 500 representatives of the 2196 cities for fair trade (FAIRTRADE, 2017) accredited throughout the planet will attend the event.

Similarly, the two universities are meeting the criteria that have been self-imposed. Although the validity of these awards for cities and universities is very short. The results are already encouraging that more organizations join and expand the activities of fair trade certification.

Intervention and pending tasks of the public sector and the academy

There are approximately 60 universities operating in Ecuador, and no more than 10 of these have academic links with the solidarity economy and with fair trade, with the exception of the two already mentioned. Tangentially there are research efforts for thesis development, but real involvement is still lacking. In regards to the public sector, the public purchase required from fair trade organizations and the popular solidarity economy an average of 3% to 5% of the annual purchases that must be made from these solidarity organizations. In 2017, 6.5% was registered (Vicepresidencia de la República, 2018). The role of training for solidarity ventures has been suggested and is a very strong aspiration for a network to be formed between the public sector. It means that the central administration, local administrations and universities work together in each territory.

Deficit of responsible consumers being ethical, ecological and supportive

Among the greatest challenges is the organization and operation of networks of responsible consumers. It means a stable demand but that will be expanded as awareness increases. Several ideas have been proposed, such as the preparation of campaigns to make fair trade known in schools, colleges, universities and corporate organizations. The emergence of organic groups for fair trade has not yet taken shape.

Challenges and the search for associative and solidarity social regional integration: South-South relationship

More than a reality, this orientation is a challenge because the fair trade products of the south are similar. In fact, their economies have similar productive structures in the region. There have been some attempts at exchange, but they have failed. In addition, to this similarity in production, the transport costs are high, markets of incipient responsible consumers and low purchasing power.

In Mercosur, which is the unit of countries of South America, appeared a great effort through the creation of the: Espacio Mercosur Solidario, the Latin American Network of Fair Trade Stores (WFTO-LA, 2018) and RELACC through a collaborative work strategy in a regional network. It identified common needs and fostered regional actions such as the Andean network of community tourism and incipient steps for the creation of the network of quinueros, cocoa and the Latin American school of solidarity economy and fair trade. The intention is to establish synergies to intervene in the market in a corporate manner.

Another action that contributed to the south-south integration was the Regional and Latin American Solidarity Fairs. One of the best known is the Latin American Solidarity Economy Fair of Santa María, Rio Grande Do Sul in Brazil (Cooperatvas de las Américas, 2017).

Although in an incipient form, there are already relationships to integrate and interact between the countries of the South. Ecuador and Brazil have already tried and Ecuador and Nicaragua signed a trade agreement that explicitly incorporated fair trade. This search of unity between countries in the region has the purpose to reach exchanges of fair trade products with the purpose that they become permanent. The Latin American Community Marketing Network, RELACC, is a bridge called to generate positive results.

The model of Quito, City of Latin American Fair Trade: from the experiences exposed to the current concretions and the near horizon

Quito is the first Latin American capital that has been recognized as a fair trade city. It complied with the six principles that were required by the CLAC. Historically, several enriching and paradigmatic experiences have been present for several decades.

An emblematic experience was born in the south of the city in 1985 with a group of idealist and grassroots youth led by a Catholic priest. They began to market food products that came from the Ecuadorian highlands. They did not imagine that they were currently working at Maquita Chushunchic. They sought justice, equity and solidarity. They found a broad field to unite fair producers and marketers with fair prices. This foundation currently leads the industrialization and external marketing of cocoa derivatives. It has achieved building a plant in the Guayas province where they produce liquors, cocoa paste and chocolate.

While it was happening in the south of the city, other important organizations such as Camari was founded in 1981, which promoted the international placement of fair trade products in foreign markets and operated in several cities of the country. In fact, they settled in Quito and opened a new store in the capital with the best city comments in 2019. The organization recognized by the national government as an emblem of fair trade Grupo Salinas opened its doors. Nowadays, they have opened more stores, cafeteria and opened other fair trade stores in Quito in May 2018. They are very functional due to the growth of their activities and the increasingly positive reception that their products have.

Sinchi Sacha, an organization dedicated to promoting handicrafts, also appears on the Quito skyline and stands out for its presence in the Plaza de San Francisco, the city's tourist heart. It is the headquarters of RELACC. To these self-managed organizations, another agency was added: the CONQUITO Local Development Agency. It was born with a horizon to meet the demands of training and support for productive activities of the private sector. When the new Constitution was issued in 2008 and declaring that Ecuador will have a social and solidarity economic system, CONQUITO incorporated the Popular and Solidarity Economy Program in 2013.

However, the Agency was always ready to develop activities for small productions such as the AGRUPAR, urban agriculture, and Innovative Solidarity Companies Program, PESI. It is ready to support the municipal public procurement, fairs organization, courses and finally the achievement that Quito has become a Latin American City for Fair Trade in 2016.

It counts on with the UTE EC University, declared a Latin American University for fair trade in 2016, which has developed research and other permanent institutional support in dissemination and promotion. It was responsible to identify the profile of consumers by applying a first consumer survey in the CAMARI store. The results indicate the following characteristics of consumers of fair trade: Ecuadorian women of an age range of 18–28 years, who work especially in the private business sector. They make their purchases on a monthly basis, usually in the afternoon since they comment that it is easier to go at this time with respect to their daily activities. In addition, their level of purchase is by units. They agree with the location of the current store, but they would like that other stores to be placed in the north and south of Quito in order to get the products easily, taking in consideration the distances from their homes and offices. They have the payment preference of cash and consider that the price is fair because the quality of the product is good.

They are mostly interested in receiving information about the products, benefits and promotions offered by Camari because most of the surveyed have not received any kind of benefit for their products. It manages a fairly efficient system "boca a boca" because most of its customers have knowledge of the company by reference, and they will recommend it to other people. For the next months, it has plans to investigate the consumer profile of the Salinerito and Maquita Cushunchic stores.

Thanks to the intellectual "minga" made by the institutions that make up the Local Committee of Quito for Fair Trade, the document "Live Fair Trade. A Basic Manual of concepts, advances and projections in Ecuador (Marcillo, 2016) can bedownloaded for free. The content is very light, and it pretends that more people know about the fair trade movement with the purpose of becoming involved as producers, marketers, funders or consumers all in an associative and supportive way. It will have the mapping of fair trade actors in the city, a basic instrument for the generation of municipal policy and the most successful planning for the coming years.

In this way, it is assured that Quito will be a permanent reference that reflects the benefits of fair trade. Therefore, many small producers not only benefit from the demand of the locality but also from that of the entire country.

Conclusions: future prospects and challenges

It is worth looking at where the efforts will be focused in order to give solutions and fulfil aspirations of the people and communities for a better well-being. There must be a global conscience to put aside consumerism and the tragedy of permanent aggression to the earth. There should be new ways of understanding consumption, which demands respect for ourselves and nature.

The fields are wide, but also the contenders are the masters of world trade and localities. An unequal confrontation that requires different weapons and they are in respect for what is produced, what is commercialized and what is consumed. But even more, the harmonious experience of associative and solidarity organizations, equitable sharing, democracy, transparency, cooperation and more values will allow local and international fair trade to consolidate.

Approximately 57 countries in the South provide Fair Trade products to 33 countries in the North; almost half of the countries in the world are involved with transactions, which amounts to approximately US $ 10,000. Fair Trade cities push the consolidation of it. According to FAITRADE, 35,000 products are offered in this commercialization. These realities are encouraging, but at the same time the challenges go in several directions. The most sensitive aspect is the development and the possible deviations that have happened in several organizations of the solidarity economy. The most commented has been the rise and fall of FAGOR (Azumendi, 2016) cooperative, the jewel in the crown of the Mondragón Group of the Basque Country. In Latin America, we have the near disappearance of SANCOR (i Prtofesinal, 2018) Cooperative of Argentina, which became the fifth dairy conglomerate worldwide.

Other directions suggest that fair trade organizations really contribute to reduce the serious consumerism that plagues the world population. For Quito as a Fair Trade city, the tasks will be to combine efforts to reach material achievements, without neglecting spiritual achievements. That values prevail over purely utilitarian aspirations. For this, fair trade is socialized in the educational units available in the Municipality. The academy will strengthen its incidence and the formation of the fair trade researchers' network in number and quality. The actors will work together and finally the biggest challenge is the creation of responsible consumers.

Among the numerous challenges will be to encourage and strengthen the local dynamics of fair trade, seeking that these products are not limited to the export market. This will require the construction of a structural and institutional support by public actors, especially for the creation of local consumer networks, promotion of consumer co-operatives, adequate legal frameworks and other alternatives. Taking into consideration the level of development achieved, there are necessary elements to create a synergy with all actors (public authorities, private actors, universities) insisting on the importance of product quality, as well as the incorporation of new practices and ethical concepts and operating principles around sustainable development policies, such as agroecology, and also with the impulse of different participatory democracy activities. The last element, which is very important, is to recommend that the principles and policies take into account the fragility of small actors, as well as the risk of creating or exacerbating dynamics of the concentration of powers of privileged actors to the detriment of the most vulnerable, which are always present to some degree.

References

Aguilar, G. (2017). *El Movimiento de Economía Social y Solidaria del Ecuador. Revista de la Academia*, *21*, 101–128.

Altieri, M. (2010). *ILSA Ed., La revolución agroecologíca en América Latina*. Bogotá, Colombia.

Asamblea Nacional. Constitución de la República del Ecuador (2008). Retrieved from https://www.asambleanacional.gob.ec/sites/default/files/documents/old/constitucion_de_bolsillo.pdf.

Asamblea Nacional. Ley Orgánica de Economía Popular y Solidaria (2011), Pub. L. No. Registro Oficial 444 de 10-may.2011 Ecuador. Retrieved from https://www.seps.gob.ec/documents/20181/25522/LEY ORGANICA DE ECONOMIA POPULAR Y SOLIDARIA actualized November 2018.pdf/66b23eef-8b87-4e3a-b0ba-194c2017e69a.

Azumendi, E. (2016, September 30). La caída de Fagor Electrodomésticos, el día que tembló Euskadi. *El Diario El Norte de España*. Retrieved from https://www.eldiario.es/norte/euskadi/caida-Fagor-Electrodomesticos-temblar-Euskadi_0_564494445.html.

CLAC. (2016). Avanzan las ciudades latinoamericanas por el comercio justo. Retrieved from http://clac-comerciojusto.org/2016/12/avanzan-las-ciudades-latinoamericanas-por-el-comercio-justo/.

Cooperatvas de las Américas. (2017). La 24 Feria de Economía Solidaria de América Latina batió récord de visitación. Retrieved from https://www.aciamericas.coop/La-24-Feria-de-Economia-Solidaria-de-America-Latina-batio-record-de-visitacion.

Cunningham, G. (2005). *La historia de Jambi Kiwa*. Retrieved from https://coady.stfx.ca/wp-content/uploads/pdfs/JAMBIspanish.pdf.

El Comercio. (2017, June 19). Así se celebra el Inti Raymi en las provincias de la Sierra. *El Comercio*. Retrieved from https://www.elcomercio.com/actualidad/celebracion-intiraymi-sierra-sol-cosecha.html

FAIRTRADE. (2017). Fairtrade para productores. Retrieved from https://info.fairtrade.net/es/producer.

Guerra, P. (2009). *El comercio justo y la economía solidaria deben ir de la mano*. Retrieved from https://www.alainet.org/es/active/29319.

i Prtofesinal. (2018). Luz verde para venta de SanCor: la asamblea acepta convertirse en S.A. Retrieved from https://www.iprofesional.com/notas/266557-sancor-adecoagro-venta-leche-adquisicion-industrias-otros-acuerdo-preventivo-extrajudicial-sancor-industrias-lacteas-Luz-verde-para-venta-de-SanCor-asamblea-acepta-convertirse-en-SA-y-transferir-90-de-las-acciones

INEC. (2019). Estadísticas mensuales 2014-2019. *Indicadores Laborales*. Retrieved from https://www.ecuadorencifras.gob.ec/empleo-septiembre-2019/

Kiwa, J. (2012). Bajo la influencia de la luna. *Riobamba*. Retrieved from https://www.youtube.com/watch?v=VxKxULarw4k.

Marcillo, C. (2016). *Vive Comercio Justo*. Retrieved from https://www.economiasolidaria.org/sites/default/files/reaslibrary_attachments/Manual-de-Comercio-Justo.pdf.

Marquez, C. (2015). *La pambamesa es el frefrigerio de moda en Riobamba. El Comercio*. https://www.elcomercio.com/actualidad/ecuador-riobamba-pambamesa-refrigerio-tradicion.html.

Mason, G., & Tapia, R. (2005). 20 años de utopias en el mundo de Goliat. (El Conejo, Ed.). *Quito*. Retrieved from https://searchworks.stanford.edu/view/6680007.

Ministerio de Comercio Exterior. (2017). Estrategia ecuatoriana de Comercio Justo 2014-2017. Retrieved from http://www.clac-comerciojusto.org/ulcj/wp-content/uploads/2014/06/Estrategia-Ecuatoriana-de-Comercio-Justo.pdf.

Portal de la Economía Solidaria. (2018). Declaración del espacio MERCOSUR Solidario. Retrieved from https://www.economiasolidaria.org/sites/default/files/reaslibrary/attachments/Mercosur_Solidario.pdf.

Vicepresidencia de la República. (2018, April 4). El 6,5% de compras públicas provienen de la economía popular. *Ecuador TV*. Retrieved from https://www.ecuadortv.ec/tourism/noticias/actualidad/el-6-5-de-compras-publicas-del-estado-proviene-de-la-economia-popular-y-solidaria.

WFTO-LA. (2018). Mapa del Comercio Justo. Retrieved from http://www.wfto-la.org/wfto-la/mapa-del-comercio-justo-en-america-latina/.

WFTO. (2019). Los 10 Principios de Comercio Justo. Retrieved from http://www.wfto-la.org/comercio-justo/wfto/10-principios-comercio-justo/#.

WordPress. (2008). La minga en movimiento. Retrieved from https://lamingaenmovimiento.wordpress.com/la-minga/.

Index

Acevedo, D. 162
Acosta, A. 5
agrarian capitalism 138
agrobusiness 137
agro-ecological peasant organizations 145
agroecology 136–7
air pollution: government policies for 67; strategies for 68–9; sustainable approaches to 68–9; urban transport and 69–70; vehicle builders and 67
Albuquerque, F. 117
Alió y Fransualdo de Azevedo 163
Alston, Philip 43
analysis of variance (ANOVA) test 199, 200, 201
Andean culture 112, 124
Andean values 214
Annan, Kofi 44
anthropic dimension 141
Ashley, L. J. 55
Association of Innovative Social Entrepreneurs (ASHOKA) 194
associative-cooperative organization (Salinas) 116–8
Atienza-Sahuquillo, Carlos 197
ayllu (community) 16–7
ayni (reciprocity) 17, 18
Aztec peoples 178

Banerjee, O. xxi
Barba-Sánchez, Virginia 197
Barkin, D. 163, 164
Barrágan, M. 125
Better Life Initiative Report (OECD) 101
Bhabha, Homi K. 37, 38, 56, 57
bio-economy 184
Bolivia: communal democracy in 25–6; decolonisation in 22–3; democratic and cultural revolution in 14; rights of nature in 20
Bonfil-Batallas, G. 94, 96, 97
Borja, P. 124
Brazil: colonization in 176; socio-economic and political conditions in 176–7
Broderick, Céire 38
broken window exercise 68
Bronstein, J. 162
Buen Vivir (BV) theory xxii, 214; *ayllu* (community) values in 3, 11, 16–7; community well-being pillars in 3, 21–2; conceptualization of 14–5, 15*f*; criticisms of 3, 26–7; as decolonial approach to development 3; decolonisation pillars in 3, 22–3; democratisation pillars in 3, 25–6; ecologist/developmentalist approach 3, 14, 15–6; economic pluralism pillars in 3, 24–5; indigenist approach 3, 14; inspired by Andean cosmovision 10–1; as new paradigm for development 7; plurinational state pillars in 3, 23–4; practice of 11, 14; rights of nature pillars in 3, 20–1; socialist/statist approach 3, 14–5; social movements and 16; *turaq* (harmony) and *hunt'ay* (complementarity) values in 3, 11, 18, 20; *yanapay* (solidarity) and *ayni* (reciprocity) values in 3, 11, 17–8
Burnett, K. A. 195

Calderon, Felipe 101
Campos Clement, V. 197
Cantillón, Richard 195

Caracterizacion Socioeconomica Nacional (CASEN) survey (Chile) 142
Cardenas, Lazaro 100
Carrasco, G. xx
Catholic church xxv, 130, 161, 179, 206, 208, 212
Cediel, G. 142
Cherán, tierra para soñar (documentary by Labaronne) 104
Chile: agro-food system in xxiv, 135–41; food inequality in 142–3; military coup in 1973 139; neoliberalism in 134–5; obesity in 142–3; return to democracy in 1990s 139; social changes in 2019 139, 143, 144; water crisis in 141–2
classic theories of development 7, 8*t*–9*t*
climate change 134–5
Colombia: biodiversity in 40; cooperatives in 193–4; *Encyclical Laudato Si* xxiv; entrepreneurship in xxv, 193–202; land rights in 39, 40–1; social crisis in 180; socio-economic and political conditions in 180–1; success factors n formation of solidarity organizations in 192–3; unemployment rates in 193; United Nations Universal Periodic Review (UPR) of 46–56; wastewater discharge taxes in xxi
Colombian National Government xxv
colonization 97
communal democracy 25–6
community-cooperative-associative organization 126
Contreras, D. xx
Convention on the Elimination of Discrimination Against Women (Bolivia) 38
cooperative entrepreneurship 194–5; economic factors in 198; environmental factors in 198; social factors in 198
Cooperative Society of Mexico 179
cooperativism xxv, 112, 114–5, 116–7, 145, 179–80, 181, 193; adaption of 124–5; as alternative to neoliberalism 181; background of 181; characteristics 181; definition 124
Corporación de Fomento de la Producción (CORFO) (Chile) 140
Cortés, Paula Martinez 41
cosmovision (worldview) 10–1
COVID-19 pandemic 140, 144, 148
Cowen, M. 4
creative destruction, concept of 192
Cubillo-Guevara, A. P 3, 14, 24, 26

decentralized autonomous governments (GADs) (Ecuador) 2109
decolonisation 3
degrowth 7, 10
democratisation 3
development: association with economic development 4–5; categorisations 4; criticisms of 5–6; definitions of 4; dimensions of 4; as key determinant of social progress 5; in Latin American context 5–6; as legacy of colonialism 5; new paradigm for 7; theories 7, 8*t*–9*t*, 10
Diaz, Porfirio 103
Di Girolamo, G. 144
Drayton, Bill 194
dual societies 97
Dubach, Jose 116
Duque, Iván 41

The Economist 93
ecosystem: biological *vs.* organizational 162–3; characteristics 162
Ecuador: citizen revolution in 14; fair-trade development model in 205–12; fair trade in xxv; as fair-trade leader in Latin America 208–9; rights of nature in 20; saline water processing in Salinas 112–30; sustainable innovation in xxiii
Ecuadorian FairTrade Strategy 209–10
El Bilali, H. 136
Elkington, John 193, 201
emergent theories of development 7, 8*t*–9*t*
EMES International Research Network 195
Emmelin, M. xx
Encyclical Laudato Si (Columbia) xxiv
entrepreneurial skills and assets (ESA) 193
entrepreneurial skills and knowledge (ESK) 193

entrepreneurship xxv, 125, 192; Austrian School definition of 195; cooperative 194–5; definition of 195; factors in success of 197–8; social 194; solidarity 196
environmental sustainability: awareness of value of and need for 80–1; Plan B platform for 83–7, 89; Play-City platform for 81–3, 88
Equitable Society of the Rochdale Pioneers (UK) 181
Escobar, A. 5, 10
Esquivel-Hernández, G 93
Esteva, G. 95, 99, 105
Eurocentric universe 5

fair trade xxv, 118, 205, 206
Fair Trade Consortium 212
Final Agreement for Ending the Conflict and Building a Stable and Lasting Peace (2016, Columbia) 40, 41
Food and Agricultural Organization (FAO) 136, 142, 143, 148
Food and Labelling and Advertising Act (2016, Chile) xxiv
Food Labelling and Advertising Act (2016, Chile) 135
Framework for the Urban Food Agenda (FAO) 136
free trade agreements (FTAs) 139
Fukuyama, F. 4
Fundación Sol 139

Gaiger, L. I. xxi
game theory (Huizinga) 81–2, 88–9
García, N. G. 197
Gartner 198
Gide, Charles 196
Gini coefficient 140
global capitalism 92, 96
global governance 41–2, 45–6
globalization 97, 136
global north (GN) 5, 7, 10
global south (GS) 5, 7, 10, 92
Global Wealth Report (2014) 93
Global Wealth Report (2019) 140
González, F. 162
Gonzalez, Maria de Jesus Patricio 95
Great Depression 138
The Great Transformations: The Political and Economic Origins of Our Times (Stiglitz) 92
Great Transition Initiative (GTI) 95
green capitalism 137
greenhouse gas (GHG) emissions 67; civil society and 67, 68; urban transport and 69–70
gross domestic product (GDP) 4, 6, 140, 144
Gruppo Salinas Development Corporation 118

Harvey, D. 92
Heidegger, Martin 175, 189
Herron, L. 197
Hidalgo-Capitán, A. L. 3, 14, 24, 26
Hiripan 100
Homo Ludens, a study of the play element in culture (Huizinga) 81
Huizinga, Johan 81
hunt'ay (complementarity) 18

Inca Empire 10
indigenous peoples: *see also* Aztec peoples; Mayan peoples.
see also pueblos originarios (Mexico); *ayllu* (community) as different to
western perspectives 17; Buen Vivir (BV) theory and 14; cosmovision of 10–1; history of solidarity of xxii; Mexican 93–4; SSE in Mexico and 178; UPR and Colombian 48–9
industrialization 138
information and communications technology (ICT) 80
Ingram, J. 146
Institute for the Promotion of Exports and Investments (PROCEUADOR) 210, 213
Institute of Popular and Solidarity Economy (IEPS) (Ecuador) 210
Inter-American Commission on Human Rights (IACHR) 40, 41, 50, 51
Inter-American Court of Human Rights (IACtHR) 40, 41, 50, 51
Intergovernmental Panel on Climate Change (IPCC) 136
internal company factors (ICF) 193, 199, 200, 201, 202
International Cooperative Alliance (ACI) 124
internationalization 136

International Labor Organization (ILO) 95, 99, 103, 105, 138, 174
International Monetary Fund (IMF) 6
International Trade Union Confederation (ITUC) 53

Keohaqne, Robert 41
knowledge and skills of entrepreneur (KSE) 199, 200, 201, 202
Kuhn, Thomas 182

Labaronne, S. 104
Lalander, R. 27
Latin America (LA): agrarian reforms in 138; cooperativism in xxv; environmental performance in xxi; income inequality in xix; land ownership and wealth and power 138; pre-Hispanic population of 97
Latin American Community Marketing Network (RELACC) 218, 219

Mälmstrom, V. H. 100
marginalization 129
Mars, M. 162
Martínez Fernández. Julia 197
Matua, Makau 46
Mayan peoples 173
McMahon, Edward 47
McMichael, P. 137
Mercado, Aristeo 103
Merida Initiative (Mexico) xxiii
methodological approach 164–5
Mexican Revolution (1910) 101, 103
Mexico: cooperativism in 179–80; at crossroads 105–6; as deadly conflict zone 92; drug wars in xxiii, 92, 101–2; indigenous peoples of 177–9; laissez-faire capitalism in 94; poverty in 93; social solidarity economy (SSE) in 177–8, 179; violence and criminality in context in 92–3
Mexico Profundo: Reclaiming a Civilization (Batalla) 94
Milan Urban Food Policy Pact (MUFPP) 136, 150
Miller, Grace 97
Modernity Coloniality Group (MCG) 5
modernization 92
monoculture 182, 184
Morales, Evo 23, 25
multi-level perspective (MLP) framework xxiv, 135, 136
multiple linear regression analysis 193, 194

National Council for the Evaluation of Social Development (CONEVAL) 93
National Environmental Information System (Chile) 141
national human rights institutions (NHRIs) 43, 44, 51
National Indigenous Council (CNI) (Mexico) 94–5
National Institute of Social Economy (INAES) of Mexico 174
nationalization 97
National Secretariat for Solidarity Economy (SENAES) (Brazil) 177
natural capital 40; access inequality to xxi; description xxi
neoliberalism 94, 134, 137, 139; SSE as alternative to 181
neo-Marxism 14
niches (as experimental environments) 143–4
Nirmal, P. 95
non-governmental organizations (NGOs) i, xix, 47, 51, 52, 55, 130
North American Free Trade Agreement (NAFTA) 92, 93, 94, 97, 101
nudge theory 68

Obrador, Andres Manuel Lopez 96
Olea, I. 147
Organic Law of Food Sovereignty (LORSA) (Ecuador) 209
organic law of popular and solidarity economy 126
Organic Law of Popular and Solidarity Economy (Ecuador) 209–10
Organization for Economic Cooperation and Development (OECD) 101, 140, 142, 143
Organization of Petroleum Exporting Countries (OPEC) 206

Pan American Health Organization (PAHO) 135
Pan American Sanitary Bureau 138
Papal Encyclical Laudato Si (2015) (Columbia) 161–71

participatory guarantee systems (PGS) (Chile) 145
Perez, A xxi
Peru: Lima-Callao metropolis as most polluted city 69, 70; Lima-Callao metropolis vehicle volume and types 71–3; sustainable transport in 73–80; vehicle emissions in xxiii, 67–88
pluralism 3
plurinational state 3, 24–5
pluriverse world 5
Polanyi, Karl 92
Polo, F. Antonio 116, 124
Pomerantz, Mark 195
Populorum Progressio Encyclical 127
postcolonialism 38
post-development approach 11
Proyecto Nasa 53
pueblos originarios (Mexico) 93, 94, 95, 105–6; challenges in post-neoliberal era 96–7; grassroots movements of 98–9; as historical agent 96
Purepechas (Tarascan) empire xxiii, 95, 99, 100; post-revolutionary resistance 103–4; struggles since revolutionary times 103; womens' rebellion 104

Quijano, Aníbal 184

Ramírez-Gallegos, R. 24
Raustiala, Kal 41
Razeto, Luis 196
Reporters Without Borders 53
resources and capabilities theory 193
Revolutionary Armed Forces of Columbia (FARC) xxv, 40
Richard, H. 126
Rivera, Diego 98
Robinson, R. B. 197
Robles, C. 138
Rocheleau, D. 95
Rodriguez, R. 97
Rubio, M. xx
Rutherford, Jonathan 39

Sachs, W. 163
Salinas de Guaranda (Ecuador) xxiii, 112, 112–30
Santos, Boaventura De Sousa 182, 183, 184
Santos, Juan Manuel 41
Saravia, P. 137
Savings and Credit Cooperative Salinas Ltd 115, 116–7
Schumpeter, J. 192
Scott, J. 97
Servicio Nacional de Meteorología e Hidrología del Perú (SENAHMI) 69
Shenton, R. 4
Simma, Bruno 43
Sixth Academy of Social and Solidarity Economy (2015) 174
Social and Solidarity Economy Movement of Ecuador (MESSE) 211
social capital 40; definition xx; erosion of by violence xx; as key for citizen support xx–xxi
social economy sector organizations (SESO) 174
social entrepreneurship 194; definition 195
social innovation: description xix; as sustainable resolution xx
social innovation ecosystems xix–xx
social solidarity economies (SSE) xxiv, 128–9, 135, 144, 146, 164, 171, 174, 177, 178, 179, 180; alternative theoretical perspective of 181–2; human relations as central to 184; internationally 188–9
sociology of emergencies 183
solidarity entrepreneurship 196; characteristics 196
solidarity management 165
solidarity micro franchises 165, 166, 168
solidarity organizations 169–70
Stavenhagen, R. 97
Stehr, A. 142
Stiglitz, Joseph E. 92
Sumak Kawsay/Suma Qamaña principles 11, 20, 27
sustainability transitions 137
sustainable development goals (SDGs) 85, 136, 202, 202; macro policies within 136–7
sustainable innovation 112, 125–6; saline water processing 112–30

Tangazoan 100
Tariacuri 100
Texal Salinas Craft Development Association 115–6

transition theories (TDs) of development 7, *8t–9t*, 10
transnational drug trafficking organizations (TDTOs) 98, 99, 101–2
Transparency International 180
triple bottom line (Elkington) 193, 201
turaq (harmony) 18

Union of Peasant Organizations of Cotacahi (UNORCAC) 211
Union of Peoples and Organization of Guerrero (UPOC) 98
United Nations (UN) 169 Convention on Indigenous and Tribal Peoples xxiii
United Nations Declaration on the Rights of Indigenous Peoples (UNDRIP) (2007) 45, 48
United Nations (UN) Millennium Developmental Goals 7
United Nations (UN) Universal Periodic Review (UPR) xxii, 37; accommodation of textual and political third space 37, 38, 39; characteristics of 37–8; Colombia and 46–56; as global governance mechanism for human rights 37, 42–3, 45–6; human rights defenders in Columbia 49–50; indigenous peoples in Columbia 48–9; land rights in Columbia 47–8; origins of 43–5

Up de Graff, Fritz W. 113
urbanization 138
urban pedagogy 69
Urban Transport Authority for Lima and Callao (ATU) 70–1

Vanhulst, J. 3
Veciana, A. 197
La Via Campesina 137
Victims and Land Restitution Act (2011, Columbia) 41, 48
Victor, David 41

Workers' Federation of Chile (FOCh) 138
Workers' Party (Brazil) 176
World Alliance for Citizen Participation (CIVICUS) 53
World Bank 6
World Fair Trade Organization (WFTO) 208, 212, 213
World Health Organisation (WHO) Global Control Automatization (GCA) (2005) 70
World Trade Organisation (WTO) 6

yanapay (solidarity) 17, 18
Yin, R. K. 164, 165

Zapata, Emiliano 98
Zapista Army of National Liberation (EZLN) 94, 96, 103